The Spirits of Sexual Perversion
Handbook

*Please visit **www.victoriouslyfree.org** or call **(347) 495-4555** for more information about this book and its author.*

The Cover Illustration

There have been many inquires about the cover illustration of this book. The reaction to the cover has varied between extremes of admiration and respect to that of downright disgust and utter offense. The one consistency in the many responses to the cover has been the intense interest and curiosity that it stirs. So for anyone who might care; here is the cover story.

The illustration is a representation of Adam and Eve in the Garden of Eden about to engage in sexual intimacy as husband and wife. The snakes represent the demons of sexual perversion approaching to pervert human intimacy. The larger snake on Eve's leg is satan, attempting to enter into Eve before Adam does. The bitten fruit on the ground is there to show that perversion contaminated human intimacy after man had initially disobeyed God. The fire represents the demons coming up out of hell but also represent God's consuming fire and His plan to destroy evil and to once again purify mankind.

Every aspect of this book was inspired by God. When I asked The Lord for the cover, what you have seen is the vision that He showed me. I really struggled when I first saw the completed illustration. I knew that many "church folk" would have a problem with it. I tried in every way that I could to have the artist conceal the shocking nudity of the beautiful bodies of Adam and Eve, without compromising the vision. It was not possible. God finally gave me peace when He helped me to understand that this book was never meant to appeal to the self-righteous and religious. The cover not only has a message in it, but it also appeals to those who are struggling with the very issues that this book addresses. Those who really want to be helped and those who want to help others are not bothered by the provocative nature of the cover because the truly mature understand the reality of sexual perversion and the necessity to no longer try to hide our need for deliverance.

In a study in *"Christianity Today"* 85% of Pastors claimed to speak on the topic of sex only once per year, but 46% of church-goers do not agree that is true claiming that it is even less than once per year! 44% of church-goers stated that they need to hear more Biblical teaching on the topic of sex. That's nearly half the church and believe me the other half need it too. Perhaps church folk ought to spend more time seeking out real people, with real testimonies, for a real deliverance to help educate the Body of Christ on a topic that most Pastors are obviously too uncomfortable to deal with. Look at the statistics on the back cover. It is time that we awake from our slumber. So... let me know when you want me to come to *your* church. I am ready and willing to come with the TRUTH that will set the masses free!

The Spirits of Sexual Perversion Handbook

By Laneen Anavah Haniah

Victoriously Free! Publishing

™

Unless otherwise indicated, all Scripture quotations are taken from the Holy Bible, New Living Translation *(NLT)*, copyright © 1996. Used by permission of Tyndale House Publishers, Inc, Wheaton, Illinois 60189. All rights reserved.

"Scripture quotations marked *(AMP)* are taken from the Amplified® Bible, Copyright © 1954, 1958, 1962, 1964, 1965, 1987 by The Lockman Foundation. Used by permission. (www.Lockman.org)"

Scripture quotations marked *(KJV)* are taken from the Holy Bible, Kings James Version. The KJV is part of the United States public domain and may be copied and quoted without restriction.

Scripture quotations marked *(MSG)* are taken from The Message, copyright © 1993, 1994, 1995, 1996, 2000, 2001, 2002. Used by permission of NavPress Publishing Group. All rights reserved.

All Hebrew and Greek Definitions have been taken from Crosswalk.com, Bible Study Tools Page. © Copyright 1995-2004, Crosswalk.com. All rights reserved. The definitions used are part of the United States Public domain and may be copied and quoted without restriction.

MERRIAM-WEBSTERCOLLEGIATE.COM has been used to retrieve all definition quotations. (www.Merriam-WebsterCollegiate.com) copyright © 2004 by Merriam-Webster, Incorporated. Included within Collegiate.com is the version quoted within the text:_Merriam-Webster's Collegiate Dictionary, Eleventh Edition copyright © 2003 by Merriam-Webster, Incorporated.

Any definition that is not placed within quotations is my own definition derived from my personal knowledge as a literary intellectual; God's wisdom given to me as a gift.

I have purposefully spelled satan's name with a lowercase 's' throughout the book. I will even break literary rules to defame him. He gets no honor in my life!

The Spirits of Sexual Perversion Handbook, 2nd Edition
Copyright © 2007 by Laneen Anavah Haniah
ISBN: 978-0-9794210-0-6
(2nd Printing; Printed in the US; www.DiggyPod.com)
Victoriously Free! Publishing
PO Box #151416
Dallas, TX 75315-1416
www.victoriouslyfree.org

All rights reserved under international copyright law. No part of this publication may be reproduced, stored in a retrieval system, or transmitted in any form or by any means – for example, electronic, photocopy, recording – without the prior written permission of the author. The only exception to this rule would be the use of brief quotations for the purpose of printed reviews, or for ministerial or personal use.

Foreword

In her search for the deep knowing of self through the mind of the Holy Spirit, Laneen A. Haniah, has traveled back into early childhood to trace beginnings of the entrance of spirits of sexual perversion, forward through the miles of dark confusion of the teen years full of illness, promiscuity and rebellion, and mapped on through the pain and shame of it all to birth onto the scene of her adulthood. She is an awesome woman of God and is a "**Now Word**" for the Church, and those that have not yet accepted Jesus as their Savior. Her book *"The Spirits of Sexual Perversion Handbook"* will cause believers and non-believers alike to take a deep and intimate look into the depth of their spiritual lives identifying and seeking deliverance from the spirits of sexual perversion that have them bound.

I have walked with The Lord for many years and have read many great works pertaining to spiritual growth and how to have a closer and more intimate relationship with my Savior. In this book, Laneen blends the ingredients of: Practical knowledge of the spirits of sexual perversion, her experiences in spiritual growth, the intimate exposure of her own past perversions and a well seasoned deliverance process. As her mother, one of her closest spiritual mentors and her friend, I can truthfully say that it caused me to delve into areas of myself that I had leaped over in my pursuit of spirituality. Most people are so deficient in awareness of how sexual perversion spirits invade and hinder growth with The Lord.

Too few of today's spiritual leaders are addressing this profound need, therefore it is with deep gratitude and respect that I recommend this book, not only as a <u>great *read*</u> for the Body of Christ but also as a <u>great *study*</u>. This is a book that every believer, regardless of his/her length of time with The Lord, should study to show themselves approved unto God a workman/woman unashamed, rightly dividing the Word of Truth to uncover the spirits of sexual perversion. *"The Spirits of Sexual Perversion Handbook"* is also a <u>timely necessity</u> for those who have not yet come into the knowledge of God, both young and old, as present day society is headed on a mad course of destruction due to these spirits which are a dominant force that permeate every aspect of this now civilization and its victims.

Laneen, thank you for being obedient to the guidance of the Holy Spirit and staying faithful to complete this assignment. Even though you were met with great persecution; even though spiritual, emotional and physical torment tried to hinder you so that this project would be aborted, you stayed on course. You are spiritually insightful and a true blessing to the Body of Christ both present and future. I touch and agree with you in the Name of Jesus, our Lord and Savior that this book will reach billions so that they too may be delivered from "the spirits of sexual perversion."

Spiritually Yours,
Evangelist Gail Thomas Wilson

Dedications

This book is dedicated to my confidant, my counselor, my comforter; my hero, my lover, my healer; my mentor, my covering, my king; my partner, my best friend and my husband; **Emmanuel Nikao Haniah**. *You have truly loved me as Christ loves the Church. You have been the Word made flesh in my life. It is through you that I have come to know The Lord more intimately, and because of your allowing yourself to be His vessel that I have been made whole. Words could never accurately express my love for you, but your actions have certainly expressed your love for me. It is time to possess the Promised Land My Love and I will follow you wherever you go.*

And also to:

The late **Bishop Moylan Jackson**. *You did not live long enough to see the greatness that your labor of love on my behalf produced, but I will remember you always. As the Father makes my name great, so shall your name and your works be known. Thank you my pastor.*

Table of Contents

Acknowledgements 1

Preface 3

Part I: Sex, Worship and Sexual Perversion 5

Warning: Before you continue To Read!!! 7

Chapter 1: Introduction – I understand what you are going through 9

Chapter 2: Why did God create sexual intimacy? 21

Chapter 3: How did sexual intimacy become so perverse? 29

Chapter 4: A warning to the 'sanctified' and to the married! 35

Chapter 5: Defining sexual perversion 45

Chapter 6: Assessment of the spirits of sexual perversion 53

    A. Fornication 53

    B. Masturbation 62

    C. Adultery 70

    D. Incest 80

    E. Homosexuality 85

    F. Prostitution 91

    G. Pornography/Sexual Fantasy 99

    H. Rape/Pedophilia 107

    I. Beastiality 114

    J. Sexual lust (Lasciviousness) 119

    K. Promiscuity 132

Poem: What Do You See When You Look at Me? 140

About the author 141

Part II: The Deliverance Process Step-by-Step 145

Chapter 7: Laying the foundation for deliverance 147

    The soul man 148

    The spirit man 151

    The flesh man 154

Summary of the foundation 156

Chapter 8: Deliverance for the soul man 159

    Step 1 – Confession/Acknowledgement 159

    Step 2 – Discovery 161

        A. Generational curses 163

        B. Involuntary exposure 165

        C. Spiritual wounds 168

        D. Voluntary exposure 171

    Step 3 – Renewing the mind 176

Chapter 9: Deliverance for the spirit man 179

    Step 4 – Confession/Admittance 179

    Step 5 – Penitence/Humility 181

    Step 6 – Confession/Exposure 184

        A. Accountability 184

        B. The power of intercession 186

    Step 7 – Forgiveness and letting go 190

        A. The act of forgiveness 191

        B. Bitterness and letting go 193

    Step 8 – Spiritual warfare: Putting on your spiritual armor 196

        A. The battle is not yours 197

        B. Your fight is not with people! 198

        C. The belt of truth 198

        D. The body armor of Righteousness 199

        E. The shoes of peace 200

        F. The shield of faith 201

        G. The helmet of salvation 202

    Step 9 – Spiritual warfare: Using your spiritual weapons 204

        A. The Sword of the Word 204

        B. The power of praise 207

  C. Christian fellowship 208

  D. Praying and fasting 214

 Step 10 – Spiritual warfare: Retreat and replenish 219

Chapter 10: Deliverance for the flesh man 225

 Step 11 – Discipline of the flesh 225

  A. Understanding why your body sins 226

  B. More about discipline 229

  C. More about fasting 232

 Step 12 – Walking after The Spirit 237

Chapter 11: Staying Victoriously Free Forever! 248

 The five greatest enemies to the deliverance process 248

  1. The struggle to be Holy 249

  2. Slothfulness 252

  3. Loneliness 255

  4. Anxiousness – not pacing yourself 258

  5. Discouragement 260

 The joy of The Lord is your strength 265

 Dealing with re-visitations 268

 The conclusion of the matter 271

 A final prayer 274

Poem: I Am Victoriously Free! 275

Epilogue: Are you a born again believer? 277

Part III: The Deliverance Workbook **283**

Appendix A: Sexual Perversion – Definitive Charts 284

Appendix B: Tracing Your Past 289

Appendix C: The Deliverance Process at a Glance 293

Appendix D: Tips on Fasting 297

Appendix E: Deliverance Journal 301

Contact the author/order the book 307

Acknowledgements

I would first of all like to acknowledge You Adonai, because You chose and ordained me, although I've been rejected by man. You are my Everything Lord. Thank You for writing this book through my hands and redeeming my life.

I thank my husband Emmanuel for being Mr. Mom, while I hid away at my computer for days on end. You have been my greatest supporter, encourager and motivator. This book could not have been written without your support. Thank you honey. Kiss!

I thank my children Ja'Keim, Nebiyah, Benjamin, Judah and Zechariah, for patiently enduring while I poured myself into this ministry. Sorry for being cranky at times my babies while I carried this baby. I promise to make it up to you (*smile*).

I especially thank my oldest son Ja'Keim. You are still my Number One Helper. You make this family wonderful and your assistance makes it possible for me to answer Yeshua's call more diligently. Thanks Honey.

I thank my Mom, Minister Gail Thomas-Wilson. You gave me my love for writing and helped me to develop this anointing. You have been like manna from Heaven during this wilderness season and at last our relationship has blossomed like a late desert bloom. Oh how beautiful it is! Thanks Mom. I owe you a shopping spree!

To my big sister Karmina Chin, who calls me the older sister (*smile*). You have encouraged and supported me all my life long so consistently and without fail. You have been more than just a sister, you have been a true friend. I thank my new brother-in-law Sean Chin too. In such a short time you have become so important to this family. I love you both.

To my little sister Jamila Wilson, Sergeant Hungry: I honor you greatly for your choice to go into the army and help protect our country. I thank you for all your support and the laughter you bring into my life. I'll see you when you get home girl. It's gonna be time for eatin' then!!!

To my spiritual mother Patricia Roubinek, I cannot even express with words the healing that you have wrought in my heart. Every time you hug me, years worth of rejection, neglect and low self-esteem literally melt away from your love. Thank you for choosing me.

To my God Mother, Yvonne Lewis: You have been such a blessing to me and my family. You loved me when I was unlovable. You have truly proven your heart. Thank you so much.

To my beautiful new found friend Jolene the most enthusiastic and inwardly adorned woman I know. I strive to be more like you.

To my destiny sister in Christ Marilyn Campbell. The call on your life is awesome and what a privilege to have you as a partner in my own call.

I give great, great thanks to Minister Jay Bailey. Jay, your invaluable computer skills made it possible for me to continue writing. You were a blessing to me when I had nothing to offer in return. I will not forget you and your wonderful wife Hope, as the Father elevates me.

I give thanks to my book cover illustrator. You believed in this vision even though you did not know me and you worked for far less than your talent is worth. You have a beautiful personality and I know that the Father is going to elevate you because of your kindness!

To my little sister in the spirit Kikelemo; I love you so much. You have stood by me and my husband in our highest highs and our lowest lows. Your loyal support means so much more to me than you understand especially in light of the many that have walked away. Ditto for your man of Yah, Jermaine.

I want to send love to my Dad and his wife, and my newest little sister Sheree. I thank you for all of your love and laughter over the years. May it continue forever.

I also want to acknowledge: Ava and Herb Benjamin because you two are so loving and kind; Pastor Virginia Surgeon for your sweet presence and exemplary walk with our Father; Reverend Paul Leacock, you never let me forget who I am; Joyce and James Collier, thanks for the encouragement; Michael Chase, I love you honey; the McDaniel's family, Jazmin, her Mom and dad, and her best friend Paulette, I love you guys; Alexis Kinloch, thank you for helping me grow; Quentris Sedeno, my IM buddy; Sister Terry O'Neal, the sweetest lady I know; all of the wonderful ladies at Highland Church; GOV of Stony Brook College and last but not least Elder James Washington for encouraging me to keep on writing when I felt unworthy.

Thanks to Ricci Dorisca the aspiring editor who worked for love instead of money.

I would also like to thank some of the leaders in the Body of Christ that have not been ashamed to share their testimony. Your openness really blessed me. Thank you for the inspiration: Prophetess Juanita Bynum-Weeks, Pastor Donnie McClurkin, Pastor Paula White, Dr. Aretha Wilson, Prophet Todd Hall, Prophet Andre Cook, and most of all Minister Emmanuel Haniah and my Mom Minister Gail Thomas-Wilson.

Lastly, I would like to acknowledge my favorite ministry leaders in the Body of Christ: Minister Emmanuel Haniah, Pastor Joel Olsteen, Joyce Myers, Bishop T.D. Jakes, Prophet Perry Stone, Pastor Benny Hinn, James and Betty Robison, Pastor Isaac Pitre, Pastor Donnie McClurkin, Prophet Todd Hall, Pastor A. R. Bernard and founders of the TBN Network® Paul and Jan Crouch. And, last but definitely not least my pastors, Larry and Tiz Huch of DFW New Beginnings Church in Irving, Texas, whom have totally radicalized my walk as a Christian and made me free to LIVE. Thank you all for the wonderful impact that you have made on my life. I am so glad that I am finally going to have some money to pour back into your lives!!!

Preface

I greet you in the name of my Lord and Savior Yeshua (Jesus). I am a person who has been delivered from numerous spirits of sexual perversion, and I am not ashamed to share my testimony. For this reason, The Lord has given me a mandate to expose the spirits of sexual perversion in the earth and help lead His people to deliverance. By unction of the Holy Spirit, I answered this mandate by writing this book. My number one heart's desire for this book is to see people totally set free from sexual addictions and perversion. My second greatest desire concerning this work is to see people restored back to true relationship with and worship of the True and Living God. My third greatest desire concerning this work is that it would create an opportunity for the total destruction of the shroud of secrecy concerning sexual sin and addictions that exist in the world and in the church. It is this secrecy that has empowered satan so greatly in this area and has kept people in bondage for so long.

I never fathomed the wealth of wisdom and revelation that the Holy Spirit was going to pour into me concerning this topic. I have discovered during the writing of this book that there is much deception concerning sexual perversion. Most people have not attained a precise understanding of exactly what sexual perversion is and are subsequently bound to continue on in a defeated life full of failure in this area. There are numerous people, sinners and saints alike, that struggle desperately with sexual perversion. In most instances, those bound by sexual perversion feel powerless, lost and trapped. Sexual perversion is a ferocious roaring lion. This book addresses some of the most confounding questions surrounding sex such as: Why did God make sex? How did I become so perverse? How can I get delivered? These and many other questions concerning the monster of sexual perversion are answered in this book.

If you are a person that is now struggling or has ever struggled with sexual sin; if you were exposed to sexual sin as a child or as an adult whether voluntarily or involuntarily; if you have ever been raped, molested or sexually abused; if you have a spouse that has been unfaithful to you; if you live a life of promiscuity that you just cannot seem to break free of; this book is for you! Did you know that even sanctified, Holy Spirit-filled Christians, married people and/or people who are not actually *performing acts* of sexual sin can still be bound by spirits of sexual perversion? Learning this was one of the most eye-opening elements of this book for me. If you fall into this category and sexual perversion is a part of your past or your family history, you need this book too. This book contains wisdom imparted directly from the mind of the God and therefore is also a vital resource for every Christian leader.

This book is a fundamental necessity for every person that will ever have to confront the spirits of sexual perversion on any front. Understanding The Lord's true purpose for sexual intimacy and satan's true purpose for sexual perversion are the foundational truths that have eluded so many of us for so long, but now these truths have been disclosed. Every essential tool has been provided or presented in this manuscript for anyone that is truly serious about going to another level, or any one that is serious about helping others to do so.

The Lord has impressed upon my spirit the urgency of getting this information into the minds of His children right away. The Body of Christ and this nation of the United States are under attack. Our greatest enemy is not terrorism. Our greatest enemy is sexual perversion. Sexual perversion can destroy as no other enemy can. Therefore, we must arm ourselves and declare the perverting of our nation and the perverting of the Church as an act of war! This book is the war plan that will lead us to victory! Read on, and get ready to enjoy the freedom of sexual deliverance because –
IT'S TIME FOR ANOTHER LEVEL!!!

PART I: SEX, WORSHIP AND SEXUAL PERVERSION

In this part of the book we are going to learn about God Almighty's true purpose for sexual intimacy, satan's true purpose for sexual perversion, how and when sexual perversion entered the earth and about the spirits themselves and how they operate. I tried to write this book as an easy read but at the same time cover all of the necessary elements. Depending on your level of Bible knowledge, this part of the book may be a little more difficult to understand at times, but I implore you not to skim through it or skip ahead. It is critically important that you understand satan's strategy in order to successfully move forward in the deliverance process. We must build a solid foundation of knowledge.

To help you successfully read through this book I suggest that you read slowly and at a time that you are very alert. Read through certain sections twice if you need to and always, ALWAYS pray beforehand for understanding every time you pick up this book. It would be a great idea to go through this process with a partner or a sponsor. You and your partner can read the book together and help one another. Spouses should partner with one another if possible. It is very important that spouses each have a personal copy of this book and read it during the same time period. (We will discuss 'why' in chapter 4.) Also, throughout the reading of this book keep a journal with you. As you read write down things that you want to remember or any revelations God may give you concerning your own life. This will be very important as you move on to **Part II** of the book which details the deliverance process. There are also assignments and activities located in *The Deliverance Workbook* that you will need your journal book for. There are a few journal pages in Appendix E (pg 301) that you can use if there is ever a time that you do not have your journal available.

Throughout the book you are going to notice that some scriptures are quoted and some are only referenced. Scriptures that are referenced but not quoted are referenced only for validation and extra study. I did not quote them because they are not essential to the revelations in this book. I therefore suggest that you do not look these scriptures up while you are reading the text because it may cause you to lose the train of thought that is being portrayed. If you want to study these extra scriptures, it would be more advantageous for you to look these scriptures up at the end of each section or chapter instead of during the reading of the body of the text. I know this book is lengthy and that might be intimidating for those of you that are short on time or not avid readers. However, the truth is that reading just nine pages a day, from this point forward in the book, will take you through to the end of **Part II** in just 30 days; about four or five pages a day will get you finished in less than two months. So do not let satan, as he surely will try to, stop you from completing this book because it cannot help you just lying around somewhere! Ok, let's get started!

***Important Note**: I occasionally use Jesus' originally given Hebrew name which is Yeshua (yeh-o-shoo-ah). I also use the Name of the Father God Almighty, which according to Exodus 6:3 KJV (also Ps 83:18, Isa 12:2 & 26:4) is Yahweh/Yah (Jehovah). He is also known by Elohim, El Shaddai, Adonai, El Elyon and many others. Yah says that we ought to exalt His Name, which is not "God" or "The Lord". These are honorable titles, but they are not His *Name*. Just in case you are wondering, I am 100% **non-denominational**. I fellowship with any and all seekers of the Living God and His Spirit, through His son Yeshua. I just want to reconnect with our Judeo-Christian roots. After all, Jesus was a Jew and so is every born again believer in Him. This is just FYI (*smile*). Thank you!*

***Another Note**: If you feel so led in your heart, please skip ahead at anytime during the reading, to the epilogue on page 277 in order to find out how you can become a born again believer in Yeshua the Messiah (Jesus Christ). That is the prerequisite requirement that must be met in order for you to truly be liberated!*

WARNING: Before you continue to read!!!

It is only fair to warn everyone before we go on that this book is not for the religious nor is it fit for the weak or faint at heart. It is not for those that dwell comfortably in darkness and have itching ears! This book is being written only for those who need it. If it offends you, then it is not for you. As you read on you will see for yourself that this book is very intimate and for mature audiences only. It is no holds barred on exposing the works of sin in my life because I want you to really be able to see yourself in some way, in my life and in my testimony. I know that if you can identify with my sins, you will be able to identify with my deliverance as well. If you cannot identify with my sins, this book may offend you, but I offer no apologies. All I can say is that if you do not like my exposure of my past then you can simply choose to not read this book. Instead, pass it along to someone who needs it. It will cause me no offense nor will it make me doubt concerning whether I should have exposed the things that you are about to read.

For those of you who may find the material in this book offensive or just utterly shocking, if the question comes to mind as you read, *"Was it really necessary to write that?"* the answer is a resounding, **yes!** I was careful only to write what the Holy Spirit led me to. As the Bible clearly states, we overcome satan by the Blood of the Lamb and the word of our testimony *(Rev 12:11)*! I choose to be an overcomer and want to help others become overcomers as well. With the loving support of my husband, I have been given the courage by the Father to reveal things about myself that are a lot less than exemplary. Writing these things is not easy but in the same respect, the person that I will be writing about that used to commit such acts is a dead woman. That is who I *was*, not who I *am*. It is a part of my history, not a part of my present and certainly not a part of my future. It is not going to make me look good, so it is fortunate that looking good in the eyes of man is not my goal. My goal is that many may be delivered from sexual sin and addiction.

This book has the gold seal of approval from my God, my husband, my spiritual leader and my self. With that being established, I can continue on with the confident assurance that I have done well, regardless of any subsequent persecution that I may suffer from what you are about to read.

Now that I have gotten that out of the way, let us continue. **_Shall we?_**

Chapter 1:
Introduction –
I understand what you are going through

I want you to know that I am writing this book because I have been there and, I understand what you're going through.

(If you have not already, please go back and read the instructions on pages 5 - 6 <u>completely</u> before continuing. These instructions are very important for your understanding!)

I am so glad that you are holding this book in your hand right now. I know that it is by divine appointment that you are doing so. We are about to take a journey together through the wisdom and insight of God the Father, into a place where deliverance lives. We will have to travel through some dense forests and some dark caves, but there shall lay a well lit path before us at all times that will lead us into the open fields of victory that are awaiting our arrival. As you read this book, I want you to feel as if you are sitting down and talking with a friend. I am here to take you by the hand and escort you where you have been longing to go. I am here to encourage and to guide you. I pray that my spirit will be a personal mentor to you and that instead of just reading a book, you will have a total life-changing experience of deliverance with someone whom you will come to call a friend.

As I mentioned in the preface, I am someone who was once bound by numerous spirits of sexual perversion. Sexual perversion has been a part of my life for as long as I can remember. Before I was even conceived, sexual perversion was already the lot assigned me by the devil through the sins of my forefathers. Sexual sin is a generational curse that can be traced back in my ancestral history as far as my great-great grand parents, although I am sure it reaches back much further. Any person who has ancestors that have been corrupted by sexual perversion, will almost always, at a very young age, be exposed to and contaminated by sexual perversion as well. This is how the devil attempts to secure his place in a person's family bloodline.

I was no exception to this rule. My parents struggled terribly with spirits of sexual perversion, as did the rest of all of the family members that were in my life. Sexually perverse acts were commonplace in my life and surroundings. I can start tracing back from the age of two when I was regularly molested by a lesbian babysitter. Then shortly afterward, I was raped by one of my male relatives. I suppose that I could have overcome these incidents with the right support system. Unfortunately though, all of the adults in my life were too busy getting high, drunk and indulging in their own sexual fetishes to even notice what was happening to me. These two incidents of molestation and my living environment were a jumpstart into a life full of sexual perversion.

My childhood memories include watching pornography, seeing people have sex in front of me, lying in bed next to people who were masturbating and being instructed on how to do it to myself, playing with sex toys, and being casually and haphazardly touched in my intimate places by male and female relatives just as a matter of habit. I certainly became a product of the environment in which I grew up. I started masturbating, developed a fond interest in pornography, took on a homosexual nature and attempted to have intercourse all starting at the age of five. If you can believe it or not, my greatest desire at the age of five was to see a male's private parts! I was absolutely obsessed with seeing a man's "pee-pee" and tenaciously pursued my goal.

Two of the greatest factors in fostering sexual addictions are rejection and insecurity. I suffered greatly from both. I can remember even at the age of four when I was in preschool that the other children did not like me. I don't know what it was about me that caused them to dislike me so much, but I was a misfit and an outcast before I even knew how to spell my own name. From the time I was six, other girls were calling me "lesbo" and "dyke". Around that same time, my Mom tried to clean up her life. She decided to get married, but the same demons of perversion, rejection and insecurity followed us right into our new lives. She had never been married before, and she did try to choose carefully, but Mom always had a hankering for picking the wrong men. She married someone that she believed to be a God-fearing family man, but he turned out to be yet another one of sexual perversion's helpless victims. Consequently, by his hand sexual perversion, abuse and molestation continued on in my household behind closed doors.

Also, during that period of time at the age of eight, I was struck with a terminal illness. The illness crippled my body and the medications that I was taking caused my face to look funny. I was viewed as an absolute freak by my peers, and thus bad matters only got worse. The doctors eventually were successful in bringing the disease that I had under control, but the medications that I had been on had ravaged my body and destroyed my reproductive system. I was crushed when I was told at the age of 10 that I would not be able to have children. Other than seeing a pee-pee *(laugh)*, getting married and having a beautiful family one day was my life's goal. I wanted to make the type of family that I did not have. How could that dream be taken away from me at such a young age? What purpose would my life hold when my heart's desire had already been thwarted?

The list of influences and abuses could go on and on, but I mention these incidents only to point out that spirits of sexual perversion had their place in my life at a very early age. By the time I hit my teen-age years, I was **out of control**. I graduated from having sex with dolls, hairbrushes and carrots, to having intercourse (unprotected) with real, live men. I didn't care about my life or health at that point. I was looking for love and acceptance in all the wrong places, and I was determined to prove those doctors wrong. I wanted to have a baby! At first, I thought sex was fun and cool, but after a while I was sick and tired of being a slave to sex. Sexual perversion had completely taken over my life, and it did not take long for me to begin to feel as if I would never be free.

I believe the depth of my sexual sins is why God has chosen me to write this book, and although this book is Bible-based and written from a Christian perspective, it is not just for Christians. This book is not only biblical, it is also practical and real, and is therefore for anyone who just like I was, is sick and tired of being a slave to sexual perversion. Even before I was a born again believer, I deeply desired to change my way of living. Many people (*like me back then*), believers and unbelievers alike, despise the sexually perverse acts that they commit. They despise the momentary pleasure that it brings them and despise themselves for continually indulging in these acts knowing how they will feel afterward. There are some sexually perverse people that do greatly enjoy their sins for a moment, but there are others that do not even get momentary pleasure out of the acts. There is no pleasure in it for them at all. Most people just feel driven to do the things that they do and are unable to stop. Why do people do what they do not want to do?

This was my story. I hated my life. I hated the way I lived. I hated what I represented. I had been raped on three different occasions because of my reputation and the way I carried myself. I knew that I was destroying myself. I knew that I was assisting to destroy others as well. I knew that there would be no happiness or peace for me if I continued on the way that I was living. Yet, I just felt helpless to stop. I knew about the risk of unwanted pregnancy. After finally realizing my dream of having a child, I got pregnant several times not wanting the baby and had even had an abortion. I knew about sexually transmitted diseases. I had contracted them eight times. I knew about HIV/AIDS. I had been tested many times and had even once been scared to death after being raped by a man who carried the disease. I knew about the likelihood of never being loved by a man because of my lifestyle. Yet, none of these grim facts successfully deterred me from my destructive behavior. Sexual perversion was all that I knew, and I just did not know how to be any other way.

After I gave my life to Jesus, I thought things would change for me. I was seriously in love with my Savior and knew how much God detests sexual sin. I was sure that since I went to church and shouted and danced and spoke in tongues that I would give up my old lifestyle. Oh, how wrong I was though! *I* was ready to give up the devil, but *the devil* was not ready to give up me. I came to church and fell on the floor and left the church and fell right back into the bed of sin. After truly giving my all to Jesus and still not being able to break free of sexual perversion, the devil had convinced me that even the power of the Almighty God Himself could not save me.

I felt so hopeless. I wanted so desperately to serve my Lord, but every time I fell into sexual sin I would be so laden with guilt that it was impossible for me to seek Him. I was convinced that He wanted nothing to do with me. There is no other sin tantamount to sexual perversion in its ability to make a person feel so utterly filthy. I thought I was too dirty to come into the presence of my Most Holy God and thus my relationship with Him was like a roller coaster. Every time I messed up I would backslide into the world, and every time the world messed me up I would slide back into the church. I wanted help, but people in the church either judged and despised me or wanted to sleep with me! I did not get any help from the preacher either. I got so tired of those indignant preachers standing behind the pulpit condemning to hell everyone that commits sexual vice, ignorantly declaring, "You would stop if you wanted to!" Only Jesus and I really knew how many nights I had begged and cried for a change in my ways, but I was just so bound that I could not get out. Those that have never really struggled with sexual sin will never understand what a prison it truly is and they therefore tend to lack compassion. I thought I would be trapped forever. Does this remind you of yourself or maybe someone you know?

I really feel blessed to be able to write this book because the truth of the matter is, sexual perversion is rampant not only among unbelievers but among church-goers as well. You would be surprised at how many of those little ol' "sanctified" mothers, dressed in all white, with skirts on down to the floor go home and masturbate; how many fire preaching bishops are cheating on their wives; how many prissy pastor's wives have gay sex partners; or how many diligent deacons are having sex with their young daughters. I used to be naïve about sexual perversion in the church, but similar spirits are attracted to one another. Because I went to church not yet delivered from these spirits, other believers that carried these same spirits were drawn to me. I experienced as much perversion in the church as I did in the world!

As a matter of fact, I encountered sexual perversion at the very first ministry that I came in contact with after giving my life to Christ. Coming into Christianity, I thought that Christian men would be different than worldly men had been so my guard was down. There was a particular minister who was one of the leaders of the ministry that I had been fellowshipping with and he was supposedly "mentoring" me at the time. I developed a serious crush on this Reverend Playa. Against God's counsel to me, I let this man know how I felt about him. His response to me was that he had another young lady that he was interested in but that he liked me more. The other young lady lived states away, and they had just begun their relationship, so it seemed like a simple enough solution to me – break it off with her and get with me! I even suggested that he date us both. In pride, I thought for sure I could win his affections over some chic that was 100's of miles away.

You have to understand that I was fresh out of the womb at that time in my walk with God. My umbilical cord had not even healed yet and let me tell you, I played right into the devils hands. Rev'ren Playa liked the idea of dating us both. He took me out on dates, led me on and played all kinds of mind games with me. It was interesting that because I perceived him to be such a "Holy man of God" that I had never once had any type of sexual thought about him at that time. I felt that to think of him that way would be disrespectful because he seemed to be so serious about The Lord, but the night that he told me that I looked like I had kissable lips, everything changed. The sexual temptation alarm went off in my spirit and it was on!

After a while of communicating with both me and the other girl, he decided that since he was "having such a hard time choosing between the two of us" that he was going to allow us to compete for him at a "win all or go home dinner". (He was the true inventor of the TV show *"The Bachelor"*!) The plan was that he, the competitor and I would all dine together, and then he would make his decision. This was to be done at a Passover dinner nonetheless! I was a very competitive person, so I was definitely up for the game. He had told me prior that he did not believe in dating. His belief was that you should meet a person, know that they are your future spouse and get engaged for marriage immediately. So I was very excited about the competition because winning meant an automatic husband for me. This is the craziness that was going through my mind anyway (*laugh*).

I spent the only little bit of money that I had buying clothes and accessories for the evening and practiced my feminine charms more everyday as the event drew near, but suddenly my hopes were thwarted. I believe the reality of what he was doing finally hit Rev'ren Playa as the day was approaching. You see, as I was to find out later, the other young lady had no idea what was going on all that time. He had never told her any such thing. He had been lying to us both. So he bailed out by calling me from work one day to tell me that he had good news, *"I have chosen my wife. I'm going to marry Diana."* he aloofly said to me. My heart dropped to the floor and shattered into a million pieces.

I had just come out of an abusive, two-year relationship with a married alcoholic, and I had set my heart on marrying this 'man of God' that I was pursuing. I just wanted to have a happy life for a change. I wanted my dreams of having a family to come true. How dare he get my hopes up just to crush me?!

As he waited silently on the other end of the phone, I mustered up a few nice words to say as I choked back the tears, but in my mind all I could think about was fighting back. I was so angry – angry at him, angry at me, angry at God. I had been walking with Jesus for nearly seven months at that time and had been upright before Him in almost every way, but that day I just wanted to be bad. I pulled my hoochie gear out of the closet – clothes that I had not worn since the day I had called Jesus' name – then I got all sexy and went to the mall. I wanted some attention and affirmation. I wanted someone to whistle at me, call me 'Shorty', ask for my number, anything. *"Please just let me know that I still got that appeal 'cuz' I don't think this Holiness thing is working!!!"* This is what I was thinking.

I am sure you have heard of *'God's timing'*, but did you know that the devil has timing too? I could not believe it when I ran into Rev Playa's daughter at the mall. She lived with him, and we were close in age. She asked me to come visit her at the house that night and have dinner with them. She had no idea what had happened, but I can't imagine that she could not see the evil in my eyes as I accepted her invitation. I'm sure she would have seen the horns atop my head if she had looked twice! Anyway, to make a long story short, I went to their house and Rev Playa and I ended up alone that night. The daughter left the house and that was the worse thing that could have happened. I still had revenge on my mind, and the only thing I could think of to do to him at that time was to tease him. I knew that men hate to be teased sexually and so I sat on the couch next to him in my sexy clothes, clothes which he had never seen me in before, and

I laid it on thick. It was not long before he was huffing and puffing and grunting and eagerly trying to finish what I had started.

Suddenly the realization of what I was doing hit me like a Mac Truck going 150 miles per hour on a highway. The way he was acting was the same way that all the men had acted. I was being set up by the devil and suddenly I realized it! I had been sexually pure for four months. This was a huge accomplishment for me. I did not want to lose Jesus because we had grown so close. I did not want to cause this minister to be in sin. I just wanted to get out of there. I was so sorry for what I had started. I told him that I had to go. I kept trying to leave, but he was pulling me back. I told him that I did not want to do it, but he was like a possessed man. It was as if he did not even hear me or see me. I didn't know what to do. I knew that it was my fault that I was there, and I did not want to make a scene because his daughter had returned home by then. I begged him to stop, but there was no daunting him. His body was set to do what he had in mind to do. So I just did what I had gotten accustomed to doing for the seven years that I had been sexually active: I turned over on my belly so I would not have to see his face, laid there numb and limp, withdrew all resistance, began the torment of self-hatred and let him pleasure himself at my expense. I felt the guilt of a million sins all at once in that moment. I did not know how I could ever be restored after that.

We had actually been there on the couch for the entire night by that time, probably about six hours. When *he* finally finished having sex (I truly was not a part of it, and the actual intercourse lasted less than two minutes) the sun was cracking the sky. With the break of day a new hope dawned in my soul. I remembered that Rev Playa had told me that if he ever had sex with a woman he would marry her. I think deep in my subconscious that had been my plan all along, and at that memory my eyes lit wide with expectation. Would he be my husband after all? Would he redeem me from the degradation of sexual perversion? I lay silently as he pushed himself off of me. I rolled myself onto the floor from the couch carefully avoiding his eyes. I lay quietly on the floor, drum rolls beat in my heart as I waited for him to comment, but what came out of his mouth I never expected.

You see, even though we were not going to have our "competition dinner" anymore, Diana was still on her way into town in just a few days.

He had let me know a few times prior that Diana was a virgin and that is what "gave her the advantage" over me. He wanted a virgin girl, not some used up single mother (even though he had been married four times already!). Yet still, I had hoped against hope that he would choose me; however, when he made the comment that he made, I understood just what he meant. Finally gaining the courage to look at him, I watched him lean back on the couch and rub his belly in the same way that people recline in their chair after eating a big, delicious meal. Looking rather satisfied, obviously not experiencing any of the torment of guilt that I was, he sighed deeply, looked me in the eyes and said with a gentle smile, *"Now when Diana comes, I'll be alright."* And with those words, I knew most certainly that even as a Christian, I was still that same ol' slut that I had always been – there would never be deliverance for me. I got up and quietly readied myself to leave. He walked me to the bus, and I just wanted him to go away. Couldn't he at least allow me to mourn my wounded pride and broken dreams privately?

After this incident occurred I tried to get help. I went to the head of the ministry and talked the matter over with him. Not out of spite, honestly. I just did not want to lose my True Lover. I was so scared. Jesus had been so good to me. How could I do this to Him? I cried and cried but avoided talking to God. I thought the ministry leader would help me be restored, but instead he blamed and rebuked me. He accused me of causing Rev Playa to fall and I was eventually ostracized from the ministry – not even allowed to come back and fellowship with them anymore. By his assessment, I was trouble and not worth the hope of redemption. That simply said to me that God did not want me anymore and so I stopped pursuing God all together.

Going full speed back into the world, my life was worse and more sexually perverse than it had ever been. The devil had me back in his camp and did not intend to let me get away ever again (or so he thought.) I thank Jesus that His Spirit living in me was greater than the spirit that is in the world and that God will never leave nor forsake His children *(1 John 4:4, Heb 13:5)*, but I remained wayward for eight months and every time I tried to come back to the church I encountered that same sexually perverse spirit in different church leaders. Single or married, young or old, pastor, elder, or minister; it did not matter who they were. I wanted counsel and they wanted sex. It was like being trapped in a maze. I knew that there was a way out, but I just could not see it. Fortunately, I never stopped wanting God back in my life, and He never stopped wanting me and so eventually He Himself restored me, Hallelujah!

I learned two important lessons though. First of all, I learned that there is a terrible veil of deception about sexual perversion in the church and secondly, I learned that the church can be the worse place to go for counseling concerning sexual sin! Very few people in the church want to be honest and just admit that they have been delivered or that they are struggling and need deliverance. The few daring souls that do "come out of the closet" are so persecuted that they often times become worse off than they were before they sought out help. Others that are in bondage observe this and opt to keep up the *appearance* of deliverance instead of putting their necks on the line for the real deal. When I would seek counsel concerning the sexual sins in my life, all I found was judgment, more perversion or uncomfortable stares with a quick offer to pray and change the subject. The wisdom in this book is the counsel that I was seeking back then. Though I had no man to teach me the Holy Spirit Himself taught me what I longed to know, and now I am going to share with you what He taught me! Hallelujah!

As you continue to read on, you will notice that this book is divided into three parts. In the first part of the book you are going to learn all about sex, worship and sexual perversion. We will answer the questions of why sex was created, how and why it was perverted, what the danger is to those who may think they do not have a problem in this area and then finally we will define sexual perversion and assess each of its demons. Some of the information may seem unnecessary, but it is very important that you understand the basic truths concerning sex and sexual perversion in order to be totally delivered.

In the second part we are going to cover the step-by-step deliverance process that the Holy Spirit has revealed. In that part of the book we will gain a basic understanding of the human make-up as it relates to deliverance, the necessary steps of the deliverance process and what you need to watch out for after you have been delivered. **Part III** is a coinciding workbook to help you along.

Throughout the book I try to take nothing for granted. I do hope to appeal to believers and non-believers as well. Therefore, the book is written with the 'total unbeliever' as well as the 'very spiritually mature, sanctified believer' in mind. Having prior biblical knowledge will help, but no matter which level you are on, you can gain powerful insights and understanding from this book. This book is easy to follow, and I am confident that you will learn something that you did not know before that will cause you to think with a new perspective concerning sexual perversion.

The devil made one of the biggest mistakes of his career by exposing me to his spirits of sexual perversion. Now that I am free and have an inside track to the real scoop, I plan to lead out as many as are willing to be liberated! Now you can get the help that you need without being persecuted. This book is not full of judgment and wrath. I will truthfully say that it is full of some bitter and hard truths to swallow, but it is also full of compassion and understanding and some real powerful information and practical answers that can lead you to victory. I come to you as one who has been there. I know the way in, and now I know the way out. My heart's desire is for you to experience the freedom, peace and joy that I now do as someone who is delivered from spirits of sexual perversion. I am a living witness of Jesus' deliverance power that can set you **totally** free from sexual perversion and even erase the stain that gets left behind. So come on and follow me as I follow Christ!

The names of most people mentioned in this book have been changed to protect their identity. Whenever possible, I received permission from family members to write about the experiences that I had with them that relate to this book. However, it was not possible in all cases. I apologize for any discomfort that I may have caused anyone.

Chapter 2:
Why did God create sexual intimacy?

We will deal with this question first because the answer to this question will lay the foundation that we need for a deeper understanding of the entire matter.

I believe that the three greatest weaknesses of humanity in the flesh are: **1) The need to eat; 2) The need to sleep; and 3) The urge to have sex.** I will not go into too much detail about these three needs because that would be another book in and of itself, but I note these three needs to emphasize how the spirits of sexual perversion work. They take advantage of one of the greatest weaknesses of the flesh and that is our God-given desire to have sex. God told Adam and Eve in the book of Genesis to, *"...Be fruitful and multiply and replenish the earth...(Gen 1:28)"* There is of course spiritual significance to what God said to them on that day, but there is also natural significance. In laymen's terms God was basically saying, *"I command you to have sex and lots of it!"* This may be a little hard to swallow because of our perception of sex. We generally think of sex as something forbidden, naughty or perverse. Let us consider it practically though.

In order for them to multiply they would have to engage in intercourse to afford conception an opportunity. Then, in order to <u>replenish</u> the earth (which is a tall order to fill for only two people), they would have had to engage in intercourse often so that they might conceive frequently. Another point to consider is the fact that when God gave this command, Adam and Eve did not wear clothing. All of us who are sexually active or have ever had sexual urges would probably agree that the absence of clothing often times stirs sexual desire. This is especially true if you are in a relationship with someone that you are highly attracted to, in love with and naked in their presence. Adam and Eve were no exception to this rule. Yahweh is a very deliberate God and all of this was by no means a coincidence! Thus, the truth of the matter is that God created us to frequently engage in and enjoy sexual intimacy.

What we have to realize is that because man was created in the image and likeness of the Lord God Almighty *(Gen 1:26)*, he was created in Holy Perfection. Everything about man was Holy and pure at the time of creation, including the act of sex. But once sin entered into the earth it perverted everything God had created on earth. How did sin enter into all of creation on earth considering that man alone committed sin? It entered into all of creation on earth because earth was under man's dominion. Once man became corrupt, all that he had dominion over became corrupt along with him. Sin had entered into man and corrupted him in his entirety. The corruption of sin caused man to be separated from Elohim the Creator and without that connection with God, all of creation and everything about it became perverse and evil. That is why David says in the book of Psalms that *"I was shapen in iniquity, and in sin did my mother conceive me. (Ps 51:5, KJV)"* The act of sex is just another part of what was perverted by sin at the fall of man.

So now we understand that God ordained sexual intimacy and that sex is not bad. But we still need to understand why He implemented sex as a part of the normal routine of mankind. It is important to understand that everything that exists in the natural exists first in the spirit realm. God has given us everything in the natural to help us understand His Kingdom and the spirit realm, which is the realm of eternity and is also where the true existence of each and every one of us lies. Therefore, God implemented sexual intimacy between man and woman to teach humanity something about the spirit realm. There are three things about the spirit realm and our relationship with God that He wanted us to learn through sexual intimacy.

The first, and I believe the most important purpose of sexual intimacy is: **To help us understand that we are to worship only *one* God – the True and Living God that created us.** Through study and revelation of the scriptures we learn that sexual intimacy in the natural is equivalent to worship in the spirit. We can see this by looking at some scriptures in the third chapter of Jeremiah. *(Keep in mind that 'Israel' and*

'Judah' were used as names for the collective chosen nation of (Yahweh/ God in the Old Testament) "⁶...*Have you seen what fickle Israel does?* **Like a wife who commits adultery**, *Israel has* **worshiped other gods** *...* ⁷*... And though her faithless sister Judah saw this,* ⁸ *she paid no attention. She saw that* **I had divorced faithless Israel** *and sent her away. But now Judah, too,* **has left me and given herself to prostitution.**" Scriptures similar to these can be found all throughout the books of the prophets. In both the Old and New Testament of the Bible the people of God are commonly referred to as "wife" or "bride" *(Isa 62:5, Jer 2:2, 2 Cor 11:2, Eph 5:23).* The Bible makes a strong and clear comparison between sex and worship. Therefore, there is no doubt that sexual intimacy in the natural is equivalent to worship in the spirit.

So we learn that just as a married person is to have sex only with their one spouse, we are to worship only our one Lord. God implemented sexual intimacy as an act to be performed between one man and one woman only. This is obvious because He took only one rib from Adam's body to create only one woman *(Gen 2:21-22).* Furthermore, there was no other man on earth that Adam had to share his wife with! Every other activity that spouses do together can be done with some one else as well. Sex is the only act that a spouse cannot do (lawfully in the sight of the True God) with any other human being. Understanding that sexual intimacy is equivalent to worship, we can easily see that this is true in our relationship with God as well.

We can interact with others in many of the same ways in which we interact with God. We talk to God – we can talk to people; we seek God – we can seek things; we praise God – we can praise accomplishments; we desire God – and we can desire people too. Performing any of these acts toward people or other pursuits is perfectly lawful in God's sight. Worship is the one thing that The Lord tells us we are to do to Him and *Him alone,* as is stated in Exodus 34:14, *"You must worship no other gods, but only The Lord, for he is a God who is passionate about his relationship with you."* So you can see how sexual intimacy between husband and wife in the natural is symbolic of spiritual intimacy (worship) between God and humanity in the spirit. Just think of how jealous and hurt a man or woman is when they know that their spouse has been unfaithful to them. Our Lord feels the same way when we worship any other god (a god can be an object, person, pursuit, or activity) beside Him.

The second lesson that we can learn from the act of lovemaking is: **the importance of worshiping God and the intimacy of it.** The most critical purpose of sexual intimacy between a husband and wife is to strengthen and re-establish the covenant bond and partnership between them. Medically we know that the first time a woman has intercourse she sheds blood. This can happen at times other than the first as well. Blood is also the driving force behind the erection and ejaculation of a man. In the Bible, we learn that the most powerful covenant that can be made is one that is established in blood *(Ex 24:8, Zech 9:11, Mat 26:28, Heb 9:18-22)*.

Taking all of this into consideration; a blood covenant was made between Adam and Eve when they first had intercourse. Through sexual intimacy they became obligated partners to one another for life. The covenant was for life because a blood or marriage covenant can only be broken by death *(1 Cor 7:39)*. Thus every time they connected their bodies and blood in intercourse they were reminded of the bond and covenant between them that had been established. We too are in a blood covenant (through the Blood of Jesus) with the Father. Just as was the case with Adam and Eve, each time we worship Him we re-establish and strengthen our bond and spiritual covenant with Him. We see a picture of this parallel even in the practice of communion where we partake of the Body and Blood of the Messiah *(Luke 22:19-20)*.

Couples must be intimate frequently and we likewise must worship God frequently. If you were to observe a couple that has poor and infrequent sexual relations you would find that couple does not understand the concepts of partnership, loyalty and commitment in marriage. (This may exclude some couples that are unable to have sex for some reason such as illness, distance, age, etcetera…, but if they are excluded it is only due to God's special grace on them.) Unsatisfactory sexual intimacy is the number one cause for infidelity. This is not because the sex is so important, but is instead because without the intimacy all other aspects of the relationship fall apart. It is so important for a married couple to have mutually enjoyable sexual intimacy. Each time they lay together they are reminded of the covenant that they made to one another as husband and wife. This bond is strengthened as time and tribulations reveal their commitment to one another. It is equally as important for us to experience mutually enjoyable worship with God to help us remember our covenant and remain faithful to Him. This is what sex teaches us about the ***importance*** of worshiping Yahweh our God.

What does it teach us about the ***intimacy*** of worshiping God though? A man and woman (idealistically that would mean a husband and wife) that are truly in love enjoy the act of sexual intimacy immensely. They consent that their bodies belong to one another *(1 Cor 7:4)* and they use every part of themselves and all five of their senses to express their love and desire. They touch, smell, taste, hear and see their spouse during sexual intimacy. Not out of a lustful desire but instead out of their love for one another, they are easily aroused sexually. Unashamed, they embrace in nakedness to explore one another in body, soul and spirit.

Through intercourse they become one in all three realms. Likewise, God wants to own us and wants us to give Him all of ourselves in worship. He wants us to be easily aroused – ready to worship Him at any moment. He does not want us to come to Him ashamed and covered, but instead He wants us in spiritual nakedness to allow Him to freely explore and touch every part of our spirits. He desires to freely and fully give Himself to us as well. He wants to reveal Himself to us. He desires oneness with us His creation, but we have to be willing to embrace Him. Who really enjoys sexual intimacy when their partner is resisting them? Only a rapist which God is not!

What is one of the few things that God seeks after? The Bible tells us in John 4:23, *"... true worshipers shall worship the Father in spirit and in truth: **<u>for the Father seeketh such to worship Him</u>**."* How important must worship be if the God who is sovereign and owns everything is actually ***seeking*** true worshipers?!! True worshipers are those that worship The Lord in spirit the same way a husband and wife who are truly in love share sexual intimacy in the natural – as in the description you just read above. God desires this type of intimacy from us in worship.

You show me a couple that lacks sexual intimacy in their relationship and I will show you a couple that is disconnected, does not know each other well soulfully or as friends, does not enjoy spending time with one another and misrepresents one another in the presence of others. It is the exact same way for believers that do not worship God intimately. Given that we are His vessels and representation here on earth, you can understand how crucial it is that we stay connected to Him through worship.

The third thing that sexual intimacy in the natural teaches us about worshiping God is: **the creative power that we have when we join together with God intimately in worship.** Sexual intimacy not only demands commitment to covenant and causes bonding and oneness, but it also gives a couple creative *power*. When we join together intimately with God in worship, we have the same creative power spiritually that an earthly husband and wife does naturally when they join together intimately with one another in sex. Why is it necessary though for us to have this creative power spiritually?

We know that God is the Creator of all things and that in the beginning He created everything that we now see through that which could not be seen – the power of Christ *(Gen chap 1, Heb 11:3)*. But afterward, He also ordained the laws of nature and He now adheres to those laws that He set in order. That means that now, in order for God to manifest what exists in the spirit realm (the unseen world) here in the earthly realm (the seen world), He must use physical vessels. Everything that ever has, does now or ever will exist here on this earth has always eternally existed in God's spiritual Kingdom. Yet by His own sovereignty, the Father chose to use us as a way to get it from "there" to "here". When we worship Him, He makes a deposit in us. His Spirit, His power and all that He is, is implanted into us. We conceive and give birth to His Kingdom and His will and cause it to be done here on earth just as it is in heaven *(Mat 6:10)*.

It is the same way that the love between a husband and wife can cause a baby to be born here on earth. The power to create a baby does not come from sperm and egg. Something more powerful that is unseen must first exist to bring that man and woman together in order for them to conceive. Sexual intimacy in a marriage ordained by God is fueled by the love that exists between the man and the woman, and it is the power of that love that brings them together. Let us consider that for a moment. In essence, the love between a husband and wife cannot be seen, heard, touched, tasted or smelt. To us that live in a seen and tangible world love is more of a "concept" than a "thing". Yet, the intangible and unseen concept of love can be manifested here on earth when the sexual intimacy that is fostered by that love causes a living, breathing human being to be conceived.

Before the baby is ever born it already exists inside of the bodies of its parents. The love that the parents share already exists too. But none of that can be seen or actually brought into manifestation until the couple comes together in sexual intimacy and the husband deposits what is in him into his wife. It is as if once the baby is born you can actually "see" the love. Everything already existed all along, but some type of physical vessel is needed to create something that can be considered "real" here on earth – something that we can see. Thus, the unseen love and the unseen baby, is manifested using our seen, physical vessels. It cannot be done any other way. In just the same way, God's unseen Kingdom is brought into a seen manifestation right here on earth through our seen, physical vessels – when we come together intimately in worship with Him.

Without sexual intimacy a couple cannot conceive a baby – they have no natural, creative power (aside from the use of modern day reproductive medical technology). Without us worshiping God intimately we cannot conceive His Kingdom – we have no spiritual, creative power! The same way that babies exist in the bodies of their parents even before they are ever born, God created us with seeds of greatness already within us. Seeds of the power, majesty, splendor, greatness and glory of His Kingdom already exist within us, but He must first enter into us and fertilize those seeds in order for them to ever become anything more – anything real.

He can only fertilize what is in us when we come together with Him intimately in worship, and then we together with the Almighty Creator of all can be used as vessels to manifest His creative power. Just think about it. God could have multiplied the earth in any way that He chose. Every so often a human being could have just grown up out of the soil like a plant. So why did He chose to do it through the process of sexual intimacy and procreation? He wanted us to understand our creative power when one with Him! How wonderful is our Lord to share with us His awesome power to create. Hallelujah!

To summarize this chapter; we learned that sexual intimacy was instituted by God and that He does intend for married couples to engage in and enjoy sexual intimacy often. We also learned that the spiritual revelation behind the institution of sex is that God wants to teach humanity about our relationship with Him through the relationship and sexual intimacy of a husband and wife. Let us not forget the three lessons that we learned which are all founded in the truth that natural sex is equivalent to spiritual worship. Those lessons are: 1) We are to worship God alone – no one or nothing else should receive our intimate worship except our Creator; 2) We learned that worshiping God is critically important in order for us to stay connected to Him and be reminded of the terms of our covenant with Him; we also learned that worship is very intimate and must be done in spirit and in truth; 3) And finally, we learned that when we worship God, we have creative power through the conception of His will and Kingdom agenda.

Chapter 3:
How did sexual intimacy become so perverse?

Understanding the origin of sexual perversion and the devil's true purpose for it is the next building block that we need to lay on our foundation.

    Now that we have a better understanding of God's *purpose* for sexual intimacy, it will be easier for us to understand how the spirits of sexual perversion operate and why. As we have now learned, the Father is actually seeking those who will worship Him in spirit and in truth *(John 4:23)*. Just like sexual intimacy is important in marriage, worship is extremely important in our relationship with God. The devil understands the importance of worship. We must be mindful of the fact that he once dwelled in the very presence of God, in Heaven *(Isa 14:12, Luke 10:18)*. He probably understands better than most Christians how important worship is to God and our relationship with Him.

    Satan's aim in introducing sexual perversion into the earth was to distort our understanding of worship. If satan can successfully pervert our ability to be sexually intimate on earth with our true mate, then he can pervert our ability to be worshipfully intimate in spirit with our True God. Our thinking about satan is much too finite. His purposes always stretch far beyond just the act of sin in the flesh. You have to remember that he too is a spirit and operates in the spirit realm, as well as the earth realm. His ultimate goal is that we be destroyed in the spirit realm more so than in the earth realm. Our flesh is just the physical vessel that he seeks to use to fulfill his true intentions.

    Once mankind was created the devil did not waste any time introducing sexual perversion to the earth. It can be traced in the Bible all the way back to the book of Genesis. I do not want to cause any confusion nor do I want to divert your attention away from your intended goal which is deliverance from sexual sin. We only need to focus on those aspects of scripture that are going to empower you toward your goal. For this reason, I am only going to trace the origins of sexual perversion back from Genesis chapter 4 and verse 19 where it tells us that Lamech married two women. Lamech was born five generations down in the bloodline of Cain (the first child born to Eve whom killed his brother Abel). The Bible does not talk much about Cain after he was cast out of God's presence *(Genesis 4:14, 16)*. He was no longer remembered because he was cast out of God's presence and the presence of Adam and Eve. He thus lost all of his rights as a son. Subsequently, the generations of Cain are barely discussed. As far as Adam's genealogy is concerned, Cain never even existed.

Yet, I noticed in the studying of the text that the bloodline of Cain is discussed briefly up until Lamech. None of any of Cain's other descendants born before Lamech are mentioned at all beside their names and the names of their sons, but Lamech is discussed in a bit more detail. The only distinction that I noted with Lamech is the fact that he had two wives. He was the first man recorded in the Bible to have more than one wife. This was obviously very significant for the Bible to make note of it. After Lamech and his children are written about in Genesis chapter 4, none of Cain's other descendants are named. When the descendants of Adam are listed in detail in chapter 5, neither Cain's name nor the names of any of his descendants are mentioned at all! This once again makes it plain that there was a distinction with Lamech and that distinction was the fact that he had two wives.

"Lamech married two women – Adah and Zillah. (Genesis 4:19)" What was so significant about Lamech having two wives and why was he the first man to do this? Lamech having two wives was significant because this was satan's first successful attempt to pervert the sexual relations between human beings. The covenant and commitment that Lamech was supposed to have with only one woman was then divided between two women. We all know that the more commitments we have the less dedicated we can be to each of them. Since marriage and sexual relations were implemented to help us understand our commitment to and relationship with God, Lamech having more than one wife introduced the

idea that if a man could have sex with more than one woman then he could also worship more than one God. It was a subtle way for satan to pervert our relationship with the Father by distorting our perception of intimacy.

Cain or any of his descendants were likely candidates to be the first to be used by satan to pervert sexual intimacy. This is because the Bible lets us know in Genesis 4:14 and 4:16 that Cain was literally *cast out* of The Lord's presence. He was no longer in the presence of God and therefore no longer able to serve or worship Him. In the book of Ecclesiastes it tells us that the whole duty of man is to fear God and to keep His commandments *(12:13)*. Once Cain was cast out of God's presence and could no longer serve and worship Him, he ceased to have a purpose for existing. His entire understanding of life on earth and relationship with his Creator was distorted. He passed this purposelessness and lack of understanding down to his descendants. Bearing in mind also that God is love *(1 John 4:8)* and without a connection to Him we are incapable of loving, sex served no purpose in the lives of Cain and his descendants (including Lamech) other than the sheer pleasure of it and its use for procreation. It was merely a physical act for them.

As we are still pondering the question of why Lamech was the first man to be used by satan to pervert sexual relations between humans, let us consider this: We learn in the Bible that all that is in the world is the lust of flesh, the lust of the eyes and the pride of life *(1 John 2:16)*. The more *detached* we become from the Father the more *attached* we become to the world, and lust begins to consume us. As I stated earlier, Lamech was a fifth generation descendant of Cain who had been cast out of God's presence. Thus Lamech was also part of the sixth generation of humanity on earth. Theologically, six is the number of mankind. Therefore Lamech's bloodline (descendants of the outcast) and his generation symbolized humanity in all of its wickedness and lustfulness completely detached from God. Because of this symbolism, I believe that Lamech was deliberately targeted by satan to be the first man to willfully pervert sexual intimacy.

I found it interesting that the Bible gives the names of Lamech's two wives. (It does not give the name of the wife of Cain or any of Cain's other descendant's wives.) Lamech's first wife's name was Adah, which translates "Ornament". She was his gift, his ornament, his beauty and his true helpmeet. She accentuated his strength and complimented his manhood. His second wife's name was Zillah, which translates "Shade". It was simply lust of the flesh that caused him to marry a second wife when he had already been joined together with his ornament. His second wife Zillah was just a shade of the glory of his first wife Adah. It is just like us who already have Yahweh, the Lord God Almighty as our very own and then seek out another god. Any other god is just a shade of His glory and pales in comparison!

The next instance of sexual perversion recorded in the Bible is in Genesis 6. In the first four verses of this chapter it is discussed how the "sons of God" made wives of the "daughters of the men". *"¹ And it came to pass, when men began to multiply on the face of the earth, and daughters were born unto them, ² That the sons of God saw the daughters of men that they were fair; and they took them wives of all which they chose."* I know that there are a lot of questions about this scripture and the use of the term "the sons of God". Who are the sons of God? Well when Jesus was on the earth He often referred to Himself as the "Son of Man" *(Mat 8:20, Mark 2:10)*. This was to indicate that He had been <u>born of the flesh</u>.

In the text that we just read, the scripture differentiates between the "sons *of God (who is of Spirit)*" and the "daughters *of men (who are of flesh)*". This is recorded to help us differentiate between *spiritual beings* and *earthly beings*. So in this text the term "sons of God" could just as easily have been translated as "spiritual beings", and the term "daughters of men" could have been translated as "earthly women". I believe that these spiritual beings were a part of the fallen angels that satan had deceived while still in Heaven *(Jude 1:6, Rev 12:4)*. God's Holy angels are just that – **HOLY**. They are ministering servants that help to further God's purposes and not to hinder them.

At any rate, when the Bible says that *"they took them wives"* that means in laymen's terms that they had sex with them. To break it down into simplest form, demon spirits had sex with human women. The devil was not satisfied with the subtle influence that he had on humanity through Lamech and the distortion of marriage. He wanted to literally <u>enter</u> into human beings and take total control of us. He accomplished this by assigning demons to have sex with and impregnate human women. To further prove this point we can look at verse 4 of the same chapter, which says, *"⁴In those days, and even afterward, giants lived on the earth, **for whenever the sons of God had intercourse with human women,** they gave birth to children who became the heroes mentioned in legends of old."*

When you think legend, when you think superhero what sort of image pops into your head? Perhaps Superman, Paul Bunion, Spiderman or the Incredible Hulk is what comes to mind. What causes those characters mentioned above to be characterized as superheroes? The fact that they all have superhuman strength is what causes them to be categorized as superheroes. These characters all operated with a supernatural power – the type of power that is not available to average human beings. These characters that I mentioned are all fictional, but my point is still proven that when the Bible says that these women *"gave birth to children who became the heroes mentioned in legends of old"*, it is a clear indication that they gave birth to children who possessed supernatural powers. Why did these children possess supernatural powers – because they were conceived with a supernatural seed. They possessed supernatural powers because they themselves were possessed with demons – conceived through the seed of demon spirits.[1] Thus, these demons of sexual perversion literally entered into and possessed mankind.

If you read on in chapter 6 of Genesis you will find that in verse five (the very next verse after demons and humans having sex is mentioned) it says, *"⁵Now The Lord observed the extent of the people's wickedness, and he saw that all their thoughts were consistently and*

---

[1] Maybe you are wondering how it is possible for demon spirits to have intercourse with human women and impregnate them. Throughout the Bible there is plenty of evidence that spirits can take on some type of physical form and function as such. In the book of Genesis satan, who is a spirit, took on the physical form of a serpent and spoke to Eve *(Rev 12:9, Gen 3:1-4)*. If he can take on the form of a serpent, what would prevent him from taking on the form of a human being and operating as such? The Lord God who is a Spirit also took on a physical form as Jesus Christ and functioned as a human being. Not only did The Lord and satan do this, but in the Old Testament angels also took on physical forms and functioned as human beings. If you read in Genesis, all of chapter 18 and chapter19 through verse 23 (I suggest the New Living Translation for better understanding) you will find proof of this. In the text, The Lord and two angels manifest themselves as human beings. They actually talk, eat, rest, walk, have their feet washed and even sleep. This is proof that spirits can manifest themselves in physical form. There are other scriptures that make reference to this point as well but the ones I have given are sufficient for the purpose of this book.

totally evil." It is not by coincidence that God makes this observation after sexual perversion becomes rampant on the earth. Satan knew just what he was doing when he perverted sexual intimacy on the earth. He distorted man's ability to understand relationship with God and man's ability to be intimate in worship with their Heavenly Father. As a result, because of the lack of worship and relationship with God, man became totally consumed with the evil nature of the flesh and the world. The only other sin mentioned up until this point in the Bible is murder. Both Cain and Lamech murdered. Other than that, the sexual perversion of mankind is the only sin that is mentioned.

How abominable must this sin be to God for it to cause Him to go on to say in the following verse, *"⁶So The Lord was sorry he had ever made them. It broke his heart. ⁷And God said, 'I will completely wipe out this human race that I have created'..."*? (He was speaking here of the coming flood that would destroy all life on earth except Noah and his family.) Yet, I do not believe that it is the act of sexual perversion itself that grieved God so much but instead what it symbolized concerning humanity and its relationship with Him. Not only did mankind turn away from intimacy with God, but mankind also turned to intimacy with the devil himself! Instead of receiving into us the Spirit of our King, we worshiped satan and received his spirit. *"...for whenever the sons of God had intercourse with human women, they gave birth to children who became the heroes mentioned in legends of old."* We received, conceived and gave birth to evil. God's precious wife gave herself to His enemy and bore His enemy's children and it *"broke his heart"*

The devil truly is a deceiver and a liar. Just imagine what it must have been like back in those days. Here these people were, just discovering the momentary pleasures of sexual perversion, not realizing that their souls were being destroyed in the process, as satan just sat back and watched with pleasure as they were all destroyed as a result of their wickedness! And so it is today as well.

Chapter 4:
A warning to the sanctified and to the married!

To you sanctified believers, whether single or married, who have sexual perversion in your family history and/or have committed these acts at some point in your past: Are you really liberated? After reading this you may think twice!

I really feel pressed in my spirit to more specifically address my sanctified brothers and sisters in Christ as well as those who are married, on this issue before I continue. As you will learn in the next chapter, each of the acts of sexual perversion is named after a demonic spirit that causes that act to take place. I cannot stress to you enough the importance of understanding that the chief assignment of every spirit of sexual perversion is <u>to distort our intimate relationship with God</u>. The act of sexual sin in the flesh itself is only a means to an end. The end is a distorted intimate relationship with God and if the spirit of sexual perversion that has been assigned to operate in your life can get to that end by a different means, it will. Distorting your relationship with God is the greater goal and the task that is most important to that spirit. As a matter of fact, I could have actually named this book, **"The Spirits of Worship Perversion"**!

What I am trying to get you to understand is that just because you may no longer, or even if you never did, *physically* commit acts of sexual perversion that **<u>does not</u>** mean that you do not have spirits of sexual perversion operating in your life!!! Let me give you a more practical example. A man who is infected with the HIV virus may not have any *physical* symptoms but yet that virus is still operating in his blood.

Although he may seem healthy, he is infected and in turn is able to infect others. Sometimes we as believers think that we are spiritually healthy just because we do not see any physical manifestation of the spirits that have us bound. In other words, if we do not commit the act of sin in the flesh then we believe that we are free of that particular sin or spirit, but this is not at all always the case.

I talked about how the act of sexual perversion taking place physically is just a method that is used by spirits of sexual perversion to achieve the greater goal of distorting our intimate relationship with God. For more clarity consider this analogy: A man's ultimate life's goal is to own a multi million dollar corporation. He maps out a plan of action to achieve this goal. His action plan includes going to college to get his masters degree, then starting a small business and finally growing that small business into a multi million dollar corporation. The man begins college but in the midst of his studies his rich uncle dies and wills to him an already established multi million dollar corporation. The man will now have to leave college in order to run this corporation or he will lose it. Should the man leave his studies to take his place as owner of the corporation? Well, what was his ultimate goal? His ultimate goal was to own a multi million dollar corporation. Has he achieved that goal? Yes he has.

His goal was never to go to college, it was to own a corporation. Going to college was only a method or a means that he was using to get to the greater goal at the end. He would be a fool to turn down the greater for the lesser! He may at some point in time return to school to get that degree if he thinks it will help him maintain his corporation or maybe even just for something extra to do. But, if he is never able to go back to college and is still able to maintain or increase the status of his multi million dollar corporation, he will certainly die content and satisfied with that part of his life. He has achieved his ultimate life's goal! It is the same with spirits of worship perversion. Their goal is not to get us to physically commit acts of sexual sin. Their ultimate goal is to distort our intimate relationship with God. If they can achieve this by a method other than luring us into sexual sin, they will most assuredly be satisfied. They will abandon the attempt to lure us into sexual sin in order to secure us in a place of distorted intimate relations with God.

I iterate to you again that what I am really trying to convey is that these spirits can be at work in your spiritual life even if they are not at work in your physical life. As I was writing this book, this is the revelation that really blew me away. I thought that I was just writing it to help those that are physically committing acts of sexual perversion. But, then the Holy Spirit began to reveal to me that many of the spirits of sexual perversion that I *thought* I was delivered from, I was not delivered from at all! Yes, it is true that I no longer physically commit the acts, but spiritually these spirits had still been at work in my life distorting my intimate relationship with my Lord. How deceived we Christians can be at times – so blind to satan's plans and purposes. Often times we are too wise in our own conceits *(Rom 11:25)* to receive an impartation of God's true wisdom!

Furthermore as I said earlier, I do not want to neglect to address married couples as well because herein can hide even more deception. These spirits can still be at work in our lives, both spiritually <u>and</u> **physically**, even when we are married. When I got married, I thought a marriage license was also a license to go buck wild in the bedroom (or any room for that matter). I thought that having 'legal' sex with my husband would be more gratifying and intimate than fornicating with other men had been. I was disappointed to find myself not feeling much different than I had when formerly engaging in sinful sex.

As I took my concerns to The Lord, He began to reveal to me how much perversity was yet in my husband and myself. Although we were married, the same spirits of sexual perversion that had influenced us before we had gotten married were still influencing us after we had gotten married. I would have all types of perverse images of my past while trying to be intimate with my husband. At times, I felt like I was still being raped. Other times I still felt like a prostitute or lesbian. Sometimes he would ask me to do something and I would feel like a fornicator all over again. I literally cried afterward on more than one occasion. It was really quite disturbing, and my husband was experiencing similar difficulties.

We began to really fast and pray about this issue, together and individually. We did not know what was wrong, but we did know that something was wrong. We knew that Holy matrimony and the undefiled marriage bed *(Heb 13:4)* had to be about more than what we were experiencing. The more we talked it out, fasted, consecrated, prayed and touched and agreed concerning our intimate lives, the more the Holy Spirit was able to reveal to us that spirits of sexual perversion yet had us bound.

At first it did not make much sense to me, and when I tried to seek counsel concerning this issue I either heard some undercover fiend say something like, *"Marriage is honorable and the bed undefiled. You can do whatever you want (followed by a devilish laugh and a wink of the eye)."* Or, I would talk to some deranged sex-hater who thought that everything sexual is dirty, married or not, and that a couple should only have sex to make babies, *"No touching, no kissing, no nothing. Just stick it in, plant the seed and get outta there as quickly as you can. Then go pray so God can cleanse ya!"* (OK, I know that sounds funny but this is really what some legalistic, religious folk believe.) The funny thing about it is that both groups of advisers had either never been married, were divorced or were in the midst of a miserable marriage. I was really turned aside by their opinionated lack of true wisdom concerning the matter. God does know how to get you to seek *His* face; I'll tell you that! *(laugh)*

As I sought God the more, the Holy Spirit began to reveal to me the ignorance surrounding the scripture, *"Marriage is honorable in all, and the bed undefiled: (Hebrews 13:4, KJV)"* If you look at the same scripture in the Amplified version of the Bible, you gain understanding of the message that the author was truly trying to convey, *"Let marriage be held in honor (esteemed worthy, precious, of great price, and especially dear) in all things. And thus let the marriage bed be undefiled (kept undishonored); for God will judge and punish the unchaste [all guilty of sexual vice] and adulterous."* Insight into this scripture brought me to understand that although the marriage bed itself is truly undefiled because God has ordained it Holy, the persons who lay down in it may not be.

In the Old Testament of the Bible it was made plain that if anything clean came in contact with something that was unclean, the clean thing then became unclean through that contact *(Lev chap 15)*. When defiled people come in contact with an undefiled marriage bed they can easily cause the bed to become defiled right along with them. And let us make no mistake here, when the scripture says *"bed"* it is expressly referring to the sexual relations of husbands and wives. Being able to break past the language barriers of the King James Version of the Bible with the help of the Amplified Version, we can clearly see that it is possible to be guilty of sexual perversion even within the confines of marriage. I am sorry to bust the bubble of those of you that thought you could do whatever, whenever and however once you get married. That is just not the case.

I am not going to be specific about what you can or cannot do sexually as a married couple. The Bible is not specific about it and I do not think that anyone has the right to add to what is written in Hebrews 13:4. What a married couple does in privacy is between them and their Lord. However, I will implore you married, Christian couples to come out from under the veil of deception that has you thinking that any and everything sexual is acceptable in the sight of God once you are married. Everything sexual is not acceptable in His sight. Neither becoming born again nor getting married is an automatic eviction notice for demons of sexual perversion that have already taken residence with us. It can happen that way and for some people it does, but that is not a given and is a very dangerous assumption to make. We have to, with deliberate effort, allow God to close the specific doors and tear down the specific strongholds that gave those spirits of sexual perversion access to us in the first place.

In order to know the truth about the defilement of our marriage bed, we must explore our motives behind doing something. God is always looking at the motives of our hearts and that is what He judges us based upon. Take for instance a position other than "missionary". If you watched a lot of pornography before marrying and said, *"Yeah, when I get married I wanna give it to my wife like that!"* and you then carry out that act once you get married, you are certainly being driven by a spirit of sexual perversion to have sex in that certain position. At the same time, if you do that same position say because your wife is pregnant and is uncomfortable in the "missionary" position and out of tender love for her you want to please her, then your motive is pure.

It was not until we understood these revelations about motives and our past acts that my husband and I finally began to recognize the cause of the problems in our sexual relations. There are some sexual acts that my husband and I engaged in during the earlier part of our marriage that after fasting, praying and seeking God, we realized were being influenced by sexually perverse spirits from our past and present. Some of the acts we stopped all together. Others, after being delivered from those spirits, we engaged in again with a new perspective and being motivated by intimacy instead of perversion and lust. No one had to tell us that we should stop doing certain things. Through our own personal relationship with God, the Holy Spirit led us.

The key factor in this is, *understanding the intent of your heart*. *Your* motives might permit you to engage in certain sexual practices that *my* motives may not permit me, and vice versa. That is why no one can give you a list of "dos and don'ts" as far as how you can have sex as a married couple. Please understand that even if you are in a plain, missionary position doing nothing extra, you might still be practicing perversion. At the same time you could be doing something unconventional and seemingly wild and yet be totally pure in God's eyes. It is not so much about what you are doing in the flesh as much as it is about what is going on in your heart while you are doing it, and what spirit is influencing or controlling you. The question is: Where did you learn that and why are you doing it?

Is your only goal to get a *good feeling*? Anyone (your spouse or anybody else, even yourself) can give you a *good feeling*. So if this is your only motivation for having sex with your spouse then you fail to understand what God's true purpose for intimacy in marriage is. Due to the fact that sex is the physical equivalent of worshiping God, it should be exceedingly tender and intimate. When we as Christians truly understand intimacy and perform it the way that God intended for us to, it invokes worship in our spirits. My husband and I now understand this and we enjoy intimacy immensely. Implementing God's Holiness into our lovemaking has transformed it from a mere flesh-gratifying experience into a supernatural experience of Holiness and worship. Yet, in order to get there we had to deal with truth, trust the Father and make sacrifices.

If you are married, even if you have been married for many years, and do not yet understand this revelation and are not experiencing lovemaking as a worshipful experience that glorifies God, then I would suggest to you that it is likely that spirits of sexual perversion are still operating in your life. Please do not allow ignorance to provide an opportunity for spirits of sexual perversion to retain a place in your marriage and in your relationship with your Lord. And, by no means should you fear what you might have to sacrifice sexually in your marriage to get delivered. I assure you that whatever my husband and I sacrificed is exceedingly outweighed by what God has given us in return! We do not think of, nor even slightly miss anything from our past that did not glorify Him.

I mentioned in the introduction to **Part I** that married couples should read this book as partners. It is important to understand that as a married couple **you must go through this deliverance process together**. We are going to learn in the next chapter that demons are transferable. Therefore, if both spouses are not cleansed simultaneously these demons will be passed back and forth between you and your spouse like an STD. This was a truth that my husband and I did not understand for quite some time. Even after much fasting and prayer individually, demons of sexual perversion still had an avenue to each of us through our contact with one another. I encourage husbands and wives to read this book together and partner with one another in deliverance. However, if you have an unbelieving spouse or your spouse is not willing or unable to go through this process with you please do not feel that it is hopeless. Once you acknowledge the problem you can simply anoint yourself, your bed and your spouse (while they are sleeping), and bind in the name of Jesus (Yeshua) any demons of sexual perversion from affecting you before and after intercourse. *(Bind the spirits out loud but not in your spouses hearing. That would be a definite turn off, [smile].)* Then continually pray for your spouse, standing in the gap for him or her. Most importantly, you must live uprightly before your spouse until they are fully delivered (and continually afterward of course!)

──

Please hear what the Spirit is saying to us my brothers and sisters in Christ. Whether we are single or married believers, there is still a great likelihood that spirits of sexual perversion are yet operative in our lives. These spirits could be manifesting themselves physically and their works could be blatantly obvious, or even more dangerously they could be manifesting themselves only spiritually while being deceptively subtle. Either way, the assignment of these spirits of sexual perversion in our lives is still the same – to distort our intimate relationship with God. If our intimate relationship with The Lord becomes distorted, everything in our lives will be distorted as well.

Without proper intimacy with God we are not strongly connected to Him. Jesus is the vine and we are the branches *(John 15:5)*. So without that connection we will not be able to produce abundant fruit – maybe no fruit at all. Anything that does not produce fruit will be cut down and burned up *(Mat 3:10)*. How we interact with God also affects how we interact with people. Therefore, a distorted relationship with Him is also going to distort our relationships with others including our spouses, children, friends and etcetera. How then will we be effective witnesses for Christ? Furthermore, we as Christians are all a part of Jesus' **One** Body. Thus, distorted relations with The Lord means distorted relations with one another as sisters and brothers in Christ as well. Consequently, each spirit of worship perversion plays an integral role in the disunity and dysfunction of the Body of Christ as a whole.

Are you beginning to understand the depth of this thing? It is about so much more than just you as an individual committing an act of sin. Satan is at war with the Body of Christ in an attempt to completely destroy us all. Even though he is already defeated, his demons of sexual perversion have an important role in his greater plan to destroy as many believers as possible. Part of what keeps us in deception concerning this issue is the confusion surrounding the question of whether or not a Christian can be *possessed* with a demon. Although there is a correct and incorrect answer to this confusion, we do not need to specifically address this issue. Do you know why we do not need to address it? – Because it does not matter. Listen, whether you are possessed, oppressed, suppressed or otherwise; whether the demon is living in you, on you or just hovering around you; it really does not matter. The effects are still devastating at any rate and the way you get delivered from these demons is basically the same regardless. You must bind every demon that is operating in your life on any level and the question of *possession* matters very little.

So how will you know if these spirits are operating in your spiritual life or your marriage? If you open your heart to receive Jesus' truth, it will be revealed to you as you read on. As I stated previously, I was not writing this book thinking that I needed to be delivered from anything of the sort. I was certain that I was victoriously free from all spirits of sexual perversion. Yet, my heart was receptive to the truth and as the Holy Spirit wrote through my hands, I realized that in some instances I was only free from the act but not the spirit.

When you begin to read Chapter 6, pay close attention to the assessment of each spirit. Be especially mindful of what is written under the heading entitled, **"Manifestation in the spirit"**, that will be listed for each spirit that is assessed. In that section the Holy Spirit exposes the behavior of believers that are operating under those particular spirits and it is written particularly with believers that may not be committing the *physical* acts of sexual sin, in mind. These sections were essentially helpful to me. It was as I wrote these sections that I most realized I was yet in need of deliverance.

In conclusion, let us understand Church that for the sake of our own soul salvation, our marriages, our personal happiness and the Body of Christ as a whole, it is so important that we allow Jesus to truly heal and deliver us in totality. If we do not allow the Holy Spirit to reveal the truth to us about our own hearts, we will be just like the person who is carrying the HIV virus but does not know it. We will be spreading infection and disease to others while we ourselves will be in danger of dying a miserable, tortuous death. God will hold us accountable for our carelessness and selfishness because He forewarns us in Jeremiah 17:9 that *"The heart is deceitful above all things, and desperately wicked..."* Deceitful above **_all_** things? Wow, what a powerful statement! Are you sure that you have not been deceived by your deceitful heart into *thinking* that you are delivered? You better be really, really sure.

Chapter 5:
≈≈≈≈≈≈≈≈≈≈
Defining sexual perversion

Having a clear understanding of exactly what sexual perversion is will strengthen the foundation that we have built thus far.

It is almost time to look at the assessments, but before we go on to the next chapter let us build on the knowledge that we have gained thus far by looking into the definitions of the words 'sexual' and 'perversion'. We do not want to leave any room for satan to deceive us. We therefore need a crystal-clear understanding of exactly what sexual perversion is. According to Merriam-Webster's On-line Collegiate Dictionary, **sexual** can be defined as *'Of, relating to, or involving sex, the sexes, or the sex organs.'* The root word of perversion is pervert. According to that same dictionary **pervert** means *'1. To lead away from the proper, right, or accepted course: corrupt. 2. To use wrongly or improperly: misuse.'* It also lets us know that the word **perversion** means *'1. The act of perverting or state of being perverted. 2. A deviant form of sexual behavior'* (www.Merriam-WebsterCollegiate.com 12/05/2004).

Therefore, for Christians who base our lives on the Law and Righteousness of God, a comprehensive definition of **sexual perversion** is "Deviation from God's ordained sexual intimacy between husband and wife; misuse of sex and/or sex organs; corruption of sexual intimacy in thought or in action as it relates to God's plan and purpose for it." Sexual perversion would include any and all sexual acts that do not take place *in privacy, between* a lawfully (*in the sight of God*) married husband and wife. Understanding the definition of sexual perversion enables us to concisely outline what behaviors fall into this category. There are ten manifestations of sexual perversion that I noted that are expressly outlined and/or described in the Bible:

    **1. Fornication, 2. Masturbation, 3. Adultery,
4. Incest, 5. Homosexuality, 6. Prostitution,
7. Pornography/Sexual fantasy, 8. Rape/Pedophilia,
9. Beastiality and 10. Sexual Lust (Lasciviousness).**

For the most part these exact terms will not be found in the King James Version of the Bible (which is the most widely used version). However, there are scriptural references that do describe these specific acts of sexual perversion in accordance with our definition and understanding of them. Coming up in the next chapter we are going to gain a better understanding of each of these acts of sexual perversion named above by doing a detailed assessment of every one. We will also assess the assisting spirit, promiscuity. Let me explain to you the lay out of the upcoming assessments in order to increase your understanding.

You will first see the name of the act listed and then there will be six headings listed under each name. The first of the six headings will be "**Definition**". Under this heading will be a brief definition of the act itself. The second heading will be "**Assignment**". The Holy Spirit revealed to me that each classification of sexual perversion is also the name of a type of demonic spirit that is responsible for causing that act of sexual sin to take place on the earth. For example, if you fornicate then "the spirit of fornication" is at work in your life. Remember, we discussed in chapter 3 that satan's purposes always go beyond just the act of sin taking place. Ultimately, he wants us to be eternally damned and tries to cause this by clouding our understanding of our relationship with the Father. Subsequently, each type of demon of sexual perversion has a very specific spiritual assignment and duty. I will discuss the assignment and duty of each of these demons under this second heading.

The third heading listed will be "**Manifestation in the natural**". In this section, I will be more specific about the spirit's assignment, give a more detailed description of the acts you may commit, discuss your mental and emotional state, your personality traits and your social interaction with others. Then there will be the fourth heading, "**Manifestation in the spirit**". Here, I will write about how the particular demon that is being discussed manifests itself in people's spiritual lives. This will include how it distorts a person's relationship with God, what bearing it has on a person's likelihood to be a Christian, how it causes people to act as believers (if they are believers) and how it affects their interaction with other believers.

Then I will share with you a little bit of my testimony and personal experiences with each of these demons under a heading listed as, "**My personal experience**". I wanted to include this section to help you understand how to trace back over your life and find the entrance wounds that allowed in these spirits. (We will talk more about this in **Part II**.) I also, as I mentioned in the intro warning, truly want you to be able to see yourself in my testimony. I know that sharing my personal experiences with you will really encourage you to press on toward deliverance. And finally, there will be a heading listed as "**Biblical references**". This section will contain information about scriptures in the Bible that you can refer to as you read about each spirit and act of sexual perversion that we discuss.

Prior to moving on to the breakdown of the different types of sexual perversion, I would like to lay a little more ground information. Just as the ten terms of sexual perversion already noted will not be found verbatim in the King James Version of the Bible, neither will you find the term "sexual perversion". This is simply due to the cultural and language differences of the era in which the King James Version was written. In the Old Testament the terms 'adultery', 'harlot(ry)' and 'whore(dom)' are often used in place of the term 'sexual perversion'. In the New Testament the term fornication, which literally translates in the Greek *'illicit sexual intercourse',* is widely used in place of the term 'sexual perversion'.

In some newer translations of the Bible you may see the terms 'sexual perversion' or 'sexual immorality'. You may even see some of the ten terms of sexual perversion noted above referred to using the same names. It all depends on what translation you are reading. What is most important though is that we are not deceived about the truth of God's Word by getting caught up into minor language issues. Any person that sincerely desires to know the truth and desires to understand the *Spirit* of God's Holy Word will successfully be led by His Holy Spirit past every language barrier.

Another term you will see in the assessments is "sexual contact", which is used in many of the definitions that you will read. I want you to have a clear understanding of exactly what this term means. Inclusive in this term is oral sex, anal sex, manual sexual stimulation, sexual stimulation using any type of object or any type of physical contact (i.e. grinding, dirty dancing, humping with or without clothes on, etcetera) that is performed **with the intent** to sexually stimulate or cause an orgasm. This does not always but can even include kissing depending on how it is done.

By worldly standards sex has to include penetration, but by God's standard of Righteousness it only has to include the motive and intent to sexually stimulate and gratify. The Father judges us by a much more strict standard, according to the motives of our hearts *(1 Sam 16:7, Jer 11:20, Heb 4:12)*. **Please be mindful that I am not saying all of the acts that are inclusive in the term 'sexual contact' are sinful**. I am simply explaining to you what the term *'sexual contact'* means. Different types of sexual contact may or may not be upright within the confines of marriage depending on your motives. As I stated earlier, what is lawful for you in your marriage is between you and your Lord.

You will also see the terms "law", "lawfully" or "legal" in some of the definitions. Often times there are conflicts between modern law and culture and biblical law and culture. When this is the case we should adhere to the laws and customs of the region and culture that we currently live in. The Bible tells us to obey the laws of the land *(Rom 13:1-3)*; therefore we are to be subject to the laws of whatever government we are currently under. The only time we are not obligated to adhere to the laws of the government is when they are blatantly and unquestionably contrary to the Word. Unfortunately, because of the evil nature of the world that we live in this is often the case. Thus ultimately, whenever we think about what is legal or lawful we should <u>first of all</u> be considering what is lawful in the sight of our God according to the Spirit of Holiness that convicts us. <u>Secondly,</u> for issues that deal specifically with the government and secular law, we should consider the laws and customs of the time and region that we live in *now*, not what *was* legal according to customs and culture in Bible times. Please bear these things in mind as you read on.

I want you to be aware that as you begin to read the assessments you will probably find that you have more than one of these spirits operating in your life. In essence, all of these spirits are under the authority of a greater demonic power and therefore they all work in conjunction with one another. However, there can only be one ruler per kingdom. Although there may be more than one spirit of sexual perversion operating in your life, only one of them is what I will call *"the strongman" (Mat 12:29)*. This is the one that has the most control and dominates within you.

Pay attention to the descriptions of how these spirits manifest themselves in your life both naturally and spiritually, and ask God to reveal to you which spirit is the strongman. This is the demon that you may experience your greatest struggles with when seeking deliverance. Also be mindful of the fact that the dominating spirit in your life can change. For example, the strongman of sexual perversion may be different now that you are married than it was when you were a single college student. You want to identify which spirit is the strongman now and what other spirits may have been the strongman at other seasons of your life. Having this knowledge will greatly assist you in the process of deliverance that we will talk about in **Part II** of the book.

The first two steps that will be discussed in the deliverance process are going to depend heavily on how closely you pay attention to these assessments. In step one you must acknowledge the sins in your life and therefore must be fully aware of what those sins are. You must be able to recognize sin as sin. In step two I will teach you how to trace back over your life and track the opening that demons entered in through. For instance, maybe a wound of sexual molestation left an opening for a spirit of homosexuality to enter your life. Or, perhaps a generational curse left an opening for incest.

Identifying the strongman (or strongmen) is necessary because knowing which spirit is the strongman will give you insight into the severity of the particular entrance that it entered in through. In other words, it will help you discover how the strongman became so strong – what weakness did it take advantage of? In this way, you will be better equipped to tear down those fortified strongholds of satan. It is a good idea to print out the '*Sexual Perversion Definitive Charts*' which can be found in Appendix A (pg 284), which is located in **The Deliverance Workbook**. Use the charts to help you keep track of which spirits are at work in your life and which ones you think may now be, or have in the past been the strongman. Each spirit's operation can be evaluated on a scale of 1 -10.

The descriptions of how these demons manifest themselves in your life are very specific. You may find that some of the personality, emotional, mental, social and spiritual descriptions listed under certain spirits only describe you to a certain extent. That is simply an indication that the particular spirit that you will be reading about is not the strongman or that you are not yet totally given over to that spirit. You should know though that the longer you allow that demon to operate in your life the more strength it will gain and the more you will become like the description that you will read. In other cases though, concerning another spirit, the descriptions may fit you almost to a tee. It will probably be almost as if I had been reading your mind, living in your heart and spying out your business! That is how you will know what the strongman in your life is. In either case, make note of this in your journal and on the evaluation charts in order to help you make your determination. (Please <u>do not</u> try to use the charts to make a determination without reading the detailed assessments in chapter six!)

As we take a look into how these demons manifest themselves in your life, some of the descriptions will be a little rough. They may even be offensive to you if you have some of these characteristics, which of course are for the most part negative. However, God corrects those whom He loves and He gives us wisdom in areas where we are ignorant *if* we allow Him to *(Heb 12:6, James 1:5)*. Please do not allow a spirit of offense to harden your heart against God's truth. People are only offended when they feel the need to defend themselves, but you need not ever defend yourself against the truth. The Bible lets us know that it is the truth that makes us free *(John 8:31-32)*.

These are demons that we are talking about, not sweet little fairies. The demons are ugly and the way that they manifest themselves in your life is ugly too! You can take comfort in knowing though that it is not so much you that is being described as much as it is the demon operating through you that is being described. These are the same truths that I had to face when going through my own deliverance process from spirits of sexual perversion. It was hard sometimes to acknowledge who I truly was as a person in bondage. Yet, I was always encouraged to continue on because I knew that however these demons were manifesting themselves in my life was not what God created me to be. I knew and understood that if I could just allow the Holy Spirit to expose my enemies to me and empower me to break free from their bondage that those ugly truths about me would change.

Please remember and be assured throughout the book that I understand what you are going through and that I am for you and not against you. Anything that is said in this book is not being said to put you down or make you feel bad or guilty. Everything that is being said is being said to expose satan and take away his power. I want to de-power satan in your life and empower you with the might of the Lord God Almighty. Reading through the definitions, assessments and breakdowns of each of these spirits and how they manifest themselves in your life will be hard at times because you will be forced to look at yourself in Jesus' bright light of truth and see yourself in a way that you never have before. But my prayers are with you and so is God. I do not want you to be afraid because you are not alone on this journey.

Why should you continue to hide the truth from yourself? You are not fooling anyone else. Everyone else sees. You are the only one shrouded in deception about who you really are. So let down your defenses down and be prepared to drink the bitter waters of truth that will follow. The end result will be sweet. I guarantee you that! As we take this journey, if you press on until the end, you will achieve your goal of deliverance and freedom!!!

♦♦

Dear Father, I pray that You will strengthen your child as he or she reads on. I pray that their hearts, ears and eyes will be open to receive whatever it is that You want to reveal to them as they read the remainder of this book. I pray that they will be encouraged and excited to read through to the end and that they will feel Your Enduring Love, mercy and grace surround them as they do. I also pray that by Your mighty power they will be fully equipped with desire, insight and understanding in order to completely obey and carry out Your instructions that will be given to them for the purpose of enabling them to be totally delivered, walking in newness of life abundantly and victoriously. In Yeshua's Mighty Name, it is so, because You Lord Yahweh Almighty have said it. Hallelujah! Thank you Yeshua!!!

♦♦

OK, let's not forget these three key points that we've learned:

1) **The definition of Sexual perversion:** "Deviation from God's ordained sexual intimacy between husband and wife; misuse of sex and/or sex organs; corruption of sexual intimacy in thought or in action as it relates to God's plan and purpose for it."

2) **What sexual perversion literally means**: any and all sexual acts that do not take place *in privacy, between* a lawfully (*in the sight of God*) married husband and wife.

3) **What sexual contact means:** oral sex, anal sex, manual sexual stimulation, sexual stimulation using any type of object or any type of physical contact (i.e. grinding, dirty dancing, humping with or without clothes on, etcetera) that is performed **with the intent** to sexually stimulate or cause an orgasm. This does not always but can even include kissing depending on how it is done.

*Please remember that I am not saying that sexual contact in necessarily wrong within the confines of marriage. I am just defining what it is. *

Now, Get ready; Get set; Let's go!!!

Chapter 6:

Assessment of the spirits of sexual perversion

Now let us get an understanding of each spirit of sexual perversion, their assignment and the affects that they have on your life. Knowledge is power!

1. Fornication

"Now the works of the flesh are manifest, which are these; Adultery, fornication, uncleanness, lasciviousness ... as I have also told you in time past, that they which do such things shall not inherit the Kingdom of God." (Gal 5:19-21, KJV)

Definition
Sexual intercourse or any type of sexual contact between partners who are not lawfully married to each other.

Assignment
The spirit of fornication is assigned to impart into us the idea that we can enjoy the pleasures of God without being committed to Him.

Manifestation in the natural
There are numerous references to fornication in the Bible. However as I mentioned earlier, biblically, fornication is a word that was used to mark a multiplicity of sexually perverse acts. This is because in essence every act of sexual perversion is actually an act of fornication since no matter which act you commit you are having sex without being married. But for our basic understanding, we commonly think of fornication as a sexual relationship between an unmarried male and female. This is the context in which I will refer to fornication in the book,

but you should be mindful of the truth that all sexually perverse acts are a type of fornication.

For the most part, in biblical culture unless you were a prostitute, an adulterous woman, a homosexual or were a victim of rape you were considered lawfully married to whomever you had intercourse with. There was usually some type of verbal agreement between the families of the bride and groom and also a ceremony. However, these measures were not required and did not always occur. Once intercourse took place, you were considered to be lawfully married.

In our culture and times today things are quite different. Sex is so loosely regarded that it holds very little significance at all. Therefore, to be lawfully married in the US money has to be paid, a license has to be obtained, paperwork has to be filed and a qualified person has to perform a ceremony. Of course, we must remember that when we are talking about what is lawful, we are first considering what is lawful in the sight of God. No matter what the government says, God only honors marriages between one man and one woman. Unless you go through all of the practical steps mentioned above, with only one person of the opposite sex, you are not lawfully married in the sight of The Lord – meaning that **_any_** sex(ual contact) you engage in is sin.

Type 1: There are three classifications of fornicators. You are a **type 1** fornicator if you are involved with someone that does not want to commit to marriage with you and yet you are willing to settle for an illicit sexual relationship with that person. In this case you are suffering from low self-esteem and lack a sense of self-worth. You probably feel like nobody loves you. You would get married if you could, but you know that you cannot make that happen. You have been or will probably be in many relationships like this because you are highly sensitive and insecure. A relationship with you becomes very tedious after a while and you are prone to being on the receiving end of a break-up. If your partner does stay with you, it is unlikely that he or she will be faithful to you because you take the fun out of being in an uncommitted relationship. This is due to your high expectations of your partner and ever-pressing desire to marry. Because each break up makes you feel that much worse about yourself, you are that much more likely to get into the same type of relationship again.

You tend to settle for less in life. You allow others to take advantage of you without much complaint. It is not that you do not desire more, you just feel like it is out of your control to make it happen for yourself. You lack the courage and motivation to try to do better. You know in your heart that you could have more if you would try, but somewhere along the way someone spoke damaging words over you and you learned to settle for less. You are full of self-pity and crave major attention. You often times over exaggerate your woes to gain notice, but even once you gain the attention of others it is still never enough.

You are probably a person that likes being sick for the attention that it can bring you. You will for example, put up the appearance of extreme illness for something as minor as a cold or a headache. People usually *tolerate* you instead of *celebrate* you. You call everyone your "friend" but in all honesty most of those so-called friends are just "putting up with you" so to speak. You are probably totally oblivious to this though. Your constant need for attention is just a turn off to most people. However, just as you cling to your non-committing sexual partner, so do you cling to others. You are a hard one to get rid of. You hate to be alone and will always try to find some way to be in the presence of others. You feel depressed and lonely when you are by yourself.

Type 2: You are a **type 2** fornicator if you find that others are not "worth the trouble" of commitment. In this case you are an arrogant, cocky person who is selfish and cares very little about the well being of others. Arrogance and pride are usually a cover for insecurity, and more than likely you are afraid of being hurt more than anything else. You may even harbor a secret desire to get married, but you would rather hurt first than be hurt. You would never say that though, instead you use people for what you can get out of them and then move on. You usually choose a **type 1** person to have sex with because being with a person like yourself is too threatening. You want to be in control of the relationship. You feel easily threatened in life in general and want to be in control of everything. You are more than willing to abuse others to make yourself feel more secure, although deep in your heart you never really do feel secure.

You feel empowered to know that you have someone at your mercy and like to exercise that power by playing a lot of mind games. Sometimes you pretend to be very warm and other times you are cold and calculating. It is all part of the game that you play (with yourself more than anyone else). You crave that sense of empowerment. People may sometimes see you as almost having a split personality because you are so unpredictable. Although you can be a really nice person, you do not want anyone trying to get too close to you and you make sure of this by readily exhibiting the dark side of your personality. You are just nice enough to keep people drawn to you, but cutting enough to let them know that they should keep their distance.

You may have been the victim of a **type 2** fornicator in the past and this is your way of avenging yourself. Undoubtedly, someone made you afraid to love. You lost something or someone dear to you and you do not want to lose again. That is why you must stay in control. As long as you do not get too attached you can give up the relationship easily without a second thought, but if your heart gets involved you will be crushed if it is taken away from you like whatever was taken from you in your past.

Type 3: You are a **type 3** fornicator if you are afraid of failure. You are currently or have been in the past, in a relationship with someone that you would like to commit to but fear that the marriage would be a failure. You fear failure in all areas of your life. You are a cautious person that is seldom willing to take risks. You also suffer from low self-esteem; you do not believe in yourself. At the same time, you exhibit a measure of selfishness because of how you hurt those that you are unwilling to commit to. You act like a spouse in many ways but refuse to give up the safety net of freedom that excuses you from the responsibility of a marriage commitment. In life you may be an irresponsible, unreliable person that often messes up everything you put your hand to. This is done intentionally since you do not put forth much effort. This is because if you never really tried then no one can ever say you failed.

Just as the **type 1**, you too are a person who is full of self-pity over the many failures of your life and you crave sympathy. You do not realize that you live in a world that you have created for yourself that you could easily get out of. You have many regrets over past decisions that you have made and opportunities that you have blown, but to you the end justifies the means. The end is that you avoid the devastation of failure. You feel that you have failed at something very important at some point in your past and you just never want to experience that heartache again. You live not to achieve your future goals but instead to avoid your past failures or the failures that you observed in the lives of others.

You live in a bubble. What a life of bondage you have created for yourself. You may even have convinced yourself that it is OK to test out the merchandise for right now because you will get married "one day", but the truth is that it is not in your heart to do so. You are the type of fornicator that will probably keep the same sexual partner for years if possible and even live together with that person as long as you do not have to get married. You tell them that you will one day, but like I said, it is not in your heart to do so. If both you and your partner are **type 3** fornicators, it is unlikely that you will ever marry or that the relationship will ever end or change. You will probably be trapped forever unless someone becomes truly born again and delivered!

These are the three types of fornicators all produced by the spirit of fornication. You could be a mix of two or even all three of these types of fornication since all of these acts are implemented by the control of the same demonic stronghold. There are also those that fornicate that do not classify as a **type 1, 2,** or **3**. For example, some engaged couples that are not believers fornicate out of deception. They do it because they do not acknowledge Jesus as Lord and are blind to the truth that it is sin. Others may be in a relationship with the awareness that fornication is a sin but still do it anyway. They either lack self-control or just do not care. Others do it strictly for the sexual pleasure of it. Although all of these persons just named commit the sin of fornication, this demon is not their strongman. It is some other demon such as sexual lust, deception or unbelief that is the mastermind behind the fornication in the lives of people like this. Most likely people who fall into these categories are under the control of the spirit of sexual lust.

Regardless of which type of fornicator you may be, you are completely devoid of any sense of loyalty. You can bail out of the relationship whenever you choose to, for whatever reason without recognizable consequence. The real deception is that as fornicators you can do what any married couple can do. You even possess the same creative power that a married person does, but your family unit will never be complete without the commitment of marriage. Therefore, reproduction for you is dysfunctional. With marriage comes a certain type of security that you lack and if you do have children you will pass that lack of security on to them. Yes, you can do what any married couple can do, but the key elements of commitment, loyalty, covenant and trust are all missing. It is like trying to have a picnic indoors. It is not a picnic because the essence of a picnic is that it is held outdoors. You may say it is love, but it is not love because the essence of love is sacrifice, loyalty and commitment.

Manifestation in the spiritual

America is a nation that is laden with fornication. We sing "God Bless America" at every major event. Yet, at the same time we allow same sex marriages, abortion, drunkenness, witchcraft…and the list goes on and on. We want the pleasures of God without making any type of sacrifice to commit to Him. A fornicator's relationship with God, whether or not they actually physically commit the act, will be one that lacks sacrifice and commitment. A **type 1** person probably wants a committed relationship with God but believes that He is not willing to give this to him or her. A **type 2** person does not feel that all the sacrifices that have to be made in order to have a relationship with God are worth it. And, a **type 3** person fears that they will fail in a relationship with God so refuse to give it their all. These people know The Lord only casually but expect Him to be available for the pleasures of life when they are in need.

Spiritual fornicators are very likely to be believers. They call it love and feel that they deserve pity and therefore believe that how they live is OK. Fornicators are people that go to church only on holidays or special occasions – or even worse club hop, sex and drink all Saturday night and sing in the choir Sunday morning! Fornicators are the worldly musicians that sing about and glorify every damnable thing in satan's kingdom and then say, *"I would like to thank God for this."* when they win a Grammy. Fornicators only pray when they are sick or in big trouble.

The ones that do spend time in church are not reliable in their church commitments. If they are a **type 1** person they may try to commit to everything in the church but always find a reason to believe it is not going to work out for them. If a **type 2** fornicator, they try to play a lot of mind games with the leadership of the church. They want leadership to feel at fault for their lack commitment. They do not show up for rehearsal but still want a part on the night of the big show. **Type 3** fornicators will jump from auxiliary to auxiliary never putting much effort into any of them. The spirit of fornication keeps them all from making a commitment to their belief in Jesus and therefore they see very little spiritual growth in their lives.

Just as is the case with fornicators in the natural, fornicators in the spirit often claim that they love Jesus. However, no one that is unwilling to truly commit to Jesus and sacrifice their life on His behalf loves Him at all: Just think about all the sacrifice and commitment that it takes to build and maintain a marriage. A married person ceases to exist as an individual. The Bible says that the two shall become one *(1 Cor 6:16)*. A spouse literally has to die to self in order to be a good husband or wife. We have to die to self if we want to be a true servant of God and become one with Him and not just once, but we must die daily *(1 Cor 15:31)*.

Every time a married person sees an area of their own desire that hinders their relationship with their spouse, they have to give it up. It is the same way in our relationship with Jesus our Lord. But fornicators refuse to make that commitment and sacrifice and do not truly love God at all. Those who are bound by this spirit are really deceived because they seem to be enjoying all the pleasures of marriage without any of the sacrifices, but if one of the partners were to die the other one would be left with nothing. People who think they can fornicate with God will be left with nothing in the end too.

My personal experience

As I mentioned earlier, I recall trying to commit fornication as early as six years of age. This spirit had so many different ways to enter into my life. Among other entrances, I was conceived in fornication and had a spiritual predisposition to participate in this sin. However, this spirit did not really take control of me until I was about fifteen, which is the age at which I first voluntarily had sexual intercourse. It all began because of the rejection and insecurity that I struggled with. A childhood illness had left me quite small for my age and when I was fifteen people often thought that I was eight or nine years old. Not only was I small, but I looked funny due to the medications that I was taking. It seemed that I did not fit in anywhere and I was so insecure about myself.

I was also lacking love in my life at that time. My Dad was not in my life. My older sister was gone. My younger sister did not like me much and my Mom and I pretty much hated each other. I was really starving for love, affection and acceptance at that time and it seemed to be a fact that all of the popular girls at school that were dating the guys that I was infatuated with, were having sex and lots of it. I was therefore convinced that fornication was going to solve my problem of loneliness and rejection. I hated being a virgin. To me it was like a disease that I carried. I was desperately – and I do mean **_desperately_** – trying to find someone to break the "curse" of virginity off of me. Not only did I want to have sex, but I wanted everyone to know that I did it and then I wanted to do it again and again with different people until the word was out that *"Laneen will give it up."*

    I was literally striving to get a reputation as a slut and you better believe that it did not take long for my plan to take effect. Initially, insecurities about my body and the fear of pain during intercourse caused me to work at a modest pace. I was still sick at that time, totally underdeveloped physically and still experiencing quite a bit of pain from the disease Lupus. However, those fears and inhibitions subsided more and more with each sexual encounter and I became stir crazy for sex before I hit seventeen. What a fool I was thinking that sex would gain me popularity. What it did was make me notorious. Girls hated me. Guys had no respect for me and adults pitied me. I had completely lost control of my life and it was too late for me to get it back. Not only did I fail to feel better about myself. I actually experienced even more rejection and greater insecurities.

    I heard this quote from a preacher once before. I don't know his name but he said:

> *"Sin always takes you further than you wanted to go;*
> *Always keeps you longer than you wanted to stay;*
> *Always costs you more than you wanted to pay."*

That is one of the most dynamic quotes I have ever heard and it proved so true in my life, especially concerning fornication.

    Throughout my years of committing fornication, I experienced being on the receiving and giving end of all three types of fornication. I would have to say that I spent most of my time as a **type 1** fornicator though. Being in **type 1** relationships often led to severe depression and many suicide attempts. It was really a vicious cycle because the more relationships like this I experienced the more likely I was to be involved in another one. My sense of self-worth diminished more and more with each experience until… well I will tell you what happened a little later because that is actually another spirit.

At any rate, before I was finally freed of this spirit I would have had sex with scores of different men. It got to the point that I did not even care anymore. I very seldom got pleasure out of the intercourse. It was just something to do. I thought that if I did it enough times I might finally come across someone who really loved me and wanted to marry me. It was like playing the lotto to me. People never really think that they are going to win, but they keep on dreaming and playing anyway. And then when they have those close calls with winning, it only drives them to play it more and more. *"Hey, you never know."* Right? That is how I felt about having sex with men.

It is funny though. The Father wanted to show me how wrong I was. The man that He sent to me as my husband and king was a serious and sincere Man of Faith. He was no virgin or no stranger to perversity, but he had been abstinent for nearly six years when we met. True, he penetrated me spiritually from the first day, but he did not penetrate me sexually until our wedding night. He knew all about my past, but he did not care. He loved the awesome Woman of Anointing that he saw when he looked into my spirit and committed to never defile that woman. I was going about it the wrong way all of those years. I thank Yeshua for His redemption, but I assure you that it took quite some time for me to learn how to receive my husband's love and not continue to act as if I was on the receiving end of yet another relationship founded in fornication.

Biblical references
Leviticus 18:20; Romans 1:24, 1 Corinthians 6:13, 18; Galatians 5:19; 1 Thessalonians 4:3 and Jude 1:7

Note: As you read on please understand that because every act of sexual perversion is also an act of fornication, each of the acts that will follow are different manifestations or categories of fornication, which means that you will have some or all of the characteristics that have been listed under the heading of fornication.

2. Masturbation

"Run away from sexual sin! No other sin so clearly affects the body as this one does. For sexual immorality is a sin against your own body." (1 Cor. 6:18)

Definition
The act of sexually stimulating oneself, usually until orgasm is achieved without another person being involved.

Assignment
The spirit of masturbation is assigned to bring us to a place where we feel like we do not need God. This spirit is all about a false sense of empowerment and control fostered by a sense of inadequacy and isolation.

Manifestation in the natural

A lot of people debate over whether or not masturbation is a sin. Many people want to confine the Word of God to our limited English language and vocabulary. Because in their hearts they desire to commit acts of sin, they feign ignorance due to the fact that every evil act is not noted in black and white in the Bible. But, the Bible tells us in Romans 1:18-19, *"¹⁸But God shows his anger from heaven against all sinful, wicked people **who push the truth away from themselves**. ¹⁹For the truth about God is known to them instinctively. God has put this knowledge in their hearts."*

Admittedly, there is no scripture in the Bible that says, "Thou shall not masturbate", but 1 Corinthians 6:18 *(NLT)*, *"Run away from sexual sin! No other sin so clearly affects the body as this one does.* **For sexual immorality is a sin against your own body."** makes it very clear that the Apostle Paul is referring to the act of sexually stimulating oneself in this scripture. Every other type of sexual sin involves another person or creature. Masturbation is the one act of sexual perversion that you commit using your own body against your own body, **"*For sexual immorality is a sin against your own body.*"** Masturbation does not just mean using your hands either. It can involve stimulating yourself with some type of object, or it can be as simple as purposefully allowing your clothing or bed covers to caress your genitals in a sexually stimulating way. It does not even have to involve touching at all. If you know how to flex and relax your genital muscles in a sexually stimulating way or how to fantasize yourself into an orgasm that too is masturbation. Remember, it is not so much what you do or how you do it, as much as it is why you do it – what is the intent of your heart?

As a masturbator you were probably teased a lot as a child and neglected by your parents in some sense. You learned to be a loner at some point in your life. Masturbation is similar to fornication in that it yields sexual pleasure without commitment but is different in that it is a totally selfish act. Therefore, if masturbation is your strongman you are undoubtedly a very selfish person in many ways. You are also a stubborn, arrogant and controlling person. Masturbation in a sense takes a bit more effort than intercourse in that you are accomplishing alone what usually takes two people to accomplish, so you are a hard worker. But, your admirable work ethic only adds to your arrogance. Being able to give that type of sexual pleasure to yourself invokes a false sense of empowerment and isolates you from the need of other people. Because you give the credit to yourself for every pleasurable thing in life, you are an unappreciative person. Your thinking is that even though someone may have helped you, you never "needed" their help anyway. As far as you are concerned, you don't "need" anyone's help.

Although you feel as if you do not need anyone, the truth is you are one of the loneliest people on earth. The isolation from people is a cover for a feeling of inadequacy. You work hard for everything in life but do not see the results that you desire. This is because masturbation leaves a void. It is like someone who uses a surrogate mother to birth a child for them. They do get a baby in the end but always carry a void from missing the experience of pregnancy and childbirth. Likewise, you achieve orgasm in the end but there is a void where the intimacy should have been. You already feel void before you start the act of masturbation and that sense of void is only magnified when the act is complete. Because of this void and your past and present woes you are full of self-pity. You feel so sorry for yourself and want to drown away your troubles in an orgasm.

The spirit of masturbation lures you further and further into a state of inadequacy. The harder you work the greater the void becomes because all of your effort is still not producing the desired result. This sense of inadequacy begins to take over all aspects of your life. The isolation from others seems like a good way to protect yourself. By performing only for yourself you can keep your inadequacy from being exposed to others and offer yourself some relief but that is a deception. The truth is, you set a standard for yourself that is so high that it is impossible to ever achieve and you judge yourself more harshly than anyone else ever would.

You make yourself devoid of the encouragement and affirmation of others by isolating yourself and spend the majority of your waking moments beating yourself down mentally and emotionally. By isolation, I do not necessarily mean that you keep people away from you physically (although you may); I mean more so emotionally and mentally. No one gets close to you. No one gets to know the real you. Then, in an attempt to make yourself feel better you masturbate seeking to escape pressures and cares through the release of orgasm, but the pleasure is fleeting. It is like unplugging a bath drain to let the water out but leaving the taps open so that more water continues to run into the tub at full speed. You never really seem to feel any lighter. You will not let anyone comfort you but you are a failure at comforting yourself.

Even in marriage you are selfish. It is hard for you to focus on making your spouse feel good in lovemaking or everyday life. Your foremost thought is always how to pleasure yourself. If one or both spouses practice masturbation they have intercourse less frequently as a couple. Masturbation trains your body to expect a certain type of feeling in order to climax and when it does not get that feeling it is not satisfied. People that are truly bound by this spirit find that even after climatic sex they still need to masturbate in order to feel satisfied. That is because masturbation desensitizes the body to the touch of others and makes it responsive to your own touch instead. The more you practice masturbation the harder it is going to be for your spouse (or another person) to please you.

Masturbation is highly addictive! You can never quite achieve what it is that you are trying to achieve in masturbation. You want that feeling of inadequacy, isolation and loneliness to go away, but it is such a trap. What you are really craving is connectedness and intimacy. The Bible says that it is not good for man to be alone *(Gen 2:18)*. Masturbating will never fill that void. The truth is, the more you do it the more inadequate you feel because your desire is never satisfied no matter how much you masturbate. You try to become more innovative with it. You use all different types of devices and aides trying to fill that void. You try to make it last longer and include sexual fantasies, but the harder you work while still not getting the desired end result, the worse you feel – the worse you feel the more you want to masturbate. The more you masturbate the more isolated, selfish, arrogant and unappreciative you become. You cannot wait to get alone to masturbate again just for the sake of that five second orgasm that makes everything go away for just a moment.

When you get right down to it, masturbation is all about control. You try to control your life through the act of masturbation and you end up being a control fanatic in general. You want to control every aspect of your life and everyone involved in your life. As a masturbator, you are convinced that the way you do it is always best. As a result you are extremely critical and seldom satisfied with what anyone does for you. It is never good enough. If you feel someone has not put in enough effort you are upset about that. If someone goes the extra mile, you feel it was not necessary, even if what they do is done in an effort to please you. If you tell people what to do for you, you are depressed because they did not do it for you without being told. But if they do it without being told you are displeased because it is not done the way you would have done it yourself. When you cannot have control of what is going on around you, you just look for a way to masturbate again. What a cycle of misery!

Manifestation in the spiritual

The spirit of masturbation is a particularly deceptive and clever one. People who do not want to accept the truth about masturbation being a sin use excuses like, *"I'm not hurting anyone; It's my body and my business; I'm not thinking about doing anything wrong; It's better than having sex with someone. It's natural to masturbate, even children do it!"* I suppose this perspective is fine if you are an unbeliever because these statements all have a ring of truth to them. However, Christians who use these excuses are missing the true intentions of the spirit that has them bound, which is to isolate them from their need of God.

The idea is – if you can give yourself sexual pleasure you can give yourself anything. Sex is something that was designed by God to be performed between two people. Sex as ordained by God is all about intimacy, selflessness and lack of control. Masturbation is about just the opposite. Spiritual masturbators are probably innumerable in the church. It is such an easy sin to pull off in secret and that makes them likely to be church-goers. How often have you heard someone talk from the pulpit about masturbation? Most people, when they do talk about it, will not even use the word 'masturbation'. It is such a secret thing.

Those under the spirit of masturbation whether believers or not, will deny the Father of the one thing He desires most and that is true worship. Worship, like sex, is all about intimacy, selflessness and losing control in the presence of your Lover. A spiritual masturbator will never do this. Instead of worshiping God they worship themselves. Even though they beat themselves down emotionally, they still exalt themselves above God. They have ungrateful spirits and often times feel like The Lord has failed them in some way. They even go so far as to say that He owes them something. That is because He does not do it like they would do it themselves and their way is of course "the best way".

Instead of relying on God to give them the desires of their hearts, they get every thing they need on their own (so they think anyway). They are used to their own touch and are not sensitive to the touch of God. They think less about how to please Him and more about what He can do to please them or about how they can please themselves. Masturbation goes totally against God's perfect plan for sexual intimacy: It does not teach us that we are to worship God alone; it does not teach us anything about being intimate with God; and it totally robs us of the creative power that we have when joined together with God in spirit.

That means that masturbators are spiritually unproductive. If they are believers you may observe them fasting, studying and praying a lot yet never quite accomplishing much in the things of the Kingdom. Their ministry work is stagnant and they seem to always have some excuse for their inadequacy in ministry. They probably want to control everything in the church. They may not forthrightly say anything because of their feelings of inadequacy and desire to isolate themselves, but in their hearts they always "have a better way" to run the church. They are too arrogant to submit to leadership. If they ever happen to get into a position of leadership they are going to be the king. They will be unappreciative for the help and honor that people try to give them and very, very critical of everyone and everything. The spirit of masturbation creates selfish people that want things their way. Ultimately this spirit isolates you from the need for God and thus causes you to be cut off from all that is inclusive when in intimate relationship with Him. It is a dangerous spirit indeed and not at all the least among the spirits of sexual perversion. Depression and loneliness will be your lot until you can break free from this spirit.

Lastly, I will say that maybe you are a Christian that masturbates without conviction. You are not buying what you've just read. You truly think that it is OK to pleasure yourself in this way. The next time you lift your hands in the air to praise your Holy God, picture how messy your hands are, stained with your own body fluids after completing your indulgent act. Then remember this verse: *"³Who shall go up into the mountain of The Lord? Or who shall stand in His Holy Place? ⁴He who has **clean hands** and a pure heart, who has not lifted himself up to falsehood or to what is false, nor sworn deceitfully. ⁵He shall receive blessing from The Lord and Righteousness from the God of his salvation. (Ps 24:3-5, AMP)"* Notice how clean hands are directly related to purity of heart. How clean are your hands after you masturbate? Are these truly the same hands that you will lift before The Lord in worship? Think about that – Selah.

My personal experience

Masturbation entered into my life mainly through involuntary exposure. It was also a generational curse. (This is actually the case for all of the spirits that I will talk about. None of them were foreign to my bloodline.) I remember trying to masturbate as early as six or seven years of age, but at that time I was really just mimicking what I saw others do. I heard and saw people masturbate on numerous occasions. The night I first really did it with any conscious understanding, I was 12. A sexual impulse was stirred in me when I heard others in my home committing fornication. Sexual impulse does play a part in why we commit acts of sexual perversion. Yet, you have to understand that some spiritual weakness must exist in order to empower and drive the flesh to commit acts of sin. Our bodies are nothing but walking figures of clay. It is what exists in the spirit realm that drives us. Sexual impulses are only used to provide an opportunity for those spiritual dark areas to be manifested.

For me, the spiritual weakness that caused me to masturbate was initially loneliness being fostered and assisted by sexual lust and curiosity. I mean the impulse was there so why not do it, right? Anyway, it seemed like it was time for me to enjoy some of the adult pleasures (or so I would call them) that I saw and heard others enjoying. After all, I had just begun to go through puberty with the evidence of vaginal secretions and everything. (This was very exciting to me because as I told you previously, I was very small and underdeveloped for my age at that time and the secretions were a good sign.) Furthermore, I was definitely a candidate for inadequacy and that was another factor that empowered the sexual impulse that was stirred in my body that night. I was ugly, nerdy and underdeveloped and had recently been dumped by my first boyfriend. I was a pretty lonely child.

Nothing climactic happened that night because I did not really know what I was doing. I did not know how to pleasure myself through masturbation for a long time. I did it periodically for a couple of years without achieving climax, just mimicking what I had seen others do. I did not really know what to touch, but once I did discover how to climax at the age of fourteen, it launched me into a real addiction. My life was so unhappy most of the time and the orgasm was such a high. It only lasted for a few moments, but it was worth it. I wanted to feel that good all of the time. Besides, I felt so sorry for myself. I was full of self-pity. I felt that I deserved to feel good, and I took advantage of it.

It eventually got to the point that I could sit there and do it right at the dinner table without my mother even knowing what was going on. I did it any and everywhere I wanted to. It was my body, and I could do it if I wanted to. At least I was not having sex; that is what I figured. But, it was not long after experiencing the pleasure of orgasm that I wanted to try real intercourse. I was soon to learn though that intercourse was a disappointment after masturbation. I did not have the same control over my body during intercourse, and men had no interest in whether or not I climaxed. So, sex became something that I did for them, but masturbation I did for me.

Something else happened that first night too that I have not yet mentioned. The proof was manifested that even when we are not taught the right way to live, God's laws are known to us all along. Here I was a 12 year old girl doing this for the first time, having grown up around this type of behavior all of my life; having seen it done, heard it done, even having been coached on how to do it when I was just seven or so. I can even remember being taught in Health Ed class that masturbation was natural, a good thing to do and nothing to be ashamed of. It was a normal part of life as far as I was concerned, and yet I felt so guilty and convicted that first time I did it. In spite of my upbringing and the influences around me, I knew that what I was doing was wrong. I prayed afterward and asked God if He was still with me. I had just months before been baptized and born again. I felt the Holy Spirit present with me, but soon I hardened my heart against the conviction I felt and continued to indulge in the act. The demonic stronghold was more powerful than the conviction it yielded and I soon became a helpless and desperate victim.

I must admit that of all of the spirits of sexual perversion that I have struggled with, masturbation was the hardest for me to be freed of. Not only the physical act but also the spiritual acts of masturbation as well. Masturbation is so powerfully addictive and so easy to fall in to. When sexual impulses come, there is always that decision to make. And then learning how to be truly intimate with my husband, allowing him to have control over my body and not expect it to feel the way that it did when I did it to myself...that was not easy. But, by the Father's grace I am daily walking out my deliverance.

The Bible says that the battle between our evil nature and the Holy Spirit that lives within us will never cease *(Gal 5:17)*. I have definitely found this to be true. I do not think that we should ever claim <u>everlasting victory</u> over any act of sin or demonic spirit. You will learn in **Part II** that deliverance is going to have to be maintained daily for the rest of your life. So instead of claiming everlasting victory, we should simply celebrate each day for the victory that it brings and be determined in our hearts to walk in victory again the next day and that is what I do in terms of my victory over masturbation.

Biblical references:
Psalm 24:3-5; 1 Corinthians 6:13, 18, 7:2-4; Ephesians 5:3; and Jude 1:7

3. Adultery

"But whoso committeth adultery with a woman lacketh understanding: he that doeth it destroyeth his own soul." (Provs 6:32, KJV)

Definition
Voluntary sexual intercourse or other sexual contact between a married person and a person other than their spouse.

Assignment
The spirit of adultery is assigned to cause us to be unfaithful to God and to selfishly use Him. This is done in an effort to eventually cause total separation from God altogether.

Manifestation in the natural

Adultery is the only act of sexual perversion that is listed as forbidden in the Ten Commandments and is mentioned by Jesus several times in the Gospels. One of the reasons that adultery is mentioned so frequently and strongly in the Bible is because, as I stated earlier, in biblical times adultery was a word that was used to describe a number of different acts of sexual perversion. There is a more significant reason for this frequent mentioning as well though. We will look into this deeper significance in a moment. First, let us take a look into the types of adulterers. There are two classifications of adulterers.

Type 1: You can be classified as a **type 1** adulterer if you have sex(ual contact) with anyone other than your legal spouse, whether that person is married or unmarried. I believe that in most cases a **type 1** adulterer's spouse is not without partial responsibility for the infidelity in the marriage. There is something very crucial that you need as a **type 1** adulterer that you should be able to get from your spouse and you are not getting it. It could be something physical, spiritual or emotional, but whatever the case may be there is a void that is not being filled. Your spouse may even be magnifying the void that is in your life.

I am not saying this to help you escape taking responsibility for your own actions, but it is important for you to understand all the tactics that the spirit of adultery is using to keep you bound. A stronghold of adultery is rarely birthed out of sexual impulse and lust alone. There is something else that you feel you need and this spirit has deceived you into thinking that cheating on your spouse is the way to get that need met.

However, there are many married individuals that experience voids and needs in their lives that do not commit adultery. So why are you so prone?

You are a person that leans and depends on others entirely too much to give you a sense of wholeness and worth. You are afraid of being alone. You are afraid of being tested and experiencing pain. You do not know what your breaking point is and you do not want to find out. You just want someone to be there for you to make it all better. You more than likely experienced a lot of let downs and instability in your childhood and thus there is a part of you that never grew up, subsequently you can display a lot of immaturity at times. This also causes you to put high expectations on the person you are cheating with. You already feel that you have been let down enough in your past and by your spouse, and so you expect your side partner to make up for what your spouse lacks. You expect people to make up for the voids in your life in general. "Everybody owes you something".

You were probably a fornicator before you got married and it is highly likely that you and your spouse committed fornication with one another before making the marriage commitment. You took the vows but never got delivered from the spirit of fornication, and now two spirits of sexual perversion have you bound. You have to lie to cover up your adulterous activities; that makes you a liar. You have to scheme and deceive to keep your adulterous activities going, and that makes you a conniver. Someone who lies and connives will easily steal, so you may even be a thief. Unfortunately, the truth is that you cannot be trusted; not only by your spouse but by people in general. This spirit can even drive you to commit murder if you feel a sexual partner who tries to interfere with your marriage is threatening your security!

You like the security of being in a committed relationship, but you are unwilling to remain loyal to that commitment. You want loyalty but are not willing to give it in return. More than likely you are reluctant to divorce your spouse and would be livid to find out that your spouse is pursuing or attracted to another person. You are a user who lives by a double standard.

Type 2: You can be classified as a **type 2** adulterer if you are an unmarried person who has sex(ual contact) with a married person. Keep in mind that you are also a **type 1** fornicator and therefore have most of the characteristics of a **type 1** fornicator, including low self-esteem and a lack of a sense of self worth. Who broke your heart in the past and made you feel justified in sleeping with another person's spouse? Someone has hurt you deeply. It could have been in your childhood or in a relationship, but someone who owed you loyalty did not give it to you. For this reason, there is a part of you that feels that you are just giving back what was dealt to you. You do not believe in yourself or the possibility that anyone could ever really love you.

Probably due to your upbringing, you are a person who lacks strong morals and integrity. On the one hand you admire the commitment of the married person that you have sex with, but on the other hand you doubt that it is really real since you do not believe that it can happen for you. Thus, due to your lack of respect for yourself you have no respect for the marriages of others. As is the case with the **type 1** adulterer, you also cannot be trusted. You will tell lies, plot and scheme to get someone else's husband or wife into your bed. You want *love* anyway and anyhow you can get it and that makes you a dangerous person. You are a backstabber of the worse kind. Depending on your level of desperation, you may even sleep with the spouses of your friends and relatives. If you have not done this, you will if you continue on in the spirit of adultery. As you continue on in adulterous affairs, you become more and more destitute in your moral standards, and this begins to affect every area of your life.

This spirit can bring you to the brink of insanity and drive you to commit murder. It just makes you feel so desperate. You experience this emotional state because having a married man or woman makes you feel as if you almost have what you want – a spouse. The problem is, he or she is not yours. You begin to feel like your desire is right within your reach and start to move in desperation to grasp hold of it. You will do anything: quit your job, start using drugs, fake suicide attempts, try to conceive an unwanted baby…or even kill!

The spirit of adultery in your life plays on that same sense of inadequacy that I talked about when discussing the spirit of masturbation. You are never really satisfied because the truth of the matter is you want your own spouse, you want that loyalty and commitment to be dedicated to you. Your adulterous affair can never give that to you, and it drives you further and further into depression, hopelessness and despair. The longer your partner continues to be in relationship with you without leaving their true spouse and making a real commitment to you, the worse you feel and the more you are convinced that no one will ever really love you. You are a moody person due to your state of hopelessness. You are very sensitive and easily agitated. Most of your associates just never know what to expect from you. You can be the life of the party one moment and then all of a sudden the reality of your situation will hit you, and you will go as limp as a cooked noodle.

If only you would allow Jesus to heal your heart from the hurts of the past and allow Him to give you the love and commitment that you are so desperately seeking, then you would have the strength and courage to walk away from this dead-end relationship. You know that it is going nowhere fast, and you do not want to be in it anyway. You just do not have the confidence to get out of it. Or, maybe you play games with yourself by jumping from one married person to another claiming that this is your way of avoiding commitment and thus avoiding getting hurt, but you know this is not true. You are lying to yourself and robbing yourself of the opportunity to acquire true happiness.

Manifestation in the spiritual

I mentioned a moment ago that adultery is mentioned frequently in the Bible because it was a word used to describe a number of different sexually perverse acts. However, there is something else that is very distinct about adultery as well. Committing adultery involves the breaking of a covenant. We talked about our covenant with God a little bit in Chapter 2. Jesus' precious Blood was brutally spilled in order to establish this covenant. As believers our whole relationship with God is based on covenant. That makes adultery a particularly detrimental sin as is noted in Proverbs 6:32, *"But whoso committeth adultery ... destroyeth his own soul."*

The Bible lets us know that adultery is particularly offensive to The Lord because He is such a faithful and ever unchanging God *(1 Cor 1:9).* We also discussed in Chapter 2 how a blood covenant can only be broken by death. That is why the scripture says that by committing adultery we destroy our own souls. We are all in blood covenant with the Father and by breaking that covenant with Him through the spirit of adultery, we are literally pronouncing ourselves dead unto Him!

The **type 1** spirit of adultery is going after those that already know God and have already made sacrifices to be committed to Him but have wandering hearts. Spiritual **type 1** adulterers who are believers come to church and 'play the role' of someone who is sanctified. They are usually the loudest praisers and most faithful attendants. They try to play God just like a natural adulterer plays their spouse. They have no real intimacy with Him and are very critical of others that do because they are envious. These types of believers pray, fast, read the Bible and preach the gospel all without Holiness. They are religious Pharisees who are satisfied to maintain the *appearance* of Holiness and are totally deceived about their fast approaching appointment with hell. They feel like God has already or will at some point let them down and are determined to keep some type of contingency plan in place.

These persons are covenant breakers and cannot be trusted by God. He wants to give them His all but already knows that they will not be loyal to Him. Thus you will see stagnancy in their spiritual lives. They will often times feign anointing because they are not willing to commit to God enough to get a real anointing. They use the same deceptive tactics in church to fool others as a physical adulterer would at home to fool their spouse. Spiritual adulterers are some of the most notorious liars. They will lie right from the pulpit and swear on the Holy Ghost without conviction. Some are so good at lying that they even begin to believe their own lies after a while.

Type 2 spiritual adulterers desire to have a real relationship with God but just do not believe that He will love them. They are most often times people who were raised in church or know of Jesus but are backsliders. If they do come to church it is just a formality. They get nothing out of it and think about any and everything but the preached Word while in church. They usually come late and leave early and spend a lot of time outside of the sanctuary while there. They may have a seeming breakthrough from time to time but immediately after service go seeking out sin. Remember, these persons are also fornicators so they have no real commitment to God and will drop Him in a hot second because they do not feel a sense of oneness with Him. He is only part time just like a married sex partner. They just do not understand that Jesus is totally willing to commit to them and be truly loyal.

These are dangerous persons for other believers to hang around because just as these adulterers in the natural will do anything to draw their partners away from their spouses, so will these spiritual adulterers do anything to draw devout believers away from serving God. They try their best to convince other believers to sin with them. They are deceptive, conniving and backstabbing members of the church. These **type 2** adulterers are very valuable to satan because of their ability to draw others away from serving God. However, to God they are like the man that His wife cheated with. His wrath is stored up against them. For **type 2** adulterers the spirit of adultery really aims to keep them from ever having a truly committed relationship with God while using them to cause others to break covenant and commitment with Him. It truly does cause them to destroy their own souls!

Whether a **type 1** or **type 2** spiritual adulterer, the spirit of adultery is working against a person's commitment to God. Remember that sex is equivalent to worship and so this spirit of adultery is aiming to influence its victims to worship other gods. Whatever it can get a person to direct their attention toward and serve will be satisfactory. This is done so deceptively though because most often times what these believers end up worshiping is their own fears, inhibitions, hang ups and issues. We as Christians often times let our past wounds and negative experiences control our lives. Whatever controls us is our master and whatever is our master is what we will serve and worship. Are you a spiritual adulterer?

My personal experience

All praises to Jesus, Christ Yeshua my Lord, I have no experience as a **type 1** adulterer. As to date, my husband and I have been faithful to one another. I do however have a lot of insight into **type 1** adulterers because as a **type 2** adulterer you learn a lot about why **type 1** adulterers cheat. In my case, I learned more specifically a lot about why husbands cheat. I definitely contribute my adulterous affairs to lack of moral values and standards. I was conceived in an adulterous affair. My biological father was a **type 1** and my mother was a **type 2**.

I was then exposed to adultery once again during the marriage of my mother and stepfather when my stepfather was unfaithful. Moral character was just not a part of my upbringing. My parents tried to *teach* me the ways of the Bible through the words that they talked, but their actions did not line up with their words. They were victims of sexual perversion just as so many others are and did not know how to get free. As a result, I learned that you do what feels good; you desperately seek for happiness wherever you can find it and if it brings you a little joy in your miserable life then it can't be wrong. *(I thank Yah that both my mother and stepfather are born again believers today. My Mother is an Elder that diligently serves The Lord now and is a tremendous blessing to my husband, children and me, but this change did not occur until I was well into my adult years.)*

In my first experience as an adulterer when I was 17, I went after a married man and initiated the affair. I found him to be attractive. I knew he was married, but I wanted him and I had him. As I said, I had no moral character and was by then "the friendly neighborhood ho" and thus was totally devoid of self worth. My relationship with this man was very painful. Having to always hear about his wife; knowing that I was second choice; working around his schedule as a husband in order to spend time with him; having to lie about our relationship, even pretending we were related in some instances – it was really very depressing. No person who loves and respects themselves would subject themselves to that type of degrading abuse. But I did not love or respect myself, so it was easy for me to settle for such a relationship.

I can remember one night that this married user took me on a trip up into the mountains with some of his *homeboys.* I have always wanted to live in the type of neighborhood that we traveled to. It was beautiful. We were at some man's house. The man was a drug addict and his wife had taken the children and left him because of his drug abuse. The drug addict rented out his house to my boyfriend for the night in return for drugs. The house was gorgeous. There was a beautiful pond on the property. Looking around, it seemed that this man had everything I wanted and I was so sad that he and his wife were separated.

Ironically, I felt no sympathy for Stanley's (my married boyfriend) wife and intended to take full advantage of the opportunity that had been given to me. Stanley and I had been seeing each other for about six months at this time and had never before kissed. Kissing is something that a lot of cheating men will only do with their wife. I had never really tried to kiss Stanley and he had not told me that I couldn't kiss him, so I went for it that night. As I moved in to kiss him, he pushed my face away from his and told me that he did not kiss any woman except his wife. Then he casually tried to redirect my kiss toward his lower extremities, which I indignantly refused. He would not kiss my mouth but wanted me to kiss his... Humph – the nerve of some men!

I was crushed as the reality of my circumstances came crashing down on me. The reality was this: I was with this married user in the home of some poor desperate crack-head whose wife had left him; I was on the run from the authorities because of a warrant and still involved in illegal activities; I had recently miscarried Stanley's child because I had been unknowingly carrying an STD for months that had damaged my uterus; Stanley's wife too was pregnant at that time which further intensified the fact that I had miscarried; and to top it all off my face was permanently scarred as a result of she and I fighting over the matter! To make it so bad, Stanley had not long since found out about the STD that I was carrying when he passed it on to his wife after contracting it from me. I should not have expected that he would have wanted to kiss me anyway! Yet still, there I lay having degrading and unfulfilling sex with this married man.

In the midst of it all, on a moonlit night, sitting beside a still pond, I tried to pretend that everything was OK. As I sat there by the pond that summer's night, after yet another sexual disappointment, Jesus was calling me. He spoke to me through the twinkling of the stars, through the rustling of the trees as a light breeze passed through them and even in the rippling waters of the pond did I hear His voice. He wanted to heal me, but I once again turned a deaf ear to Him. It was only a few days afterward that I attempted suicide for the first time. I overdosed on sleeping pills. Stanley found me and took me to the hospital in time. They pumped my stomach and locked me up in the state mental institution. Was I so foolish that I really thought this was a better plan than turning my life over to Jesus? What fools we are in sin!

After about two years Stanley and I broke up, and I thought I would never go the route of adultery again because two, almost fatal suicide attempts on my part came out of that relationship. But, then my heart was badly broken by another man. After that heartbreak, I made it a point to go after married men from that time on. I told myself that it was a safe way to keep my heart from getting involved since I would know from the beginning that the man was already in a relationship with someone else. There is too much to tell. My adulterous relationships went on and on and on. In my heart of hearts I knew I was wrong, but I refused to acknowledge that truth. I proclaimed that if a man's wife was too much of a fool to hold on to him, then I had every right to step in and get out of it what I could.

I thought for sure that once I became a believer that I would no longer have sex with married men, but I was wrong. Unlike before when I was in sin, after becoming a believer I admitted and understood that it was not right for me to commit adultery. I did not want to do it anymore. However, the spirit of adultery worked me over really well with a married man (the assistant pastor of my church none-the-less) that would not stop pursuing me until he got what he wanted. Unlike the other instances, I knew this man's wife – not well, but I knew her still. She was a very nice sister in the church whom I admired very much.

I really did not want to commit adultery with this man, but I did not know about demonic deliverance at that time and thus did not rebuke the many spirits of sexual perversion that yet had me bound. This man was not like the others. He spent time with me. He made me feel loved, wanted and desired. I was so desperate for that type of affection that I felt as if I just could not resist his advances toward me. It was all deception though; I assure you it was. The utter evil in his heart was painfully exposed before it was all said and done. I do not believe in regrets, but I can say that having a sexual affair with that woman's husband was by far the worse thing that I have ever done. Even after repenting and moving on, it still haunted me for many years to come; and yes, as the scripture says, it did destroy a part of my soul!

I am glad for the testimony though, so that I may use it to help others avoid making the same mistake. That experience marked the beginning of my understanding of the truth about spirits of sexual perversion because it was actually the first time that I committed a sexual sin and really did not want to. That experience provoked me to seek deliverance and thus helped me get to the point of being able to write this book. Therefore, in spite of the pain it caused all of us that were involved, I know God allowed it and I am eternally thankful for the experience. Yet in the past, I often wondered if I would ever truly be released from the internal shame of committing adultery with that man. I also lived in fear for many years that my husband would cheat on me with one of my close friends or relatives as repayment for that sin. I implore you with all my heart to please stay away from all types of adulterous affairs. The consequences will linger on for years to come.

*Note: I ask that you would please pray for the man that I just mentioned and his wife as well. He is a pastor and she an Evangelist. In honor of Righteousness I confessed my sin to the wife. Her husband has never confessed nor repented of his sin and she is very unforgiving and bitter toward me to this day. She was (still is in eternity I believe) one of the most dynamic Christians I ever met. I truly desire to see her husband repent and both of their relationships with God and assignments in His Kingdom be restored. Please pray to this end. Our standing in the gap for them can allow The Lord to restore them and this will truly do my heart well and be a testament of the Father's great grace!

Biblical references
Leviticus 18:18, 20, 20:10 & 12; Exodus 20:14; Deuteronomy 5:18; and Galatians 5:19

4. Incest

"None of you shall approach to any that is near of kin to him, to uncover their nakedness: I am The Lord." (Lev 18:6, KJV)

Definition

Sexual intercourse or other sexual contact between persons so closely related that law or custom forbids their marriage.

Assignment

The spirit of incest is assigned to cause us to have a distorted relationship with God, not being able to correctly perceive Him or keep Him in proper perspective in our hearts.

Manifestation in the natural

You are a committer of incest if you have sex(ual contact) with a close family member. As an incestor you have a difficult time appropriately relating to other people. You lack understanding of what love really is and have warped concepts concerning life in general. This is undoubtedly due to a misrepresentation of love in your childhood. Someone who claimed that they loved you did not express or exhibit love as it ought to be, but because you trusted them you accepted their display as true love.

You cannot quite put your finger on it, but you know that something is wrong with you. You may often hear people tell you that you are crazy, that something is wrong with you, that your mind is not right or some similar comment. You are probably so used to hearing it by now that you do not even bother to refute it, and it does not move you much at all. You just accept it to be true, even though you still do not know why it is true. You are a withdrawn individual that feels rejected. Due to this you are reluctant to seek out new relationships and that is part of why you prefer to "keep it in the family".

The family member or members that you are in relationship with probably made you feel special when no one else did. Most committers of incest do not have sexual relations with more than one member of the family, unless they are being sexually abused. However, you may be with more than one family member in a non-abusive sexual relationship if the other relationship is not working out for some reason. Whatever the case may be, there is a sense of 'being in love' that is present within you. Often times being the victim of molestation over a long period of time can lead to this sense of being in love. One of my family members was regularly molested by her biological father. She was eventually convinced that she was in love with him and did not want to end her sexual relations with him even when she became an adult. The spirit of incest is really aiming to make you feel like you are in love.

Incest is not an act that is derived out of lust as much as it is derived out of a warped sense of love. You feel incomplete and being connected to this family member intimately gives you a sense of wholeness. It is like they fill in the missing parts. This is especially true if you have been molested by someone at a very young age. People who are molested at a young age tend to define themselves in terms of that molestation. You know that it's not right, but then you say, *"Can it really be wrong?"* because it is what you have been built on. Whether or not you have been molested, your related sex partner is the "only person in the world" who understands you, who accepts you the way that you are, and who does not make you live up to a false standard of expectations, and you feel loved and received by him or her.

You have been hurt so often that for the most part you are not even willing to give anyone else a chance. Being in the relationship has taught you to live a life of secrecy. Everything is always a secret with you. You probably do not even like to tell your age. You are a paranoid person that is always fearful of being discovered. You tend to think that people are always plotting against you (and your sexual partner). Friendships do not usually last long with you unless it is with a really naïve and unsuspecting person who is not a threat or someone who knows about and accepts your relationship of incest. You cannot allow anyone else to get too close to you or they might "find you out".

If you have other family members, you may be constantly at odds with them and try to stir up a lot of strife. You do not want your sexual partner to be drawn to or form intimate relations with anyone else in the family beside yourself. You portray everyone in a negative light to him or her because you are an outrageously jealous person. You are jealous of everyone and everything, and you try to destroy anything that makes you feel insecure or inadequate. You are particularly destructive if and when your sexual partner attempts to be in relationship with another person.

If your acts of incest are motivated out of violent lust instead of warped love (like raping a young nephew or sister) that type of perversion would fall more under the category of pedophilia/rape. There are also instances where it is just sexual lust that causes you to desire sexual relations with a family member. In this case you are probably being controlled by the spirit of lasciviousness as opposed to incest. However, the spirit of incest is still involved and your sexual relationship could eventually develop into one that is similar to the one described above. Spirits of sexual perversion work in conjunction with one another and once one enters in, it will open the door for others to join it. The bottom line of incest though is that you are never going to understand what love truly is as long as you are bound by this spirit.

Manifestation in the spiritual

Most people who physically commit the act of incest will not have a relationship with Jesus. These are broken, bitter and confused people who want to give **all** of their love to the family member that they are involved with. If committers of incest do have any type of relationship with God at all, it is a twisted one. Spiritual and physical incestors are highly likely to be involved in occultism and new age religion since they lack understanding of who God really is. Their perception of God is just as warped as their perception of love.

Those that are believers, that have the spirit of incest operating in them spiritually, are either totally deceived or always feel condemned and guilty. Just like how in the natural committers of incest are very jealous about their sexual partners, victims of spiritual incest are very jealous about God. They try to *possess* God and do not like to see others have a relationship with Him because they want Him all to themselves. They think that Christianity is some type of exclusive club for them and God alone. They are probably also the types that frown on fellowship with other members and other ministries. To them, their church is the best and only church; their pastor is the best and only pastor. They like to keep their circle small and intimate. They are really into cliques and clubs and their clique is the best and only clique worth being a part of!

These types of believers are not productive members of the Body of Christ because they reject unity unless it is with their own little group. Medically, we know that when close relatives conceive they usually miscarry or give birth to deformed children. As it is in the natural, so it is in the spiritual – whatever these believers produce is either unlikely to survive or is deformed. Not only are they themselves unproductive, but they also try to keep others from producing or try to destroy what others do produce.

They are so green with envy to see anyone else grow spiritually or be elevated in ministry and the things of the Kingdom of God. They spread much discord and disunity in the church and yet keep that air of secrecy about them. They are deceptively defiant and proclaim boldly that they have done nothing wrong. They are so far from God that they have not even begun to know who He is. Be careful of this spirit because it is deceptively disguised in love, but if you operate under this spirit there is no real love in you, and you probably do not have any fellowship with God at all.

My personal experience

Other than generational influences and the rape that occurred when I was two that I mentioned earlier, incest first entered into my life through involuntary exposure when I was five. I had a cousin that I was very close to that enticed me to perform oral sex on her. She was only nine at the time, so I can by no means say that she molested me. She had no idea what she was even doing. She was just curious. I really looked up to her, so I did not mind doing what she asked me to even though I thought it was gross at the time (*laugh*). Irregardless of the innocence of the situation, the spirit of incest now had a foothold in my life. However, the foothold never became a stronghold. I believe that God just intervened. I can remember desiring to have more serious relationships with cousins and other family members. I had a very handsome uncle that I really wanted to have sex with. I flirted with him often but nothing ever came of any of it.

There was an occasion when the spirit of incest really did almost have me when I began to pursue another very close family member. She and I had been through a lot together. At that time of our lives we were really getting a lot closer to one another. We had committed a lot of sexual sins together, not with each other but just as 'partners in crime' so to speak. The forbiddeness of seeing each other naked began to lose its grip on me. I was totally sold out to sin at that time of my life and was totally given over to my flesh and whatever it lusted after. Committing acts of sexual perversion together with this family member began to desensitize me to the fact that she was my relative and made me more aware of her as a sexual being. It was as if I was feeling like, *"We do everything else together. Why not have sex too?"*

We were really close and I felt like I loved her a lot. I just wanted to secure our relationship and satisfy my sexual desires at the same time. I had convinced myself that there was nothing wrong with it. I thank God for His sovereignty and wisdom. He had allowed this relative, when she was five, to witness one of her uncles having sex with her mother. It really disturbed her. She never forgot it, and it haunts her even to this day. For this reason, when I approached her about having sex, although she was not angry with me, she quickly and firmly refused. The horror of that memory that was etched in her soul would not let her even consider the possibility. I continued to pursue her for a time, but she never relented. As time passed on and I became involved in other acts of sexual perversion, the desire just went away.

I thank Yeshua for keeping me when I did not want to be kept. I am sure that I would have committed incest if I could have gotten my way, if not with this relative then with someone else. However, the Father just never allowed the opportunities to be available. I believe that this is because He really needed to preserve my spirit in this area so that I would be able to effectively receive His love when the day arose. Furthermore, she and I have remained close over the years without having the shadow of such an experience hanging over our relationship. Our relationship has been very important to us both. This is just further proof that God is always in control, even when we are in sin.

Biblical references
Leviticus 18:6-7, and 20:17

5. Homosexuality

"Do not practice homosexuality... it is a detestable sin." (Lev 18:22)

Definition

Strong attraction toward persons of the same sex; sexual intercourse or other sexual contact with persons of the same sex.

Assignment

The spirit of homosexuality is designed to make us devoid of understanding our true identity in God and prevent us from being able to conceive and give birth to His will.

Manifestation in the natural

First of all let me say that if you are still a *closet gay*, you are not yet totally given over to this spirit. Once it completely has you, you will go public with the news. But, even if you are a *closet gay* person this description still applies to you in most instances. Homosexuals are another group of people that have experienced a lot of rejection. The greater percentage of all gay people were victims of rape, molestation or some other form of abuse in their lifetime. You are probably no exception.

You feel as if having a relationship with someone of the same sex will enable you to finally be understood. You are seeking someone who can relate to you and your pain. The spirit of homosexuality thrives on low-self esteem, rejection, low self-worth and identity crisis. You have been rejected in some way and therefore feel bad about yourself. You harbor all of these characteristics. You currently or at some point in the past were convinced that you are 'good for nothing' and worthless. Thus it is (or was) easy for you to desire to be someone or something else. These feelings may be hidden and suppressed but they are there and that is what is empowering this spirit of homosexuality in your life.

Some homosexuals believe that they were born gay. If you fall into this category perhaps homosexuality is a generational demon that was passed down to you. It could also just be indicative of the fact that feelings of rejection and worthlessness were imparted to you at such a young age that you can't ever remember a time that you felt good about yourself or had confidence. It might also be the case that sexual abuse by someone of the same sex occurred in your life at a young age that you may or may not remember. Other gays say that it is just a choice that they made for themselves at some point in their life. If you fall into this category you did at one time believe in yourself. You had an understanding of who you were once upon a time and wanted to try and work at being a successful you. However, somewhere down the road your hopes were thwarted. In any event, I assure you that God did not make you gay. Circumstances made you gay; satan made you gay; but you were certainly not created gay by the Lord God of Holiness.

It is almost hard for me to write this section because most homosexuals have such great inner strength that they are sometimes not even aware of. You are stubborn and defiant, but these two qualities have made you a survivor. On the other hand, they also make you very hard to minister to. In your past, with much negativity, others tried to define who you were and who you would become. One day you said *"I'm not going to take it anymore!"* and you began to search out for yourself who you really were. Homosexuality is what you settled upon, and now you are determined to not let anyone dissuade you. Most others would have crumbled under the pressure of the hardships that you have endured, but through homosexuality you found a way to survive and you are not going to let anyone take that away from you. For this reason, you are a very strong person but also extremely argumentative.

You will boldly stand against friends, family members and all of society for what you believe in, which is "your right to be *you*". You have finally found your niche in life and you are staying in it! Like I said, you are stubborn and defiant but for you it is all about survival and maintaining your sanity. Circumstances made you feel as if this is the only way. You have and will continue to sacrifice greatly in order to secure your lifestyle. For instance, you know that you can never produce a baby with your gay partner, in most places you will never be considered legally married and you will have to face day in and day out the taunts, discrimination and abuse of a society that cast its eyes down on gays. None-the-less, it is all worth it to you in return for the acceptance that you have been longing for.

Even before you were gay, you have always been considered an outcast, a freak or a reject so now you have found a way to be accepted as such amongst your own kind. It is not acceptance by everyone, but it is enough for you. This defiance and boldness is what the public sees – a happy, successful person that can accomplish anything any heterosexual person can. But, on the inside there is turmoil. That little child within you is still crying out for real acceptance as a "normal" person. That person that was abused is still hurt, angry and confused. You are still unsure of who you are no matter how much you say that you have got it all together. You will play the role as long as you have to, but if there were really a way out, you would take it. Somewhere inside of you, you wonder what it would be like to be "straight". You probably still remember childhood ambitions to have a normal spouse and live a traditional American family life. You suppress these feelings, but they are there.

Often times nobody knows but feelings of depression and suicide hit you so strongly. You just want to give up the facade and take off the mask, but you still do not know who lives underneath it all. Homosexuals have the highest suicide rate among any other group of Americans. The average life expectancy for a homosexual is said to be less than 50 years of age. You do not "live" you merely "exist" and that spirit that has you bound is hoping that in the end, you will give up and die never understanding how awesome you truly are just the way God made you (which is heterosexual not gay).

I am sorry that so many "so-called" Christians are mean and abusive toward you and other gays. I have heard preachers use words like "fag" and "butch" right from the pulpit. It breaks my heart and incites righteous indignation within me. This is not the love of Jesus, who showed compassion to the masses of people no matter what their sin was. In spite of these evil and deceived people, please know that God loves you. He does not approve of your lifestyle, but He does love you just the way that you are. The taunts of these hateful people are not a reflection of how Jesus feels about you nor are they a reflection of His love and desire for you. He just wants to take you in His arms and make you whole. Please ignore them. Give Christ Jesus a chance to redeem and restore your life!

Manifestation in the spiritual

Many natural homosexuals are atheist due to their anger toward God for the abuse they have suffered in their lifetime, but there are plenty that claim belief in 'God' as well. Believers that are bound by the spirit of homosexuality are unproductive. The spirit of homosexuality comes strongly against a believer's ability to produce in the spirit. If two people of the same sex lay together, the creative power of intimacy is made null and void. Orgasm may still cause the body to go through the process that enables conception, but there is no sperm and egg to come together. Not being able to produce is what spiritual homosexuality is all about. These believers may possibly even have large ministries, but they do not produce spiritually and do not bear the fruits of the Holy Spirit. They are carnally minded and shallow-spirited believers that will tolerate just about anything in the church.

The spirit of homosexuality not only seeks to destroy humanity's ability to conceive and give birth to God's Kingdom, but also to distort their understanding of who they are in Christ. Spiritual homosexuals do not perceive or accept their true identity. They are blind to the greatness and glory with which God created them. Because they are unable to see any greatness or worth in who they truly are, they try to be something that they are not. This is what ultimately causes them to be unproductive; they do not believe in themselves or their ability to produce anything of worth. This identity crisis causes most spiritual homosexuals to be double-minded hypocrites. They don't really know who they are in Christ and are forever trying on a new personality and way of living.

There is often times an over-exaggerated effort to prove that they are "happy" and "confident". That means that they are often times showy and loud. They want to prove that they have it all together and great effort is put into this. They hope that their air of togetherness and confidence will gain them acceptance and often times it does. The spirit that operates within them blinds them to the truth that the God who created them is the only one that will ever truly know and understand who they are.

None-the-less, they are some of the most loved people in the church at times. That is why they are often given positions of leadership. Other believers that lack discernment and/or the willingness to stand for Holy integrity will elevate homosexuals because they are well-liked by others. This is the case when it comes to homosexuals committing the physical act and those that are only spiritually bound homosexuals. Just as is the case with natural homosexuals, spiritual homosexuals harbor those feelings of rejection and uncertainty deep within. They too are depressed and on the brink of losing it all at any moment.

My personal experience

As with many of the other spirits of sexual perversion,

homosexuality is one that entered my life when I was a baby through sexual abuse and my family history. I do not know a single female member of my family on my mother's side that has not been involved in some type of homosexual relationship. One might have said that it was just "in our blood". To strengthen the foothold that the spirit of homosexuality already had in my life through my family bloodline, this demon also had one of its other victims molest me at the age of two. The molester was a gay baby sitter and from what I was told, the molestation happened on a regular basis over an extended period of time. I have no mental memory of it, although I am sure my spirit remembers the incident.

    I already shared with you my first voluntary act of homosexuality in the last section on incest. It happened with an older, female cousin when I was five. Although I did not remember the incident from when I was two at the time that I had sex with my cousin, it just seemed that homosexuality was a part of who I was. I did not even see anything morally wrong with it back then. It had been imparted in me at such a young age that it was just my nature to be gay. I did not mind it at all. Through lifestyle choices and indiscretion, those that raised me taught me that such behavior was OK. At around the age of seven, I began to "flirt" with other girls. I was often called gay, lesbo or dyke. I did not like the stigma of being called names so I curtailed my flirtation and adopted the idea that homosexuality was freaky and unacceptable, but that was not how I truly felt about it. In my heart I always wanted to be with females, I just did not want the rejection that I knew would come along with it.

    My refusal to accept homosexuality did nothing to restrain rejection in my life, and so I became more defiant and strong-spirited as I got older. People did not seem to accept me no matter what I did, so I might as well have just did what I wanted to. As I became more and more sold out to sexual sin, I could no longer resist the enticement of homosexuality. I began to hang out with a gay young lady and suddenly the opportunity that the spirit of homosexuality had been waiting for finally arrived. All of those suppressed temptations that I had been harboring from childhood finally played out. From that point on, I was involved in numerous gay relationships. I aggressively pursued other females and particularly liked "breaking in" first timers.

    I can say though that this is another one of those areas where God "kept a leash on me". Even though I was aggressive and the more male-like person in these gay relationships, I always kept a feminine appearance and I preferred women who did likewise. Furthermore, although I liked being with women very much, I never really lost my desire for men. I just wanted the best of both worlds. Yet there was a time, right before I gave my life wholeheartedly to Jesus, that I was ready to take homosexuality to a new level in my life. I had been so hurt by so many different men at that point in my life that I'd just had enough. The thought of sex with a male literally sickened me. There were times that just thinking of it brought my food up. I did not think I would ever be able to have sex with a man again and I did not care to anymore. It would have been so easy for me at that time of my life to completely sell out to homosexuality.

I had never once in all of the many, many sexual encounters I'd had with men, ever been given an orgasm by a man. Sex was never gratifying for me. It was just something that I did. The only climactic, sexually satisfying experience that I ever had besides masturbating happened when being sexual with a female. Furthermore, not only had I never had a man that sexually satisfied me, I also never had a man that was nice to me; never had a man that took care of me; never had a man that treated me tenderly; never had a man that understood and supported me; never had a man that loved or cared about me; never had a man that adored and honored me; I had been physically abused by several different men; I had no father figure in my life at that time… I mean, I just really did not see any purpose for men in my life at all!

The only reason that I had held onto them for so long was because of my deep longing to have a beautiful, happy, traditional family one day. But, the cruelty of life had long since killed that dream. I had no hope left in me for marriage and so for the first time in my life, instead of just having a female playmate, I had a 'girlfriend'. I was ready to kiss men good-bye forever right along with my dreams of being a wife and mother, but God saw my pain and intercepted the relationship. Shortly afterward, I was in His bosom and ready to sell out completely to Him instead, and sell out completely to Him I did indeed! Hallelujah!!!

Biblical references
Leviticus 18:22, 20:13; Deuteronomy 22:5, Judges 19:22-23; and Romans 1:24, 26-27

6. Prostitution

"A prostitute is a dangerous trap; a promiscuous woman is as dangerous as falling into a narrow well." (Prov 23:27)

Definition
The act of offering oneself as a sexual partner in return for monetary compensation or some other favor or gift.

Assignment
The spirit of prostitution is assigned to affect our ability to see our value in Christ or simply as human beings, therefore causing us to sell ourselves short.

Manifestation in the natural

When we think of prostitution we usually envision a Vegas back street with scantily dressed women walking up and down it wearing wigs, popping gum and running to any car that stops nearby saying, *"Hey baby! Can I show you a good time?"* That is definitely a true depiction of prostitution, but it is not the only one. The spirit of prostitution also has you bound if you get into a relationship with a person just for material or financial gain or the status of the person. Even if you marry the person, the spirit of prostitution is still in your life because of your motive for marrying them. This manifestation of prostitution is very prevalent in the worlds of professional sports, politics and entertainment.

Being a stripper is also a form of prostitution. As a stripper, in exchange for money, you are performing sexually explicit moves for others to view. Those that are watching watch intently for the purpose of being sexually stimulated and pay money to do so. Remember, sexual perversion is about a lot more than penetration. Just the intent to sexually stimulate makes you guilty before The Lord. Furthermore, if you consider yourself a model or actor/actress because you pose nude or perform pornography for money, please do not be deceived. The spirit of prostitution also brings on these acts. The spirit of prostitution also binds any male who behaves in any of the aforementioned ways.

A prostitute, by all of the above descriptions, fails to see his or her true value. Why would you sell off something as priceless as your sexual intimacy? Sex is the most intimate act that a person can involve themselves in and is the act that creates the greatest vulnerability. As a prostitute, you have no sense of self-respect or self worth and do not at all value your life. That explains why you are willing time and time again to put your life in danger (by being alone with deranged people that you do not know, by living a dangerous lifestyle, by risking the contraction of AIDS or some other disease, etcetera). To onlookers, prostitution seems like an easy lifestyle to get out of, but you feel hopelessly trapped in a life full of use and abuse.

The entrapment comes not because of an inability to just walk away from it and do something different but comes instead from the inability to recognize any value in yourself. More than likely, you believe that there just is no way out and you probably do not seek a way out. That is because prostitution is addictive. It is a high in its own right and provides a false sense of being in control. The temporary escape that it provides from your shattered self-image, allowing you to feel valuable since someone is willing to pay money to spend time with you, is an addictive entrapment. You are in control (so it seems) when you are able to bargain what your sexuality is worth and demand your payment.

Prostitution can enter into a person's life through wounds of abuse whether verbal, physical, sexual or just emotional. The sense of entrapment that you feel now bound by a life of prostitution, is the same sense of entrapment that you felt at the time of your life when you were being abused. It is unfortunate that you were deceived into a life of prostitution by this spirit because the lifestyle that you are living increases the likelihood that you will now be abused again and again and again. Abuse causes us to feel like we are defective and anything defective lacks value. The initial abuses that you suffered before prostitution entered your life began to diminish your value in your own eyes, and the more abuse you suffer the less and less value you will see in yourself.

Prostitutes are usually hypocrites because they always have to present themselves a certain way in order to look appealing to a potential buyer. Yet, they seldom match internally what you see externally. You have learned to live a life of fantasy and falsehood, a life of pretense, not knowing who you truly are. You become whatever will earn you a buck or a gift for that moment. To others you may seem really tough and hard but that is just more pretense. You have to appear this way because you live a competitive and dangerous lifestyle. Although you appear tough outwardly, inwardly you are more fragile than an empty eggshell. It is not unlikely that you are a victim of drug or alcohol addiction because often times *a high* is needed to help you keep up the guise and escape your reality.

What is your reality? Your reality is a life that is full of torment. You don't desire to live the lifestyle that you are living. You would give up the financial gain that it provides for you in an instant if you could discover any value in yourself other than your sexuality. Sometimes you convince yourself that you are really providing an important public service that helps people. Other times you say that prostitution is your way to make a living in a tough world. But like I said, your life is all about pretense and the longer you indulge in this lifestyle, the less you are able to differentiate between what is real and what is pretense. Whereas many of the other acts of sexual perversion make a person feel that they are in control, prostitution makes you feel helplessly out of control (*outside of the temporary upper-hand that you sometimes have when engaged in the negotiation of a trick*).

You are not a loyal person to friends or family because you do not form meaningful bonds. You are unappreciative and selfish because you only perform for what you will gain and then you move on. It prevents you from ever really connecting emotionally. Even with those that you are not performing acts of prostitution with, you have a hard time bonding and connecting. You are so used to spending only a few fantasy filled moments with individuals that you are always expecting every relationship to end abruptly. Even if you have children, you cannot escape the feeling that "it will all be over soon". No matter what occurs in your life whether you enjoy it or despise it, you are still bound by the sense that it will all be over with soon. This sense that "all is temporary" takes away the enjoyment of the good times in life but helps you endure the rough times in life. However, it leaves you without any stability whatsoever and devoid of any sense of reality.

Our bodies are the only (tangible) things on this earth that truly belong to us as human beings. From birth until death, no matter what else we may gain or lose in life, our bodies should always be our very own. That makes it a priceless value to us. Yet, you sell your own body and therefore you have given up the only thing of value that you ever truly owned. It leaves you with nothing and you are constantly down on yourself and beating yourself up because of this. It makes you almost insane to think about it and that is why you try not to. I iterate again that your life is one that is full of pretense, lacks stability and is totally out of control. All you want is your value back, but how can that happen? Take heart, because you too can be victoriously free! Your body was never really yours anyway. It was bought with the Blood of Jesus, and belongs to Him *(1Cor 6:20, 1 Cor 7:23)*. He has redeemed you and will also restore all to you if you will just turn to Him wholeheartedly!

Manifestation in the spiritual

Natural prostitutes are highly unlikely to practice any regular religious beliefs. They just do not see the point in *wasting God's time* on someone of no value like themselves. Besides, if there even is such a deity, he would only be temporary pretense to them. Believers that operate under the spirit of prostitution spiritually have very little stability in their walk with God. One month they want to be a praise dancer, the next a minister, the next a missionary and the next a Sunday school teacher. Just like natural prostitutes, spiritual prostitutes fail to see their true value in Christ. For this reason, they allow people to pimp their spiritual gifts and abuse them.

They probably have been abused in life and in ministry. They will settle for less out of people, life and even God when they are worth so much more. They usually find it hard to say no to anything that might benefit them in some way, even if it is not conducive to their growth in the anointing. Although they are most often times the type of people that will do anything for anyone, they are always looking for something in return. They feel that an injustice has been done them if they do not get their payoff and you will see the ugly come out of them in this event. They are secretive, deceptive and hypocritical and unfortunately cannot be trusted.

They would like to have a relationship with God but are unable to receive or return His unconditional love. They believe in their hearts that it is not real and will not last. Jesus is just a momentary pleasure for them just like everything else in life. They perceive Him to be a fake and a phony, a user just like everyone else. They will not even give Him a chance because they are afraid. This feeling is what will keep many natural prostitutes from even going to church, but if they do go, they still retain these feelings toward God. Failing to realize their true value in Christ is what causes them to believe that God does not and could not ever truly love them or have any need of them. They feel trapped in a life being lived beneath their means as sons and daughters of The King.

Just like a prostitute in the natural lives a life of pretense, so do spiritual prostitutes. The longer a believer operates under the spirit of prostitution the more detached they become from God's truth. It becomes easier and easier to pretend that they are an evangelist, a pastor or a prophet. It is easy for them to pretend that they live a consecrated, Holy life that is pleasing to God. However, the truth of the matter is that they probably live wretched lives that are full of the most treacherous sins; and they know it too. Yet, they have to keep up the front. They must always look appealing and continue to advertise what they are selling. Such believers are at risk of becoming part of non-Christian religions and cults that claim belief in God but have little to no Holiness standard. That is because this would be a more comfortable setting for them. They are putting their spiritual lives in danger, but since they see little to no value in themselves it really does not matter to them. They feel as if they might as well get out of it what they can. It is so sad that they are blind to the great value that they truly possess.

My personal experience

Prostitution is another sin that runs deep in my ancestry. Furthermore, I experienced many abuses in my lifetime – early on and throughout. Thus, I was a prime candidate to fall victim to this spirit. My earliest memory of this spirit manifesting itself in my life was when I was 14. There was a guy that I was dating that I did not like much at all. I was all prepared to break up with him on a particular day and the next thing you know he gives me a gold necklace. That was a big deal for a 14 year old girl that did not own a single piece of authentic jewelry, and so I stayed with him just for that reason. I was not sexually active with men at that time of my life, but this was definitely the early stage of a spiritual bondage that would later have a stronger presence in my life. That presence showed up even more when later I began to date a notorious drug dealer. I got into the relationship thinking only of what I could gain out of it.

Yet, these manifestations were mild in comparison to what was coming. I told you before that these spirits are all interconnected. Once one enters your life, they may all enter your life. For me, prostitution really took advantage of the workings of fornication in my life. I mentioned to you when we dealt with fornication that being in those **type 1** relationships really diminish your sense of self worth. This was certainly the case with me. As I got into more and more of those **type 1** relationships of fornication and I suffered more and more abuse, the less and less value I could see in myself. Looking back over my life, I know exactly when the deadly blow for prostitution's stronghold was inflicted. Remember when writing about my personal experiences with fornication I wrote *"…well I will tell you what happened a little later because that is actually another spirit"*? This is the spirit that I was talking about. Let me tell you how it really gained its stronghold in my life.

    I was dating this guy that I just swore was the finest thing on this planet. He looked good; he smelt good and even talked a good game. I was in love child (for the 130th time, *laugh*). Knowing what I know now, I realize that he was sent by satan to utterly destroy me. As a matter of fact, I am almost convinced that satan himself possessed this guy just to finish me off. I do not want to be too explicit and so I cannot really do the story justice, but just let me paint somewhat of a picture for you. Marco would cheat on me with 20 different girls and then publicly curse me out and call me a slut for just talking to someone on the street. Because he knew of my past, he used it against me. Even though he was living off of me, in my house, eating my food, without offering any help or support at all, he would often talk to me about his "real" girlfriend. He would throw in my face the fact that he took her virginity as opposed to my whorish past. During intercourse he would call me degrading sexual names and say things like *"You are too nasty for me to penetrate you."* and would then make me perform other sexual acts instead.

    I had never really performed oral sex before (besides that incident with my cousin and I had not yet gotten into lesbianism at this time). Not performing oral sex was a reflection of my sinner's morals. Sinner's morals crack me up. When in sin we say stupid things like, *"I won't steal from my friends. I only steal from people I don't know." "I'll only have sex with a married man if his wife is treating him bad." "I'll murder someone but I'll never lie because my word is bond, Son!"* My sinner's moral was that I would not perform oral sex.

Any man who could breathe could have intercourse with me, but I would not do oral. After the harsh reality of having a reputation as a *'loose girl'* hit me when I was a teenager, I wanted to do damage control. I figured that I could at least stand tall and say *"Ilk, I don't do that!"* Men talk so badly about girls who do oral. I had a lot of male friends and I know that 'barber shop talk' well. But Marco debased me beneath the line of my own, already low, moral standards. He got me to do a lot of things that I said I would never do. He was so emotionally and verbally abusive that when he finished with me, I had no soul left. Whatever value I had left in me when I met satan in the person of Marco was completely abolished after knowing him. The wound of abuse that he left in me was so large that prostitution easily stepped in and took a seat. During my relationship with him, I was drawn deeper into the sin of prostitution and I eventually became a stripper at the age of 20.

I did not see "exotic dancing" as prostitution at that time of my life because I was blind to the truth. I would have been mad to hear you say such a thing to me, but it should have been obvious to me. I can remember being upset to find out that some of the joints that I danced in had a "no touching" rule. The men were not allowed to touch the dancers. I chose not to dance at those clubs because I knew that touching would get me a bigger tip and I wanted that money. I also preferred dancing totally in the nude. What was the point of letting a piece of string on my tush stand between me and another $100 or so? Many of the other girls did not share my boldness or viewpoint. They did not like to be touched and wanted to keep some of their clothes on. That should have been a clue to me that I was headed down a dark path because I never really had any inhibitions.

As I danced more and more, the customers began to notice that I was "willing to go the distance" so to speak. I was approached after coming off of stage with "offers to make extra money". At first I was opposed because like I said, stripping and prostituting were two totally different things to me. Sex for money went against my sinner's morals. (Most strippers that do not "do extras" will be outraged to hear you classify them as prostitutes.) However, as my self-respect diminished the more and my own value continually decreased in my eyes, I relented and began to fulfill off-stage requests. By this time, I had also gotten into homosexuality and so I even got into doing live lesbian performances and posing with other females for pornography magazines. I am sure I would have done movies and whatever else I was presented with if the opportunities had been made available because I was really far gone by then.

Even though I kept pursuing the idea, God stopped it from working out and prostitution never became my strongman. Even after my horrific relationship with Marco ended, I was still drawn back into fornication. The spirit of fornication still held kingship in my life and intended to hold on to its position as the head of my life by sending a particular man my way. This man would have nothing to do with me if I continued on in prostitution, so I dropped the lifestyle all together to be with him. Truly, I know God allowed this man to be sent to me even though our relationship was sinful. The relationship with this guy was the channel used to save me from a life of prostitution when I was yet too stubborn to call on the name of Jesus for help. At about the same time I met the guy, I had seriously considered going out of state to become a full fledged street prostitute. I was enticed to do this by the same gay girl that I had been hanging out with, who was also the young lady that introduced me to stripping. This man that I started dating was a domestically abusive alcoholic. He left me broken and bruised, but I thank Yeshua that He stopped me from doing what I had considered.

Biblical references
Genesis 38:24; Leviticus 19:29; Deuteronomy 22:21, 23:17-18; and Proverbs 23:27

7. Pornography/Sexual fantasy

"But I say, anyone who even looks at a woman with lust in his eye has already committed adultery with her in his heart." (Mat. 5:28)

"If your sinful nature controls your mind, there is death. But if the Holy Spirit controls your mind, there is life and peace." (Romans 8:6)

Definition
Pornography – Pictures, writings or films involving sexual intercourse and/or other sexual activity, designed to arouse sexual excitement.

Definition
Sexual fantasy – Indulging in mental images that are of a sexual nature.

Assignment
The spirit of pornography/sexual fantasy wants to control our minds, thus preventing us from taking on the mind of Christ and enjoying God's blessings of abundant life prosperity. If satan can successfully control our minds, he can control our entire lives!

Manifestation in the natural

When it comes to sexual perversion, the devil wanted to make sure that he did not leave anybody out! There are some people that are just too shy or inhibited to actually engage in sex with a partner. There are also those that are physically incapable of having sexual intercourse, but even those that fall into these categories must still be on guard against sexual perversion. The spirit of pornography and sexual fantasy is especially assigned to make sure that even those that do not physically have sex will still suffer some degree of sexual perversion.

This is only one aspect of this spirit though. It affects almost everyone who is involved in sexual sin because it has a very important assignment, which is to corrupt the mind. These two acts, pornography and sexual fantasy, fall under the same heading because they are controlled by just one spirit. That spirit's intent is to fill the victims mind with sexual images. Sexually stimulating thoughts can be fed into our minds directly from within the evil that already resides in our hearts or it can also penetrate our minds from an outside source – pornography. Let us just clarify what types of acts would fall under the category of the sin of pornography.

Pornography includes any type of movie, book, magazine, radio show, live show, internet site or even a letter or conversation that is designed to feed sexual images to the mind. According to our society a particular amount of sexual activity has to be included in any of the above in order for it to be classified as *pornographic*. However, God's standards are much higher. No amount of pornography is acceptable. That means that even that nice romance novel, that letter or sexual poem that you wrote to or received from someone you were dating and even sitcoms or other shows that have <u>any degree</u> of sexual undertones in them all fall under the category of pornography. *Even over-indulgent conversations between husband and wife that stir sexual images, <u>at times other than when they are actually engaged in the act of sexual intimacy,</u> are induced by the spirit of pornography!* (And yes sinful pornography is still ***<u>sinful pornography,</u>*** even if you are watching it with your spouse!) Kind of makes you think doesn't it?

Sexual fantasy would be any sexual thought that you intentionally meditate on and allow to arouse you. The greater of the two when it comes to pornography and sexual fantasy is definitely the sexual fantasy. This is because sexual fantasy corrupts not only the mind but the heart. Pornography is only used as a method to get you to the point of committing sexual fantasy. It becomes sexual fantasy once you actually take the bait and begin to meditate on the sexual images that have been fed into your mind. Sexual fantasy is not a passing thought. We all struggle with strange and fleeting thoughts and images at times. It is only sexual fantasy when you really begin to entertain and meditate on the thought. When you spend minutes, hours, maybe even days imagining on sexual acts; when you turn a thought into an entire and detailed fantasy – that is how you can tell that you are bound by sexual fantasy. As I stated earlier, sexual fantasy can be brought on by pornography or it can be stirred up from within you. You are definitely in a greater level of bondage if the images are being fed to your mind from within your heart (*Mat 15:19*).

Pornography is another sin that some would argue is acceptable, especially when used as a tool to stir passions before having sex with one's spouse, but Jesus tells us in Matthew 5:28 that if we even **look** at a person with lust in our hearts that we have already sinned. The Apostle Paul also tells us in Ephesians 5:12 that, *"It is shameful even to talk about the things that ungodly people do in secret."* If it is shameful for us to even talk about these things, how much more shameful to think about and even look at these things? These scriptures make it clear that pornography is not acceptable in God's sight. You have to understand that the five senses are the gateways to our minds. Pornography uses these gateways, and although there may be no direct danger in looking at it or listening to it, there is great danger in thinking about it. What we think about is what we will eventually become!

If the spirit of pornography/sexual fantasy is your strongman, you are a daydreamer for sure. You would rather be alone than with people because you get so much enjoyment out of engaging in sexual fantasies. You get more enjoyment out of fantasy than any other activity in life. Sexual fantasy is another spirit that will drive you into isolation. The spirit of sexual fantasy is connected to other spirits of fantasy. If you daydream about sexual fantasies, you probably daydream about other things as well. You are probably just a daydreamer in general. For this reason, you are a person that is detached from reality. It is hard for you to decipher what is false and what is real.

Because of your constant fantasizing, you get very little accomplished in life. You spend more time fantasizing than you do planning and putting plans into action. You are probably a poor housekeeper. Everything around you is junky and disorderly, but this does not matter to you because you live in a land that exists within your mind and there in that land everything is what you want it to be. In your natural life things are totally out of your control. Your career, education, health, relationships and living arrangements – every aspect of your life may be completely out of control, but in your land of fantasy you have got it all under control. An out of control life may have been the open door that allowed this spirit access to you. You wanted to exist somewhere that you could be in control.

Although sexual fantasy is a really opportune sexual sin for those that for some reason are incapable or unwilling to engage in sexual sin with a partner, it does not stop there. Most people that are bound by sexual fantasy also engage in other acts of sexual perversion. If you were to survey those that commit any of the other acts of sexual perversion, you would be hard pressed to find even one that does not engage in sexual fantasy. The images in your mind create a craving in your body that longs to be fulfilled. Masturbation is probably the sin you commit most frequently in conjunction with the sexual fantasy because it allows you to maintain that sense of control. However, it will not stop there. Although the spirit of sexual fantasy can cause you to isolate yourself, it can also drive you to seek out fulfillment of your fantasies.

Whatever it is that you are fantasizing about, whether it is child molestation, rape, sex with animals, homosexuality, and etcetera – if you are drawn deep enough into the fantasy, you will become detached enough from reality to think that you can do it and still be in control. Sexual fantasy can get so bad that it can lead you into a state of psychosis where the real world ceases to exist for you. You will get to the point that you are committing all types of crazy and dangerous, possibly illegal acts without realizing the consequences or affects of those acts. You will be completely unaware of what is going on around you in the real world because the act itself is of no significance to you. It is the fantasy that you are playing out, that consists of the act, that is driving you and bringing you pleasure.

This is such a dangerous, dangerous spirit. If you are bound by this spirit, whether in the form of pornography or sexual fantasy, if you still have enough presence of mind to understand what I am saying, I beg you to put this book down right now and repent. Ask Jesus to save you from this spirit! You could be just days or even moments away from completely losing your grip on reality; destined to rot away in insanity like so many lost souls wandering the streets homeless and behaving strangely.

Manifestation in the spiritual

Believers that are bound by the spirit of sexual fantasy are easily distracted from the things of God. These believers, like many bound by some of the other spirits of sexual perversion, are more likely to become involved in some type of occultism because of their detachment from reality. They bear little or even no fruit at all. Their lives are full of carnality and evil. Even many sinners will note their behavior and say, *"Aren't you supposed to be a Christian?"* They totally lack the character of Christ and have no Light. They are dull in their spiritual hearing, dim in their spiritual eyes and their hearts are hardened.

Because of their inability to hear and perceive the Word of God, they are often subject to confusion and double-mindedness. These people are stagnant in their growth and remain spiritually immature even after being in church for many years. They get very little accomplished, if anything at all, because they spend more time fantasizing about how their life in Christ is going to be than actually working toward applying the principles of the Words of the Bible to their lives. They are inactive in church. They probably have a lot of good ideas about how the church should be run but never any realistic plans for bringing these ideas to past. Their faith is dead because it is not coupled with works.

They are perverse in their thinking concerning the things of God. Instead of accepting God as He is, for whom He is, they attempt to make Him fit into their mental image of *what He should be*. They do likewise with God's Kingdom and His ways. When they worship, it is not done to please Jesus. It is done so that they can fulfill whatever fantasy they have concocted in their minds about what worship should be. Therefore, they are selfish worshipers that care nothing for how their worship affects God. They do it to satisfy the craving that is created when they fantasize and dream their dreams. Truthfully, individuals like this are hopelessly bound in all areas of their walk with God until they determine to use His mighty weapons to cast down imaginations, tear down the strong holds in their mind and bring every thought captive into obedience to Christ *(2 Cor 10:4-5)*.

When I consider the importance of the mind, I understand that this is even one of the more detrimental spirits of sexual perversion, if not **the most detrimental**. Pornography and sexual fantasy cause us to meditate on those things which are offensive to God and destructive to our spirits, and believers that are bound by this spirit do likewise meditate on things that are such. The Bible lets us know that the person who meditates on the Word of God day and night is the person that will be empowered with obedience and will therefore enjoy The Lord's blessings *(Josh 1:8, Ps 1:2-3)*.

How can we meditate on acts of sexual perversion or anything that is contrary to Righteousness and meditate on the Holy Word of God at the same time? It is not possible! Our Christian walk is so heavily controlled by what goes on in our minds. Furthermore, what we think about is definitely affected by what we see and hear. It is by the renewing of our minds that we are transformed into the express image of Christ – into living epistles. The mind is where the battle between Holiness and evil is fought within us and if satan wins there, he wins all together!

In the book of Romans 8:5 it tells us, *"Those who are dominated by the sinful nature think about sinful things, but those who are controlled by the Holy Spirit think about things that please the Spirit."* If a person's thoughts are of sinful things and/or they indulge in watching, reading and listening to sinful things or even talking about them, then they are still dominated by their sinful nature and are yet the enemy of God. Just think about your walk with Christ and the times you have sinned. How many times have you sinned without first thinking about it? People that are bound by this spirit are constantly feeding their flesh, their eyes and their ears, with carnality and things that are offensive to God. They are constantly meditating on things contrary to God's nature of Holiness. Their entire minds are corrupt and perverse and so are their spirits. They are full of evil and none of Christ!

My personal experience

As I mentioned earlier, the spiritual strongman in your life can change from time to time. There is always a power struggle going on in the spirit realm between different demons that want to control you. I think that I can say that before fornication was my strongman, it was definitely pornography and sexual fantasy. I was exposed to pornography at a very young age. It was all around me in the form of books, magazines, movies and sex toys. In addition to that, sexually explicit acts were often performed in front of me and spoken to me. Pornography is just another one of those things that was always a part of my life.

The sexual fantasies actually started out as just a spirit of fantasy and daydreaming. It was of course only natural for my fantasies to take on a sexual nature with all of the pornographic images that had been implanted into my spirit. My fantasies started to take on a sexual nature at around age six when a serious first grade crush stirred up sexual lust in me. I would go home everyday from school and fantasize about having 'sex' with little Joey. I did not even understand what sex was at that time. All I knew is that it involved exposed genitals that had to come in contact and a lot of grinding and squealing noises *(laugh)*.

All year, I had been trying to get Joey to *'mess'* with me. Joey being a normal six year old, thought the idea was gross of course, but I still pursued him hotly anyway. Toward the end of the year, when I found out that he would not be back to that school the next year, I knew that I had to make my move. On the last day of school I dressed myself in a mini-skirt with no stockings. My Mom did not want me to wear the skirt because it was too small for me and quite short, but that was the whole point. Thus, I did what I did best – I manipulated the situation until I got what I wanted. What mother would think that her six year old is planning on going to school to try and have sex in the playground? So, my Mom let me wear the mini-skirt.

When the class went outside that day, I was chasing Joey all around the playground. He was running from me like the plague! As time was winding down and recess was coming to a close, I started to feel desperate. As a result I caught Joey, pushed him to the ground, pulled up my skirt and sat right on top of him in a sexual position. I even somehow managed to partially expose his penis by pulling on his shorts. I was grinding on him and trying to kiss him. I was totally serious about having sex with this kid. The fact is that I had fantasized about it for so long that I was willing to do anything to fulfill that fantasy. I knew that I could get in trouble for what I was doing. Not to mention that Joey did not at that time like me, nor had he ever at any time in the past liked me! However, I had lost my grip on reality. The fantasy was driving me.

After that experience, I continued to fantasize on and off throughout the years about sexual things, but it was more for amusement than anything else because I still was not experiencing any type of physical sexual impulses at that time. As I approached puberty and was still being exposed to pornography, mostly by way of romance novels at this time, I really began to indulge in sexual fantasy. At that time, I would fantasize often. I began to write my own romance novels in my head and I was the main character. My personal belief is that Christians have no business reading romance novels. It only stirs passions and incites imaginations and longings that cannot be Righteously fulfilled. We have to keep our minds totally focused on God and our Kingdom assignment. I had not yet learned this truth about romance novels at that time though. At any rate, once my body began to experience sexual impulses, and I had discovered the ecstasy of climaxing, I often read romance novels, fantasized and then masturbated. Since I found myself to be an unattractive young lady, fantasizing that I was desirable and beautiful did bring me much pleasure and a great sense of control.

Sexual fantasy did not remain in the top position for long. Sexual fantasy opened the door to masturbation and masturbation led me to fornication. Once fornication took over, there was no turning back. I still indulged in sexual fantasy often, but it was no longer the dominating spirit in my life. However, as I mentioned earlier, there are different spirits of fantasy. They are not all sexual in nature. Although sexual fantasy lost ground with me, fantasizing and daydreaming in general remained to be a powerful stronghold in my life. The fact that all spirits of fantasy are connected is just one more reason that the spirit of sexual fantasy is so very dangerous. We should be meditating on the truth of God's Word and the visions He gives us; not some vain fantasy. Idleness of mind will make you a target for satan every time!

Biblical references
Leviticus 19:2; Josh 1:8; Ps 1:1-3, Matthew 5:28, 15:19; Romans 1:21, 8:5-7, 12:2; 1 Corinthians 2:16; 2 Corinthians 10:5; Ephesians 5:12; Philippians 2:5; and 2 Timothy 4:5

8. Rape / Pedophilia
"Our enemies rape the women and young girls in Jerusalem and throughout the towns of Judah." (Lam 5:11)

"But if any man think that he behaveth himself uncomely toward his virgin, <u>if she pass the flower of her age</u>, and need so require, let him do what he will, he sinneth not: let them marry." (1 Cor 7:36 KJV)

Definition
Rape – The act of forcing another person to involuntarily submit to sexual intercourse or other sexual contact.

Definition
Pedophilia – Sexual intercourse or any type of sexual contact with someone not of legal consenting age; also including but not exclusive to rape.

Assignment
This spirit's assignment is to give committers a false sense of control through manipulation and violence. This spirit is assigned not only to distort relationship with God in the committer of this crime but also in the victim.

Manifestation in the natural
The spirit of pedophilia and rape is a particularly violent one. With every other act of sexual perversion except this one, all those involved in the act of sin are involved willingly. This spirit is not only sexually perverse and violent, but it is also a thief because it is taking away without authorization something that does not belong to it. If you are now or have ever been bound by this spirit, I want you to rest assured that this offense is no worse in God's sight than any other sin. The Blood of Jesus is able to thoroughly cleanse us of all sins, even those that are called detestable and are considered an abomination. This book is not being written to single any one out, to judge anyone or make anyone feel bad, including you. Society at large may try to make you feel as if there is no hope for you and that you are the lowest form of life on the planet. However, the Father is seeking you out to heal you and cleanse you. He understands that you are driven by demons that feed off of the unhealed wounds of the past that still ache within you.

Studies have proven that sex offenders are the most unlikely category of criminals to be rehabilitated. This is true but not because you are unable to be rehabilitated. The reason that rehabilitation is so hard for you is because of the depths of self-condemnation that you experience. Even if others forgive you, you are seldom able to forgive yourself. Often times, the depth of guilt experienced by people who are bound by this spirit prevent them from ever being healed. This means that, like so many of the other spirits of sexual perversion, this one too makes you feel trapped – caught in a never ending and deadly cycle. Yet, if you are willing to open your heart to the love, healing and forgiveness of Jesus Christ, our Lord Yeshua, you will become a new person. You do not have to live like this one more day!

If rape/pedophilia is your strongman, then you are a bully who takes advantage of those that are too weak to defend themselves. Rapist and pedophiles (those that molest and rape children) are manipulative, lonely people. Just like committers of incest, you have experienced severe rejection in your lifetime. Your intention, especially for pedophiles, is not to hurt your victim. You just want to steal back the love that you were denied. You were starved for love, affection, affirmation and nurturing as a child, and you want to be compensated for that loss. You are just taking what you feel should have rightfully been yours in the first place.

Children make an easy target because they are so naïve, loving, kind, trusting and forgiving. Not every pedophile violently rapes their victims. You may or may not. For the most part, you would rather them come willingly because the aim is not to hurt but instead is to experience love. However, if the victim is being uncooperative a situation can easily turn into a violent rape because child molestation and rape are acts that are both induced by the same spirit. An uncooperative victim causes you to experience rejection all over again. In your mind, you are just trying to show this person love and they are rejecting your love. It makes you very angry.

Not every rapist molests children either. If you are not a child molester but rapist only, you were abused at some point in your life too. Pedophiles and rapist are both after a sense of control, but the need is different. A pedophile wants a friend and a lover. Pedophiles rarely see their victims as *victims*. But as a rapist, you have lost all hope that love exists. You do not want a friend or a lover. You do not believe in love anymore. You became angry and bitter because of all of the neglect that you suffered. You gave up hope at some point in your life and stopped caring. All you want now is revenge and control. You want to take revenge on somebody for the hardships and abuse that you have suffered in your lifetime. At some point in your past, someone made you feel weak and helpless. They took control away from you and now you desperately want to experience the sensation of control. You are often times just overwhelmed by the urge to be in control. These compulsions are what usually drive you to rape.

Regardless of which category you fall into, whether a pedophile or a rapist, someone violated you and now you want to redeem yourself by doing the same thing to another. It is just that two different methods are used. As a pedophile you want to control using manipulation and mental power. As a rapist you want to control using physical strength. In both cases, the goal is to control someone else the same way that you yourself were once controlled, and in controlling that person you want to force them to restore to you something that has been stolen away. Regardless of how you approach it, you are never satisfied after committing your acts of sexual perversion. What was taken from you can never be given back to you. No matter how many you may molest or rape that void is never filled. After the reality of what you have done hits home, you still feel weak and helpless and also ashamed.

After you victimize, you feel the exact same way that you did when you yourself were violated and abused in your past, except even worse. The abuse you suffered could have been sexual in nature, but that does not have to be the case. Any act of abuse makes you feel powerless and weak. You could have been bullied or picked on in school. Perhaps you were abandoned or neglected by your parents. A relative may have physically abused you or you may have been sexually abused. No matter what type of abuse it is that you suffered, the end result was this spirit of rape/pedophilia entering into your life. You are after a sense of fulfillment and acceptance, but the guilt that follows your acts of perversion serves only to drive you further into degradation, isolation and deviance.

Socially, you are a sneaky, eerie type of person. You give people a weird feeling. You may be very withdrawn, or you could be extremely outgoing. It depends on the depth of deception that you are in. In any event, you have a short temper and are easily frazzled. Especially true for pedophiles, you are a nervous person who is easily spooked. It is that deep sense of guilt that keeps you feeling this way. If you are the outgoing type, more common amongst rapist, then you want to be forthrightly in control of everything. Usually, your guilt is so deeply buried within you that you cannot even comprehend or acknowledge that you have done something wrong. In this case, you are a cocky and arrogant person. You have an intimidating demeanor about you that makes others leery about challenging you.

If you are the withdrawn type, you too want to be in control but you accomplish this craftily and subtly through manipulation. Secretly, you take great pleasure in your ability to fool and control people. However, guilt is ever looming over you and you are depressed. You try to stop what you are doing, but the guiltier you feel, the more helpless you feel. It only facilitates your sexual sins because that sense of helplessness causes you to continually and desperately seek out empowerment and control through molestation.

Rape/pedophilia may not be your strongman even if you commit these acts. It might be sexual lust or sexual fantasy which both greatly foster acts of rape and pedophilia. You should be remembering to use the Sexual Perversion Definitive Charts to help you determine this. It is important that you understand which spirits are driving you and which one is in control. This will help you in the deliverance process. Also, the spirit of pride is always operative in a rapist. Pride, violence and sexual lust combined will make a rapist out of you every time, so beware!

Manifestation in the spiritual

Some of the most famous pedophiles and rapists in history have been either satan worshipers or atheists. They are angry, bitter people often angry even at God. Commonly, this is the case because they themselves were victims of this type of crime at some point in their own lives. For those that are spiritually bound by this demon, it manifests itself in their spiritual lives by causing them to have a relationship with God that is shrouded in deception. Remember, this spirit makes victims out of the weaker, so such a person will not try to victimize God but will instead try to operate on His level.

They see themselves as a God in their own right. They force

weaker believers to worship them instead of God – the same way that natural pedophiles and rapist force weaker persons to have sex with them. Believers that have this spirit operating in them try to manipulate other believers into their way of thinking. They are highly defensive and take it very personally if you do not agree with them. You will usually find them surrounding themselves with young, immature Christians that are easily controlled. Preachers or leaders with this spirit actually expect to be worshiped. They do not see it that way, but that is the truth of the matter.

These believers most often times will have an entourage of *"yes"* men and women around them, who agree with everything they say and do. They are prime candidates for satan to use to start new cults. Occultism is all about mind control, deception and empowerment of the leader. Likewise, that is what this spirit is all about. Just like a rapist utterly violates a person's rights and tries to steal from them, believers with this spirit do the same thing amongst other believers. They are constantly speaking into the lives of others trying to control everything they do. They want their voice to be the loudest voice that others hear. They are seeking revenge against someone and they take it out on God and His children. They are deceived individuals with a distorted understanding of God and His Kingdom.

Victims are left not being able to trust people or God. They are rebellious at home and rebellious in the church. They too are angry and bitter. They feel dejected, dirty and worthless. It is very hard for them to receive Jesus' love and to believe that His promises are for them. They are the type of believers that no matter how much you minister to them and how much love you try to show them, they are always discouraged, down and depressed. But beware victims because you are the most likely people to become victimizers! That is how this spirit is able to maintain such a strong presence.

My personal experience:

Being raped or molested is a terrible experience for anyone to have to go through. I know what it is like to be both raped and molested. I know what it is like to have a pedophile living in the home with you. I know what it feels like to be violated and robbed of what is rightfully and sacredly yours. I know what it is like to be tricked, lied to and betrayed by someone you love. I know what it is like to experience the fear that your victimizer will kill you when he is finished. Yes, I know what it feels like. I have experienced it more than once or even twice.

The nightmares do not soon go away. You remember the look in their eyes, the smell of their breath and the touch of their skin. You remember the press of their body on yours. You remember the fear, the panic and the helplessness. It seems that you cannot get over the disgust of it. You try to wash it away, but you never feel quite clean. You become worthless and dirty in your eyes and you feel that can never be changed. You have been robbed and violated and even the thief himself cannot return to you what has been stolen.

You remember the confusion and the anger that follows. The anger stays with you and sometimes turns into bitterness. The distrust lingers on and on until you are completely bound by it. If you have ever been raped or molested then you need to ask God to totally heal you and be willing to receive His healing. I know that it seems impossible that you can ever be restored. I do know how you feel, but the devil is a liar! You can be completely healed and restored and you must! (I will detail spiritual healing in the next part of the book.)

It is so easy for you to go from being the victim to the victimizer. I never actually acted out the sin of pedophilia or rape (unless you consider what I did to Joey in the first grade rape! *Laugh*) However, I know that this spirit's presence was in my life. I remember discovering this two year old boy that I was babysitting playing with his genitals. I laughed and told him that he should keep doing it and then walked away as if I had never seen a thing. I did this because I had heard that frequent masturbation at a young age would promote penal growth. That is a very inappropriate thought to have about a toddler. I can also remember times that I had sexual thoughts about my own children. I never actually lusted after them but sexual images would pop into my mind at times when I was handling them. Sometimes I did not even want to bathe or change my children because of my disgust and fear for having such thoughts. (I know that sounds terrible, but I told you in the introduction that it is no holds barred on exposing sexual sin in my past. My desire is not to look good, it is to bring deliverance.)

This spirit manifested itself in another way in my relationship with my children as well. Not only did I have sexual thoughts toward them, but

I was also very abusive to them at a point in time. It really disturbed me. I could not understand why I was having those thoughts or acting the way that I was. My greater struggle though, with this spirit, was the effect that it had on me as a victim in the spiritual manifestations of it. I was such a controlling and manipulating person, which contributed to my involvement in witchcraft (another form of this spirit). It was not until the Holy Spirit revealed to me the things that I am writing to you in this book that it all finally made sense to me. I needed to allow Jesus to heal those wounds, give me peace and forgiveness, and fill the voids that had been left in my heart. It is a terrible thing to happen to anyone, but Jesus, Yeshua can and will heal you if you allow Him to. I know because He healed me.

If you have already committed this offense, I beg of you that you get help at once. You have, and will continue to, destroy so many lives by allowing this spirit to operate through you. Not only are you hurting the persons you victimize, but you will also be responsible for everyone that they victimize. Father God loves you and will forgive you. He understands why you behave the way that you do and He wants to help you. He knows that you are hurting and that you yourself were victimized so badly. Although what was taken from you as a child can never be given back to you, God can restore all that is missing within you.

The Bible says that *"He will restore the years (Joel 2:25)..."* He wants to heal you and set you free and restore <u>all</u> back to you. Please do not hurt anyone else. Just give God a chance. He loves you. I now feel comfortable around all children. I know that they are safe because Yeshua has made me whole. Once I understood that it is the Holy Spirit and not me that needs to be in control and furthermore understood that God is so good in my present that my past does not matter, it was then that I was able to be truly liberated and you too can be victoriously free! (***Please follow <u>ALL</u> steps in the deliverance process thoroughly.***)

Biblical references
Leviticus 18:10; Lamentations 5:11; Judges 19:22-30; Ezekiel 22:11; and 1 Corinthians 7:36

9. Beastiality

"A man must never defile himself by having sexual intercourse with an animal, and a woman must never present herself to a male animal in order to have intercourse with it; this is a terrible perversion." (Leviticus 18:23)

Definition
Sexual intercourse or any type of sexual contact with an animal.

Assignment
This spirit is assigned to draw people completely away from God. It aims to take them to the point of no return.

Manifestation in the natural

There is not really too much to say about this sin because the act itself needs no explanation. If the spirit of beastiality is your strongman, you would probably never even pick up a book like this unless by the power of the Holy Spirit. (*There is a reason why I say this. Read on and I will explain.*) However, I can still appeal to those that are operating under this spirit if it is not yet your strongman. What the act itself entails does not need to be explained, but the question of *'Why?'* must be answered.

This spirit can enter into your life through a generational curse. It can enter in through sexual lust or a hatred for The Lord. Exposure to satanism and occultism can also bring this spirit on. Having an unnaturally hateful person in your life at a vulnerable time can also leave an opening for this spirit. As this spirit takes over your life more, you will become a mean and hateful person who is mentally warped. You will have no respect for people, God, or any of His creation. You will not care about the environment or starving children in Africa. You just will not care *period*.

Once beastiality becomes your strongman, you will be inherently evil with no desire to repent or be restored back to normalcy. You will have no natural love within you for people, not even your parents or children. You will haphazardly hurt others without remorse. You will even get to the point of shunning humanity altogether because after a while you will lose your identity as a human being. You will lack natural affection and even the most basic moral principles and human values will be foreign to you. You will have no regard for other's feelings or appreciation for what others may try to do for you. As I stated earlier, this spirit can truly take you to the point of no return and that is why I say if beastiality is your strongman, I would be surprised to find you are even reading this book.

If you are reading this book and beastiality is your strongman, maybe you just picked it up out of curiosity, or perhaps you are not so far gone as of yet. Either way, you are in a good place having this book in your hands. The fact that you have continued to read it shows that you do still care somewhere deep in your heart. The part of you that longs for your true Creator is crying out for deliverance and if you want it, you can have it starting today, starting even right now! Please do not let that conviction that you feel pass away from you. If it does, it may be too late.

People that are involved in acts of beastiality are just too ashamed to admit it most of the times, which means that you refuse to seek help. You are even ashamed before God, although He already knows what you are doing. Do not let the spirit of guilt and condemnation cause you to perish. Conviction comes from the Holy Spirit of Jesus, but condemnation and guilt come from satan. Conviction motivates and moves you to pursue liberation, while condemnation paralyzes you in a prison of shame and guilt. Satan wants us to feel too ashamed to seek out deliverance, but do not be fooled. God still loves you and He wants to help you. Do not wait until it is too late! Go to the epilogue on page 277 and find out how to become born again and then continue to read this book. Find someone you trust or even a clergyman that you do not know to confide in. Repent before God in the name of Jesus, Yeshua and get prayer. He can and will break this stronghold off of your life.

Manifestation in the spiritual

The spirit of beastiality is empowered by the insatiable lust of the flesh that is in the world. The Bible calls this sin a *"terrible perversion"*. What is so terrible about this sin? Most people just find the thought of it detestable, but what really makes this sin so terrible is how inordinate and unnatural it is. Having sex with animals is a common practice in most satanic cults and that gives evidence to this spirit's assignment.

Man was created to worship God – to fellowship with and have communion with Him. That is why we are the only creatures on earth created in His likeness and His image *(Gen 1:27)*. Any type of sexual perversion is a deviation from God's intended purpose for mankind and is against His nature, but having sex with an animal is as far away from the natural order of creation as one can possibly get. We were created to have dominion over the animals of the earth, not to submit to them and become one with them through intercourse.

Anyone _sold out_ to the spirit of beastiality utterly hates the Lord God and has no relationship with Him at all aside from their hatred of Him. But, for believers that are not totally sold out to this spirit, yet have somehow fell victim to it to some degree, whether physically or just spiritually, their relationship with God is distorted in specific ways. Similar to the spirit of homosexuality, this spirit also affects our ability to produce spiritually and blinds us to our identity in Christ. However, this spirit goes a step further and distorts our identity as human beings.

As I stated previously, only man was created in the likeness and image of God, Elohim. To have sex with an animal prevents an individual from being able to even identify with humanity and therefore almost hopelessly thwarts their hopes of ever being one with God and His Son or taking on His nature. Therefore in believers, this spirit's aim is to create totally sold out satan worshipers. Just as there can be no greater deviation in nature from having sex with your spouse to that of having sex with an animal, so there can be no greater deviation in spirit from worshiping The Lord God to willfully worshiping satan.

These believers have a "love-hate" relationship with God, but they can't go on like this forever. They are lukewarm most of the time and if a change is not made, God will spew them out of His mouth *(Rev 3:16)*. Half of the time they do not even want to be bothered with Christianity. When they do, they have trouble fitting in and lack a sense of belonging and connectedness. They are ashamed about the way they feel toward God at times; too ashamed to let anyone else know about it. Because so many believers are so judgmental, if those operating under a spirit of beastiality ever have tried to confide in anyone, they were probably ridiculed and judged and pushed that much more into isolation.

Yet, it is hard for other believers to understand how someone could be so unnaturally disconnected from God. For this reason, those under this spirit do not enjoy fellowshipping with the saints and avoid church functions and gatherings. They have a very warped and unnatural interpretation of scripture and the Heavenly Kingdom, and this is all due to their inability to identify and be one with God. If you see any signs of this spirit operating in your walk with God, bind it now and seek out prayer from someone who is seasoned and mature in love. If you do not soon get delivered, you probably never will!

My personal experience

This is another sin that can be traced back in my ancestry, but I have very little personal experience with the sin of beastiality. I do however, have an experience to share. I mentioned earlier that this spirit can enter your life if you are exposed to someone who is unnaturally hateful. This was the case for me. I actually already had an opening for this spirit because I had been involved in witchcraft and satanic rituals as a child, but the manifestations did not begin until I got into a relationship with a domestic abuser. This man was extremely abusive and extremely hateful. He had six daughters and his five year old he particularly hated. He would frequently say to me, *"I can't stand that f*%king, b#$tch!"* I could not understand how someone could hate their own child so much. He hated old people, white people, children, animals, babies, his own parents and siblings – he just hated every one and everything, including me and my son. He especially hated anything that had to do with church or God. I could not even watch a Christian TV program with the volume turned all the way down, without getting cursed out by him.

So anyway, we were living together during our relationship and at that time we brought two cats home. (He only allowed it because of a serious mice infestation.) It was then that I began to fantasize about acts of beastiality. I began to strongly desire to watch animals have sex and found myself to be sexually stimulated by this activity. I also, at times had fantasies about my cats. At one point, I had begun to fantasize about the way they would have sex with one another and used these fantasies to stimulate myself during intercourse. I know that living with him afforded an opportunity for this spirit because I'd had four cats prior to these two cats and had never had such temptations.

Ironically, this spirit's manifestations subsided after my relationship with him ended but resurfaced after I had become a married, born again believer that really loved Jesus. As the Bible says, the heart is desperately wicked and deceitful above all things. We never really know what is lingering deep down on the inside of us. That is why we must allow God to reveal it all to us through fasting and prayer. In this way, we can bind each spirit and be truly liberated. At any rate, the beastiality fantasies started occurring again when I brought home two new cats from an animal shelter after getting married (another rodent problem, *laugh*!).

The cats were very strange from the beginning. We had family worship every night in the house and one of the cats utterly hated it when we would sing and praise God. He would always go as far away from us as he could and hide somewhere until we were finished. I do not know if the cat was evil or had been used in satanic rituals (they were all black cats) or what, but somehow the spirit of beastiality was being stirred within me. They were both male cats, and I was disgusted to find them having intercourse with one another once they came of age. I had never seen anything like it. *Gay cats?* However, as disgusted as I was, I found myself also to be sexually stimulated by it. Fortunately though, I realized what was going on and I was not going to take any chances with having those spooky cats in the house. I got rid of them both! God kept me once again.

To add knowledge to my limited experiences in this area, I was fortunate enough to meet a young Christian man that truly loves The Lord, who was once bound by the spirit of beastiality. Amazingly, he had shared his testimony about beastiality in front of the entire congregation during a tent revival one night. I was so touched that I began to cry. I could see a healing taking place in his spirit that night as he overcame the devil with the word of his testimony. I am sure he experienced a backlash afterward. Many are just not ready for that type of truth, but the victory that took place in the spirit that night cannot be erased by any means.

I had the opportunity to interview the young man before writing this section of the book, in order to gain some more insight into this spirit. I thank him for sharing with others and myself the powerful insight and truth that he did. I hope that more will follow his example of boldness and courage unto the glory of God. I know that because of his testimony being able to add knowledge to this book, he will be rewarded by the Father for those that get delivered as a result of it. In all though, I believe that the bottom line for beastiality is this: if you love Jesus even just a little bit, it will be hard for this spirit to really get a foothold on you, but if you are angry or bitter toward Him, you better watch out because this spirit could easily manifest itself in your life!

Biblical references
Leviticus 18:23, and 20:15-16

10. Sexual Lust (Lasciviousness)
"For all that is in the world, the lust of the flesh, and the lust of the eyes, and the pride of life, is not of the Father, but is of the world." (1 John 2:16)

*"Now the works of the flesh are manifest, which are these; Adultery, fornication, uncleanness, **lasciviousness**," (Gal 5:19 KJV)*

Definition
Lust – Desire, craving, longing, desire for what is forbidden, lust.

Sexual lust – Craving, longing, or desire to achieve sexual gratification through acts of sexual perversion.

Lasciviousness – Extreme sexual lust; sexual lust completely unbridled and totally unrestrained; the insatiableness of lust that will drive one to create endless new ways to commit sexual perversion. All acts of sexual perversion that are not mentioned by name within the assessments fall under the category of lasciviousness (i.e. orgies, sado masochism, sex with demons, etcetera...)

Assignment
This spirit is assigned to make its victim feel a complete loss of control over their bodies and desperately driven to satisfy an evil desire – to totally consume an individual's mind, body and soul until the person is unable to pursue God and is totally sold out to the sinful desires of the flesh.

Manifestation in the natural
Have you been unable to identify your strongman as of yet? Maybe you have seen yourself in several of the spirits but you have not yet been able to pinpoint exactly which one is really dominating in you. It is probably because sexual lust is your strongman. Sexual lust is a strong spirit but cannot easily be identified as the strongman because it cannot operate alone. Before I explain why, let me make sure there is no confusion concerning the difference between sexual lust and sexual impulse. Sexual impulse is the physical urge to be sexually gratified and is not in and of itself a sin. Almost every human being was created by God to experience sexual urges at some point in their life. The spirit of sexual lust goes beyond just the natural inbred urge to be sexually gratified. Sexual

lust is when we actually begin to desire acts of sexual perversion to fulfill those urges. We must exercise discipline to prevent sexual impulses from turning into sexual lust.

The reason that I say that sexual lust cannot operate alone is because the sensation of lust itself is not an *act* of sexual perversion. Lust, whether sexual or otherwise, is a sin in its own right. Just the fact that lust is present in one's heart is evidence that evil and sin resides within that person. The Bible says that lust is not of the Father but of the world *(1 John 2:16)*. Lust is not just a desire for something. It is a desire for something that is evil and contrary to Holiness and Righteousness. However, the spirit of sexual lust must work in conjunction with some other evil spirit in order for an actual *act* of sin in the flesh to take place. It must manifest itself through some particular *act* of sexual perversion and that is what makes sexual lust so difficult to identify as the strongman.

If sexual lust is your strongman, you are dealing with the greater stronghold of *"lust of the flesh"* that is in the world. Sexual lust is just another manifestation of that greater demon of lust in general that operates within the entire earth. If this is the dominating spirit in your life, it may be the case that no particular act of sexual perversion is your favorite. Sexual lust drives you to seek out sexual gratification in whatever vice is available to you at that time, whether it is fornication, masturbation, beastiality, incest or whatever. It does not matter. You just want to satisfy that craving.

The spirit of sexual lust can drive you to commit any act of sexual perversion. You may still have a favorite act of sexual perversion. You may even turn your nose up at other acts, but you have to understand that lust just wants the craving to be satisfied. If at the time lust consumes you, your preferable act of sexual perversion cannot be performed for some reason, you will settle for whatever other act is available – even acts you swore you would never commit. Sexual lust will drive you to do things that you never dreamed you would. Sexual lust is that spirit that causes you to have sex with the ugliest person you know, even though you are not attracted to them. It is the spirit that will cause you to commit homosexuality, even though you have always been homophobic. It is the spirit that will cause you to cheat on your spouse, even though your marriage is solid and your spouse a dream. Lust will cause you to do anything, anywhere, anytime without any thought of the consequences that may follow.

Have you committed acts of sexual perversion that are not listed in the assessments? Acts such as sex with dead people, orgies, multiple partners in one night, swinging, sex with demons, or sado masochism? These acts do not each have their own individual category because the Bible does not expressly describe them. Because lust is never satisfied, the world will never cease to think of new ways to pervert intimacy and so the Bible just sums it all up with one word – lasciviousness. Whatever you are into that may have not yet been named, it is all implemented by the spirit of sexual lust. Sexual lust **is** your strongman. However, if sexual lust has already gotten to the stage of lasciviousness in your life you are in a greater level of bondage and it is unlikely that you would even be reading this book (*unless you thought you might get some new ideas!*)

Lasciviousness is an insane lust, and only a sane and sound mind can consciously choose to accept Jesus as Lord and servitude to God.[2] To put it plainly, lasciviousness is extreme lust. It is lust completely unrestrained and totally out of control. Most people involved in acts of lasciviousness have been exposed to satanism, occultism or witchcraft. This exposure may have been intentional and obvious (*i.e. voodoo, spells, incantations, calling on demonic powers*) or intentional but out of ignorance (*i.e. horoscopes, physics, deceptive religious group, mind control, manipulation*). Either way, lasciviousness only occurs in the lives of people who have with hostility, alienated themselves from The Lord. They have intentionally rebelled and pledged allegiance to satan – if not by their words, certainly by their actions!

In the case of lasciviousness or otherwise, sexual lust makes your flesh burn. This spirit can actually convince you that you are going to literally die if you do not do something to satisfy the craving immediately. It makes you restless. It takes over your mind and your body all at once. It is an ambushing spirit that likes to attack you suddenly. It will lie dormant

---

[2] If this does describe you and you are somehow by the Mercies of the Almighty God reading this book, I beg of you to accept Yeshua (Jesus) as your Lord and Savior right now. You can turn to page 277 to find out how, or just pray to re-dedicate yourself to Him if you already once knew Him but then turned away. He must be seeking after you to have given you the fortitude to read this book. Please open the door of your heart to Him.

and then suddenly attack you at a time that you feel unprepared to deal with it. It will then incite some act of sexual perversion in order that your lusting can be satisfied. Sexual lust often works closely with sexual fantasy. This is because the desires of lust are most easily fostered and empowered by sexual fantasy.

In most cases, the other spirits of sexual perversion cannot operate in your life without the assistance of sexual lust. The *desire* to commit the act of sin is what finally causes most people to fall. This is not always the case though. Some people commit acts of sexual perversion and do not at all desire the act itself and/or get no enjoyment out of it. In these cases, it is the desperate need to fill a spiritual void that drives a person to commit acts of sexual perversion, without sexual lust being present. *(Of course, if this is the case then sexual lust is not their strongman.)* If sexual lust does dominate within you then you are undoubtedly an impatient, restless, greedy, desperate, untrustworthy, selfish and envious person. These traits are manifested because if sexual lust is present in your life, other manifestations of lust are present as well. Lustful people are impatient and greedy. They are restless and anxious to get their lust satisfied.

You have to understand that **lust can never be satisfied**. Lust is **all** that is in the world. This whole world's system is founded in lust and it always wants immediate gratification and it will never be satiated. Therefore, if the spirit of sexual lust binds you, you are a greedy, impatient individual that is never satisfied and is always restlessly trying to fulfill your desires. You are so desperate to satisfy your lust that you will beg, borrow or steal. As I stated previously, this spirit makes you feel as if you absolutely cannot survive unless the craving is satisfied.

That sense of "a need to survive" creates the feeling of desperation within you and thus you cannot be trusted. You cannot be trusted because you will do anything to satisfy your own greedy craving. That breeds selfishness in you. You do not care who you have to hurt or let down or hinder in order to satisfy your lust. It could be your children, your friends, your family, your employer or anyone else. Anyone or anything that is standing in the way of you satisfying your lust is going to be crushed. You are loyal to no one because lust is a slave driver. You are allowed to serve only it. You can be unreliable because of this and do not make a good friend to people. Lust is a covetous spirit and thus you are an envious person. You are never satisfied with what you have and always want what someone else has. Lust makes you think that you have to have what they have and drives you to go after it. But no matter how much you have, you always want more. You are never satisfied.

As I already stated, sexual lust makes your flesh burn and that is why the Apostle Paul says in the Bible that it is better to marry than to burn with lust *(1 Cor 7:9)*. He was not encouraging people to just find any old Tom, Dick or Harry, or any old Sue, Jane or Mary; but he knew how dangerous this spirit of sexual lust is. Most of these other spirits that we have discussed take over your life somewhat slowly. You can see what is happening with the other spirits and regain control before it is too late. But not lust. Lust blind sides you. You never know that it is coming and by the time you realize it, it is often times too late. Sexual lust will cause your life to spiral out of control so fast that you will not even be able to remember exactly how and when it happened. You will just know that you are now lost in blinding darkness and trapped within your own evil desires and the consequences thereof. Lust is all that is in the world. Lust is the spirit of the world. Lust is the soul of satan.

Manifestation in the spiritual

Sexual lust is the most likely spirit of sexual perversion, to be the strongman of a Spirit-filled believer. This is because more than any other spirit, sexual lust plays on our natural inclination toward sexual desire. Every other spirit of sexual perversion operates out of some spiritual void or wound within us. As we get closer to God and those voids are filled, those spirits no longer have a place to reside, are cast down and become inoperative. But sexual lust is an opportunist. It thrives on desires that were naturally given to us by God that will never go away. Therefore, lust will always have a channel through which to operate. Lust does not care if you are a believer or not. It is going to try to take advantage of you.

As a Christian, lust cannot ***utterly control*** your life because you have Jesus' Spirit, so it will not be the overall dominating spirit of your entire life, but it will be as far as sexual sin is concerned. As I already mentioned, lust is the spirit of world. Therefore, *if lust completely dominates you or has gotten so out of hand that is has become lasciviousness*, you are not truly a born again believer in Jesus. You may be a believer, but you are not a born again believer, you are not a Christian at all. You cannot be a true child of God and be dominated by the spirit of satan. *"... If anyone loves the world, love for the Father is not in him. (1 John 2:15a, AMP)"*

This may sound harsh to you if you have been considering yourself to be a Christian, but if any type of lust **_controls and dominates_** your life you are not of God the Father and do not at all have His Spirit. The above scripture and many others in the Bible prove it. You belong to satan and are not a part of the covenant of reconciliation that was established in the Blood of Jesus. Your eternity will be spent with your father the devil if you do not repent wholeheartedly and let Jesus clean your spirit. Please do not be offended by this statement, but instead examine yourself truly and read the Holy Word of God in order that you may see yourself in the Light of His truth. God can cleanse you and save you, but you must be aware of your utter need for His intervention! Does lust control and dominate you?

As for those that are truly born again believers, I warn you that the weaker you are spiritually, the more carnally minded you are as a believer, the more likely you are to be dragged into sexual sin by this spirit. If many believers were to tell the truth, they would have to admit that they are often times struck by sexual lust even during church services and personal devotional time. During our pursuit of intimacy with God, we become extremely susceptible to this spirit because of the parallel between natural sex and spiritual worship. Because often times our spirits are already perverted, we do not know how to detach the two. We become very vulnerable when attempting to worship. As I stated earlier, sexual lust is an ambushing and opportunistic spirit. It waits until your own natural sexual urges are stirred and then attacks!

Not only during attempted worship, but it can be a situation as innocent as one washing their genitals while taking a shower and the next thing you know a sexual urge arises. The urge itself is not bad, but if sexual lust is operative in your life it will seize that opportunity and consume you with burning lust inciting the act of masturbation. A sister in church may be kneeling at the altar for prayer and her breasts become exposed causing a stir in your body. That stir is not wrong, but lust will attempt to seize that moment and turn it into a sexual fantasy. Maybe some perverse person on your job touches your butt one day and walks away. Lust will have you to follow after the person and commit adultery. Every believer, no matter how mature or sincere in his or her walk with God, is susceptible to this spirit. Why? Because we all experience spiritual lows and walk carnally after the flesh at times.

If you are a believer that is really struggling with the spirit of sexual lust, it would come as a surprise to me if you are not actually *acting* out some other sin of sexual perversion. It could be fornication, homosexuality or even perversely motivated sex with your spouse. It could be any of the acts that we've discussed, but regardless of the act the bottom line is that lust is a powerful spirit and it usually is able to manifest itself in some sexually perverse *act*. If sexual lust is your sexual strongman, I must warn you that you have quite a battle on your hands. Then too the Spirit of Victory is living in you if you are willing to submit! Yet, you should not take this situation lightly because you are in a very dangerous place. Lust is the foundation of every sin on earth that has ever been committed or ever will be committed. *"But every man is tempted, when he is drawn away of his own lust, and enticed.* ***Then when lust hath conceived, it bringeth forth sin:*** *and sin, when it is finished, bringeth forth death. (James 1:14-15, KJV)"* Satan lusted after God's throne and Power in Heaven and that caused him to sin. Eve lusted after the forbidden fruit in the garden and that caused her to sin. Cain lusted after Abel's relationship with God, and thus he sinned. Sin begins and ends with lust.

As believers, sexual lust wants to do much more than just cause us to commit acts of sexual perversion. We can be believers that truly love The Lord and really want to serve Him and yet struggle with some evil desires. We may not always act out these desires, but the fact that they are present within us is evidence that evil still resides in our hearts. We already learned that sexual lust is actually under the authority of that stronger demonic ruler of lust. Ultimately, it is this stronger spirit of lust that is in the world that aims to control us. When lust is in our hearts, it causes us to desire things that are against God's Righteousness.

The more we yield to God and delight ourselves in Him, by meditating on and studying His Word, the more our desires will change. If we continue to give into lust by failing to exercise discipline and self-control and failing to build up our spirit man in the things of the Kingdom, we will be led into more acts of sin. Sin causes separation from God and separation from Him leads to death. Lust wants us to be totally separated from our Creator, be sold out to the pleasures of this world and die spiritually. It wants us to be totally consumed mind, body and spirit with the pleasures of this world and desperately driven to fulfill our evil desires.

Lust is always aiming to become lasciviousness within us and lasciviousness often times takes people to the point of no return. This is because lust is the spirit of the world, and satan is the spirit of the world. Satan hates God and if you continue to indulge in lust you will come to hate Him as well. We can look into the Bible and find two instances of lasciviousness taking a people to the point of no return. *"²And many will follow their immoral ways and lascivious doings...⁵And He spared not the ancient world...when He brought a flood upon the world of ungodly [people]. (2 Pet 2:2a; 5a, c; AMP)"* In these verses of scripture, the Bible talks about the flood in the days of Noah. What was going on in those days? Lasciviousness – people were having sex with demons. Sexual lust had gotten completely out of control and it was said of that people *"⁵Now The Lord observed the extent of the people's wickedness, and he saw that all their thoughts were consistently and totally evil. (Gen 6:5)"* He then destroyed every wicked person on the earth because they loved lust but hated Him.

Then again we see God destroy an entire geographical location that was inhabited by a lascivious people. *"⁷[The wicked are sentenced to suffer] just as Sodom and Gomorrah and the adjacent towns – which likewise gave themselves over to impurity and indulged in unnatural vice and sensual perversity — (they) are laid out [in plain sight] as an exhibit of perpetual punishment [to warn] of everlasting fire. (Jude 1:7, AMP)"* The Lord said of these people, *"...the shriek [of the sins] of Sodom and Gomorrah is great and their sin is exceedingly grievous. (Gen 18:20b, AMP)"* If you read the entire context story about these two scriptures in Genesis chapter 19, you will see that these people were unnaturally wicked in their sexually perverse acts. Just as the people in Noah's day, they too desired to have sex with angels. They had no regard or reverence for the Lord God or His Holy beings. In both of these instances, lasciviousness had taken the people beyond the point of no return and the end result for them was eternal damnation. This is what sexual lust wants to do to you!

A believer that is operating under the spirit of lust will always try to find some excuse to fulfill their evil desires. They are good for misinterpreting the Word of God into something that will support the fulfillment of their lust. They are very opinionated and are blinded by lust from the truth. They are impatient and lack faith. They always want immediate answers and immediate gratification. They will not be able to maintain a close personal walk with the Father because their lust always drags them into sin, which separates them from Him. They are seldom at peace because they are always restless about having their desires met right away. At times, when they are winning the battle, they may be very spiritual and fruitful, but when they are losing you will see a stark difference in their personality. They ride a spiritual roller coaster and lack stability in their walk with God due to the frequency of them falling into sin when consumed by lust. They are greedy for position and prestige in the church. They are the ones that preach for filthy lucre and manipulate people for their own personal gain.

These are dangerous people to put into leadership positions because they are greedy and selfish. They lead according to what will cause them to prosper and be benefited. They have no concern for the needs of the people. You may note these believers coveting the gifts or positions of others due to envy because they are never satisfied with what they have. They are often gifted but seldom anointed. The anointing is only given to those whom God can trust and those operating in lust cannot be trusted. They are desperate to satisfy their own desires. Even if their desire is concerning some ministerial pursuit, it is still not according to God's will because their motives are not right. Since it is not God's will, His blessing is not on it and you will see them moving in desperation, severely compromising the principles and Word of God in order to fulfill their lustful pursuits.

I believe that sexual lust is the most dangerous of all of the spirits of sexual perversion because 1) you can be whole in Christ and still be confronted with and fall into lust; 2) it can lead you into all other acts of sexual perversion; 3) it takes advantage of our natural desires and everyday needs; 4) it can so quickly take over your life; 5) it can never be permanently shut out because of how it comes in; discipline and self-control must be there everyday, and finally; 6) it can lead you right into bondage to the greater spirit of lust which is the spirit of the world and the soul satan. It can overtake you with lasciviousness and doom you to eternal damnation. *"...Then when lust hath conceived, it bringeth forth sin: and sin, when it is finished, bringeth forth death."* If you lust you will eventually die. Please take your deliverance seriously. Go after it violently starting right now!

My personal experience

There is not anyone that has committed acts of sexual perversion that does not have a personal experience with sexual lust. Lust is more than just a generational curse. It is a mankind curse. If you are a human being, lust runs in your family. For me, sexual lust was prevalent in my life from the time I started puberty – the transition from girlhood to womanhood. It was present with me when I committed masturbation that night when I was twelve. That was my first *conscious* act of sexual perversion and sexual lust was there, taking advantage of the sexual impulse that had been stirred in my body. Because I was young and inexperienced, I did not know how to sexually gratify myself through masturbation. Not being able to satisfy the craving only perpetuated lust in my life because part of what drives lust is the fact that it can never be satisfied.

When I became sexually active with men, the stronghold of sexual lust increased. I can remember being eighteen and having sex with this guy that I found to be ugly as sin. He had been trying to get with me for a long time, but I was dating one of his best friends at the time. Besides, he was scrawny looking, always wore bummy clothes, he was not very intelligent and his breath was kicking! Although he was a nice guy, there was nothing at all physically appealing about him. To top it all off because no girl really wanted to be with him, he was known for having sex with prostitutes. He and I sold drugs together and therefore spent a lot of late night hours in close proximity, and so I had witnessed him sleeping with prostitutes with my very own eyes.

But like I said, when you are dealing with lust nothing else matters. I was high on drugs the day I had sex with him. Drugs and alcohol cause you to lose control of your mind and thus weaken the restraints you would normally hold yourself to. Intoxicating substances and lust are great buddies, believe me. Since the guy knew that I liked to smoke, he came to my house and used the drugs as a way to gain my attention. Soon we were high, talking and laughing up a storm. Then my guard was down and the next thing you know we were touching and lust suddenly seized me. I was so repulsed at the site of the guy or even the thought of having sex with him that I turned my back to him, but I was *burning with lust*. I was going to explode if I did not do it (this is what lust told me). I had to have sex and he was the only one there. He did not even have any protection with him and even knowing that he frequently slept with prostitutes, I still had sex with him, my backside to him so I would not have to see his face, without using a condom!

Lust will kill you my friend! I wonder how many AIDS victims are really dying of sexual lust. In spite of the fact that I contracted an STD from that guy after having sex with him that day, it did not slow me down or make me any more cautious. I cannot even count the number of times I had sex with some unsavory character that I hardly knew because of sexual lust. If they did not ask, I did not even bother with condemns. Lust is not looking out for your best interest. Most of us know that condoms lessen sensation and compromise spontaneity and lust is greedy. It wants ultimate and immediate gratification.

There were days that I snuck guys into my house and times that I did not come home at night when I was still a teenager. I knew that my Mom was going to flip out on me, but I did it because of lust. I had sex outside on the streets, at other people's houses, in rooms crowded with people, in cars, in bars – where ever lust consumed me that is where I did it. I would have sex anywhere, anytime, anyplace, with just about anyone. I did it because of sexual lust. I desperately had to fulfill my lusting. That is why I found myself to be with STDs so often. It is only by the enduring tender mercies of the Father that I did not end up with HIV or AIDS. I should surely be dead right now. He has been so good to me. (Hallelujah! That is why most people don't understand my praise! Thank you Yeshua! Glory!!!)

Most of the times I had sex, fornication was still in control of me, but it would not have been able to operate without the assistance of sexual lust. However, once I became a born again believer, after some time, fornication lost its grip on me. So did homosexuality and all of the other spirits of sexual perversion. *(Except masturbation, which I still did not acknowledge as sin at that time.)* Those many spirits of sexual perversion still hovered around me, but they did not have the same free reign that they had once had. However, I did not understand what sexual lust really meant back then and it was the spirit of lust that kept its claws locked around me for the longest time to come. The reason that sexual lust is the last spirit of sexual perversion that I list for an assessment *(promiscuity is only an assisting spirit),* is because it is the last one the Holy Spirit revealed to me. I did not understand sexual lust until I started writing this book.

Not too long before I started writing the book, I had gone on a very long fast and consecration. During that time, God told me to fast from sex with my husband for 40 days. My husband agreed and so I said with my lips, *"I will obey you Lord."* But in my heart, I wanted to have sex with my husband. One night during the fast, I was pursuing my husband sexually. I was thinking in my mind as I was stirring his passions, *"This is my husband. Why should I have to fast from sex with him? We have fasted and abstained from sex so many times already Lord. I have been pregnant three times in the last three years. I've missed out on enough sex. This is my husband. I love him...blah, blah, blah..."* This was my mental rationalization for attempting to disobey my Lord. But, as I was working on getting my hubby's fire started, I heard the voice of the Father speak to me so clearly. He said to me, ***"I said no! If you can't say no to your husband, you will not be able to say no to any man! I AM trying to clean your spirit!!"*** I moved away from my husband so quickly, you might have thought that he had cut the cheese Honey!

Jesus wanted to get sexual lust out of my heart. It is one thing for lust to operate as an outside influence trying to control your flesh, but it is another thing altogether when it is on the inside of you. Lust was still in my heart and I had no idea. I had not even so much as masturbated for a very long time, so I could not see it. But it was lingering deep down inside just waiting for an opportunity to take over me, and it was even showing itself in my sexual relations with my husband. We did not realize it though. When The Lord began to deal with the sexual lust in my heart, He did not just take it out of me all at once. It was almost a one year long process. Exposing the spirit of lust just stirred it up and caused it to manifest itself more blatantly. Once stirred, God allowed me to *struggle* with the spirit of sexual lust until I fully understood how it operates.

He perfected me in my failures and gave me the wisdom I needed to be able to teach you about this spirit. My struggle has now become your gain. The most important thing that you need to understand about sexual lust, especially as a believer, is that every other act of sexual perversion is derived out of some spiritual wound, void or need. However, sexual lust is derived out of the sin nature of the flesh itself. It is a lust of the flesh and it thrives on our inbred desires, needs and urges as human beings. Because we are encased in flesh, lust will always have an opportunity to attack us. Even if your heart is made clean, your flesh will never be clean. That is why we must crucify the flesh. Dead flesh cannot be used.

After Jesus began to fill the spiritual voids in my life, I was liberated from the many spirits of sexual perversion that had me bound; including the strongman of fornication. But when all other spirits of sexual perversion lost power in my life, sexual lust still remained. Because I did not understand lust or how it operated, I kept focusing in on the actual *acts* of sexual sin that I was committing. I tried fasting and praying and binding. Yet, my focus was always on the act and never the spirit of sexual lust and that is the mistake you must avoid making. As you go into **Part II** of the book and begin to learn how to close doors on spirits so that they cannot return, you are going to have to learn how to examine your behavior. You may still sometimes fall, even after being delivered from (let us say for example) masturbation. When that happens, you must be able to determine whether you have not truly been delivered from masturbation, or whether you have been delivered but are just under an attack from lust.

Is it the *spirit* of masturbation or just the *act* of masturbation? If you are sure that you have truly been delivered from the spirit of masturbation and you are then suddenly consumed with temptation one day and fall, you will know that the fall is due to sexual lust. You must learn to distinguish between an _act of perversion_ and a _spirit of perversion_. It is important to know what spirit you are dealing with because deliverance from lust has to be approached a little differently. Once you read **Part II**, know in advance that Steps 11 and 12 are going to be the main keys to walking in victory over sexual lust. We will talk about this more later.

Biblical references
Romans 1:28-31, 1 Corinthians 10:8, Galatians 5:19-21, 1 Thessalonians 4:4-5, James 1:14-15, 2 Peter 1:4-6, and 1 John 2:16-17

11. Promiscuity

"Why spill the water of your springs in public, having sex with just anyone?" (Prov 5:16)

Definition
Lacking discrimination or selectivity, especially when referring to a number of different sexual partners.

Assignment
Promiscuity is not an actual spirit of sexual perversion. It is an assisting spirit. Its assignment is to assist other demon spirits (sexual demons as well as other types) in gaining access to your life. Ultimately, it is assigned to distract and confuse you.

Manifestation in the natural

The last spirit that I want to talk about before we go on to **Part II** of the book is promiscuity. Promiscuity cannot in and of itself be the sexual strongman nor is it an actual act of sexual perversion. Promiscuity is a spirit that acts as an assistant to the other demons of sexual perversion. Promiscuity is not assigned to any one particular spirit. It will work with any of the other spirits of sexual perversion that may be operating in your life, if it is given the opportunity to. There are of course some acts of sexual perversion that are less likely to induce promiscuity, such as the act of incest which causes you to focus in on just one person. And there are some other acts of sexual perversion that are more likely to induce promiscuity such as prostitution. Sexual lust facilitates promiscuity greatly. Remember, lust is never satisfied and causes you to want to commit more and more acts of sexual perversion. Therefore, promiscuity will usually come along with sexual lust if lust is your strongman. However, in most cases no matter which spirit of sexual perversion is your strongman, promiscuity is going to be operating in your life to at least some degree.

The moment you move on to your second sexual partner, unless your spouse has died and you have remarried, promiscuity has entered your life because truly you were created to have sex with only one partner. Promiscuity's assignment is to cause you to commit acts of sexual perversion with as many different partners as possible. Once promiscuity can find an opportunity to operate in your life, its job is to open the door for other demon spirits so that they may build new strongholds within your spirit. The Bible teaches us that the act of sex actually causes two people to become one *(1 Cor 6:16)*. You are literally joining yourself together with whomever you commit acts of sexual perversion with. That means that when you commit an act of perversion with someone, whatever spirit oppresses that person will then have access to you through your connection with him or her. In this way more and more spirits of sexual perversion can gain access to you.

Something that we have not talked about yet is the fact that the names that I have listed for these spirits of sexual perversion are just headings. There is not only **one** spirit of prostitution operating in the earth or only **one** spirit of homosexuality operating in the earth. For each heading or title name that I have given you for the different acts of sexual perversion, there are innumerable spirits that operate in the earth under that heading, each attempting to carry out the specifications of the assignment. Furthermore, each spirit will operate within the limitations or greatness of its power because there are different levels of power among demons. *(We can read about this in the Bible in Ephesians 6:12 and Matthew 12:45.)* In actuality, it is possible for you to have two, three or even more spirits of the same kind operating in you all at once, each functioning with a characteristic rank of power. *(Mark 5:9, 16:9 [some Bibles do not have Mark 16:9])* I am sure that I must have had a legion of demons that went by the name of fornication operating in me. That is why it was always able to remain the strongman until I got married.

I tell you this to help you understand that promiscuity will not only open doors to spirits and acts of sexual perversion you have never committed before, but that it can also enable spirits of sexual perversion that are already operating in your life to manifest themselves more strongly. For instance, I already had a spirit of prostitution operating in my life as early as age fourteen. It was not a very strong spirit though and had only accomplished influencing me into being a stripper. However, after making sexual contact with a street prostitute, the spirit of prostitution gained a stronger presence in my life. The sexual connection that I made with the street prostitute gave a stronger spirit of prostitution entranceway into my life and that new more powerful spirit began to work along with the one that was already present. Consequently, I went from just dancing on stage, to fulfilling off-stage request, to making plans to go out of town to work a street corner in Atlanta.

Even though promiscuity is not an actual act of sexual perversion and is only an assisting spirit, it is a very dangerous spirit. Just think of all of the demons you are exposing yourself to when you have sex with different people. You are literally having sex with, and opening the door to, every demon of perversion that is in the persons you have sex or sexual contact with. That means that if you are strictly heterosexual and then have sex with someone who is homosexual, homosexuality now has a doorway into your life. You may then see that act manifested in your life at some later time. What makes it so bad is that it is not only spirits of sexual perversion that gain entrance into your life through sexual contact, but any type of demon that is operating in the life of the person you connect with will now have access to you. It could be anger, hatred, addiction, manipulation or witchcraft; a demon of any kind could enter into you causing you to take on a person's spirit and nature.

Have you ever done something that was really uncharacteristic for you and just asked yourself the question, *"Where did that come from? Why in the world did I do that?"* A lot of times these are the workings of demon spirits that have been transferred into your life from someone you had sex with. I started smoking cigarettes when I was fifteen, just months after being in an on-going sexual relationship with a guy that smoked, even though I had always hated cigarettes. I started selling drugs shortly after getting into an on-going sexual relationship with a guy who sold drugs. I began to crave violence after being in a sexual relationship with a man who loved death and murder. The list could go on and on. Through our sexual contact, I picked up their demons and their spiritual weaknesses.

It having already been established that two people actually become one through sex, (not only in body but in spirit as well) you have to understand that you are not only receiving spirits but giving spirits as well. That is why promiscuity can bring about emptiness and confusion in your life. You are taking into yourself things that should not be there and giving away the things that should (pieces of your heart and soul). Having sex with many different people is like taking a large number of different jigsaw puzzles and mixing them all up. Let's say for example, you and every person you have sex with are each represented by a 5,000 piece jigsaw puzzle. Now think of approximately how many people you have had sex with. Now think of mixing all of those different puzzles together and trying to sort them out!

Bear in mind that if the people you have had sex with, have already had sex with others then they were already jumbled up when you met them. And the people they had sex with may have been jumbled up already too. Oh my Lord, what chaos and confusion this causes. Your whole spirit consists of the fragmented pieces of the many wounded, wicked and dysfunctional spirits you have had sex with. You do not even possess all of your own fragments anymore and yet you contain a multitude of fragmented mess that should not be there. This is a picture of such complex confusion that only the Holy Spirit will be able to sort you out and put you back together.

That is why if you have promiscuity operating in your life, you are suffering from an identity crisis. One of the most common non-sexual spirits that you are going to see in conjunction with promiscuity is confusion. Because confusion is in your life, you cannot really define who you are. You really do not know what you are or what you want to be. And this is especially true if you became promiscuous at a young age because when you are young you have not yet had a chance to finish developing into a whole person. You have not even successfully defined yourself as an individual, as opposed to being defined as someone's son or daughter. You have not discovered yourself, nor have you had a chance to perfect and polish who you are. Therefore, the effects of promiscuity can lock you into a place of immaturity and stunt your mental and emotional growth.

So promiscuity's assignment is to work in conjunction with other spirits of sexual perversion in order to bring you under greater oppression and new types of bondage. It takes its assignment as an assisting spirit very seriously and you better take it seriously too. You are losing more of yourself every time you have sex. You are becoming more mentally confused each time you connect with someone. One of the most detrimental impacts of promiscuity is that the effects of its workings in your life extend long beyond the sexual experience.

Referring back to the example of the jigsaw puzzles, you can stop mixing new puzzles into the jumbled mess but that is not going to cause the ones that have already been mixed together to automatically sort themselves out. The pieces of your soul will still be scattered across the earth and you will not know what in you is really you or really a fragment of someone else. The demons and habits that you pick up through the workings of promiscuity will stay with you for years, maybe even for life. Only by allowing God to come in and make you whole once again and restore you back to His image and likeness can you be healed.

Manifestation in the spiritual

I did not list many personality traits in the last section on promiscuity because pinpointing the personality traits of promiscuity is not so easy. This is because a promiscuous person has the traits of so many different human souls and demons. It could really manifest itself in an endless number of ways, but the most common way is confusion. Also, promiscuity is going to have the same effect on your personality both naturally and spiritually because it manifests itself more as a personality type than an actual act. Therefore, I chose to list some of the more common personality traits of promiscuity in this section.

If you are a sexually active person that has sex with more than one partner, than the fact that promiscuity is operating in your life is obvious, but just as is the case with each of the other demons we have discussed, this spirit can still work in your life even if you are not committing any *acts* of sexual perversion. Because it is not an act, promiscuity often manifests itself as a seemingly harmless personality type that is often ignored. If you are a believer that is not sexually active you may not consider this spirit to be a threat, but promiscuity is about more than just sex with a lot of different people. Just look again at the definition, *"Lacking discrimination or selectivity..."* If you are a person that never really has a favorite anything, if you instead of choosing one take them all, if you are in love with someone new every month, if one week this show is your favorite and the next week it is another show, if you change friends often, if you just do not care who you hang out with; if you feel a need to be a part of everyone and everything; you have a spirit of promiscuity operating in your life.

Being choosy about whom you let into your life is important in and out of Christ, but as a believer selectivity is even more important. We are often warned in the Bible of the dangers of false prophets and doctrines *(2 Pet 2:1-3)*. We are also admonished to separate ourselves from other believers that are not walking uprightly before God *(1 Cor 5:11)*. We are definitely strictly charged to sanctify ourselves from the world *(2 Cor 6:17)*. Promiscuity will hinder a believer's ability to do all of these things. There are a number of different ways that spirits can gain access to your life. Sex is only one of those ways. Promiscuity does not have to work only through sexual relationships. It can work through friendships, fellowships, teachings and activities. Promiscuity wants you to expose and connect yourself to as many different things, people and entities as possible. Maximum exposure yields the greatest opportunity for new demonic influences to enter your life.

Promiscuity is going to affect a person's prayer, their study and their worship because promiscuity drives them to connect with things and people and leaves them with no quality time for God. Not spending that quality time with Him is going to leave them confused about His true call on their life. In church they are going to be truly indecisive about everything. They are not going to be sure if they want to sing or dance or usher or even be in church at all. Or, they will be unsure if they are called to be an evangelist or a teacher or a pastor. Not being able to make a decision about what is or is not for them, in terms of ministry work, will keep them all over the church trying to do everything. They will be totally misplaced and completely ineffective in the work of the Kingdom.

Having an indiscriminate nature is also going to leave them open to believe just about anything. It will furthermore stifle their ability to discern spirits. They will accept just about anything or anyone – anything goes with them. A person is not able to watch and pray when this spirit is operative in their life because they are too busy trying to be a part of everything. They have to be in the mix of everything. This spirit's greatest assignment is to ultimately bring about confusion in your life and keep you busy and distracted. Thus, these believers are the people, leaders included, that have to always be at someone else's church or have someone else at their church. These believers are constantly running and gunning and talking about the need to preach out or *'fellowship'*. Preaching and fellowshipping is important but it should not come before your intimate relationship with God! The dangers of this assisting spirit are very real. Examine yourself and make sure promiscuity is not in your life.

My personal experience

Well... what can I say? I have to expose myself once again, but I do so for the benefit of the readers that are truly seeking deliverance. Promiscuity was a serious stronghold in my life and it really did a job on me. Before I was finally married, I had committed acts of sexual perversion with over 200 different men and women. Promiscuity was of course in my family history. Growing up, Mom dibbled and dabbled in everything. She was a Pentecostal, a Jehovah's Witness, a Baptist, a Muslim, a Five Percenter, a Seven Day Adventist and a New Age Religionist at one point. I did not know what to believe when I got older. However, I think what really allowed promiscuity into my life were the wounds of rejection that I carried.

When a person experiences rejection, they begin to feel desperate to connect with anyone and anything. I suffered rejection from the time I was just a toddler. I can remember not being liked by the other children when I was only in Pre-school. I did not even know why the kids did not like me, but I was just never liked by my peers. This seemed to only get worse as I got older, especially after I got sick. By the time I started having sex, I just wanted to be a part of anything or anyone that wanted to be a part of me. There was a point in my life when guys would literally get up from intercourse with me and inform the boys on the block that they *"were finished"* and someone else would come. For a long time, I just did not care anymore. I was so confused about who I was and why I was alive. I was just a mess.

Sexual perversion is so rampant on the earth now-a-days that my number of 200 in a lifetime may seem modest in comparison to many. I remember one disturbing episode of a talk show where a woman wanted to set a world record by having sex with 300 men consecutively. She had sex with 300 men in just one day as the cameras were rolling! Clips from her escapade were taped and aired on television. She was in tears most of the time because she was swollen, raw and bleeding, but she accomplished her goal. Now that is what I call confused. (I hope she will read this book one day and receive healing if she hasn't already been healed. And no, I do not watch talk shows like that anymore, *laugh*!)

Even in light of this woman's accomplishment, me having sexual contact with over 200 people in my lifetime is certainly nothing to wink at, especially considering that we were created to have sex with only one person! I was actually amazed when I sat down and thought about it. I could not believe that I had been with so many different people. The numbers can add up so easily without you even realizing it. If you have sex with a new person every month for 10 years (that is how long I was sexually active before I got married) then you have had sex with 120 people already. If you make that two new people every month for 10 years, you have reached 280. Maybe if you sit down and do the calculations, you will find that you are not as far behind me as you think!

At any rate, I cannot even describe to you how worthless and used up I felt when it was all said and done. I did not know that I was giving a part of myself away every time I had sex. I did not know what was happening to me, but I knew that I felt so scattered and empty. I felt all warped and twisted inside. I couldn't even begin to fathom the remote possibility of me ever being whole again. How could all of the missing and scattered pieces ever be replaced? I did not think any decent man would ever want to marry me, and I did not feel worthy of love or respect.

When I first met my husband, I was very honest with him about my sexual past. At the time we met, Jesus had already begun to cleanse me and I just wanted to be delivered and made whole at any cost. I was not about to have this man enter into a marriage covenant with me not understanding my struggles. There is a prophet in the Bible named Hosea that was commanded by The Lord to marry a prostitute whose name was Gomer *(Hos 1:2-3)*. My husband was titled as a Prophet when I met him and so once I knew and understood that he was willing to accept and love me the way that I was, I used to tease him and say that he was Hosea and I was Gomer.

It is something though. He knew that although I was "joking", in my heart I really did see myself as a prostitute. He never found my little joke funny. He always immediately corrected me and said something like, *"No, you are a virtuous woman of God, my Queen Esther."* God knew just what it would take to heal me and restore to me all that I had foolishly squandered away. I Thank my Almighty and Loving Creator for His mercy in returning to me all of the scattered pieces of my heart. Hallelujah!!!

Biblical references
Duet 22: 21; Provs 5:15-23, Matthew 7:6, 10:16, and 1 Thessalonians 5:6

What Do You See When You Look at Me?

What do you see when you look at me?
A nasty girl, a freak – spending my life making men peak?
But you don't see the words that made my heart weak
You don't see the hatred that made my life bleak.
Look more closely and please let me speak.

What do you see when you look at me?
A harlot and a whore? A slut who wants more?
But you don't see the abuse behind the closed door.
You don't see the child that none would adore.
Look more deeply, please I implore.

What do you see when you look at me?
A fool? A lust-filled cesspool using every sex tool?
But you don't see my upbringing,
The teachings of my generational school.
You don't see the influences by which devised I this self-rule.
Take a second look cuz your judgment's not cool.

What do you see when you look at me?
A home-wrecker? A family divider?
A treacherous b%#tch, a black widow spider?
But you don't see the deceit,
the slick words of those lying tongue gliders.
You don't see the innocence,
The youth that was stolen by the many rough riders.
You might try to look again, but you're still an outsider.

What do you see when you look at me?
A hopeless case, irreconcilable defection?
A dangerous enemy devoid of direction?
But you don't see the rejection,
You don't know my loneliness or the lack of affection.

But thanks be to God that by Jesus' resurrection
I'm still His selection; by His Blood I have protection
Despite your deflection I will still receive perfection
Because when all is said and done I am yet His election!

What do I see when I look at me?
I see restoration and I see victory!
What does God see when He looks at me,
That is all that matters and He sees glory!

About the Author

Laneen Anavah Haniah was born on July 2, 1975 in Poughkeepsie, NY. One of three daughters that were raised by a single mother, she learned early from her Mom Elder Gail Thomas-Wilson that perseverance and determination could enable her to overcome any obstacle. That lesson would be one that she would desperately cling to when at the age of eight she was struck with a life-threatening illness called Lupus, which had been designed to kill her. Everyday became a struggle for survival, but she battled on until she saw the 21st birthday that doctors said she would never see.

Laneen was blessed enough to be slightly familiarized with church as a child but never had a solid foundation in Christ. For Laneen, lacking that real relationship with Jesus became the tool that the enemy used to lure her into every trap that he could possibly set for her. He surely intended to accomplish what Lupus had not been able to – Laneen Haniah's early demise. As a teenager and young adult she used and sold drugs, drank alcohol, lived a life full of promiscuity, practiced witchcraft, was involved in gangs, was stabbed, held a gunpoint on four separate occasions and even incarcerated. The treachery of these and many other trials caused her to attempt suicide on numerous occasions and to spend time in several mental institutions.

On September 29, 1997, Laneen sat sobbing bitterly on her living room floor planning to attempt suicide once again. However, because He drew her, she ended up calling on The Lord instead. Yeshua the Messiah, heard her cry and entered into her heart. Her life would never be the same. Although there were yet many hardships ahead, she had a new determination – to serve her Savior Yeshua with all her heart and to make the devil pay for all he had done to her.

As a testament to her relentless pursuit of God, just two and a half years later, the late Bishop Moylan Jackson, whom she credits with discovering the unpolished greatness in her and to whom she is forever endeared, licensed her as an Evangelist at Good Shepherd Church of God in Christ. She then went on to become a recognized minister at the, *Beginning Anew Life! Worship Center*, following the anointed tutelage of Prophet Andre

Cook. She has since gone on to answer the call through a strong prayer and fasting life, bearing the Fruit of the Holy Spirit, preaching the gospel, teaching seminars on sexual perversion and mentoring young adults.

The Haniah family currently has membership at DFW New Beginnings Church located in Irving, Texas, where Larry and Tiz Huch are the Pastors. Laneen and her husband Emmanuel are owners of a business called *PREP Consultant Services*, which writes and coordinates character education, behavior modification and student achievement advocacy programs for educational, youth and religious institutions, as well as for individual parents. Laneen is also the owner of a newly founded publishing company named *Victoriously Free! Publishing*. As an anointed author and sharp business woman, she founded this company in order to publish her first completed book entitled, **"The Spirits of Sexual Perversion Handbook"**©. She plans to continue to liberate Yahweh's people through the anointing of authorship that He has given her and to help other aspiring authors do the same.

Despite these many accomplishments, Laneen's foremost focus is none of these things. Because of the tender mercies of the Father, she has been blessed to marry her true soul mate and has gone on to defy doctors once again by giving birth to six beautiful children, which doctors said she would never be able to have: Ja'Keim Emmanuel age 12, Nebiyah Av'va age 6, Benjamin Naim age 5, Judah Jimmy-Lee age 4, Zechariah Maxwell age 3, Mi'Kara Gail age 7 months. This family that The Lord has given to her is what she treasures most in life and that is why above all else her focus is on her greatest call – that of perfecting the ministry of a Proverbs 31 Woman.

Prophetess Laneen Anavah Haniah believes that her testimony is her greatest weapon against satan and tenaciously uses it to overcome him – never ashamed to share it in all truth. One of her favorite scriptures is *"I tell you, her sins – and they are many – have been forgiven, so she has shown me much love. But a person who is forgiven little shows only little love. (Luke 7:47)"* She loves this scripture because she knows that the many sins that she has been forgiven of enables her to love her Lord much more than she could have come to love Him by any other means. She hopes that her testimony will encourage every person that is bound by sin and sexual addictions to, with hopeful expectation, pursue a relationship with The Lord Yeshua and a testimony of victory. She is a living witness of His boundless grace and shows her appreciation to Him by striving to maintain a consecrated life that brings Him glory.

God is no respecter of persons. If He did it in Laneen's life, He can do it in yours too! If you would like to contact Laneen to share your testimony of victory with her, she would love to hear from you. She would also appreciate any help that you can offer in terms of helping to push the vision of this book. Because this book is being self-published, financial resources for marketing are starting off very limited. It would be a great help if you would bring this book and her website, www.victoriouslyfree.org, to the attention of everyone you know, especially those that would be able to open more doors to help enable this book to reach the world. We will also gladly accept donations of any amount. **Please refer to the contact information located on page 307 of this book.** *Thank you so much.*

PART II: THE DELIVERANCE PROCESS STEP-BY-STEP

Now that you have learned so much about the spirits of sexual perversion, I am sure that you are eager to learn how you can be freed from these demons. In this part of the book we will discuss the deliverance process at length. We are going to talk about the necessity of a triune deliverance, discuss the 12 steps of the deliverance process and the necessary measures for maintaining deliverance. In **Part I**, I shared a lot of personal testimonies of defeat to sexual perversion with you. Now you will learn firsthand how I was transformed from the woman you have been reading about into the woman that I am today!

I did not know about a "deliverance process" when Jesus bought me into His Light. I kind of just haphazardly stumbled through this thing, so it seemed. Although my steps were being ordered by the Holy Spirit all the while, I did not get to enjoy the advantage of a step-by-step guideline such as this one and therefore lacked understanding of the process that I was ensuing. I learned through trial and error. It was difficult and frustrating and that is why I am glad to be able to lend you this invaluable tool. Traveling the road behind me will be easier because the way has already been paved. So now, let us get down to the real business of deliverance!

I am going to remind you once again to not read too fast, keep your journal with you or use the journal space at the back of the book if you do not have yours with you and ALWAYS REMEMBER TO PRAY BEFORE READING! Please be sure to do the exercises that you will be directed to do which are located in **The Deliverance Workbook** appendixes (pg 283). They will really help you move forward more successfully. If you are still reading with a partner, you and your partner can work on the exercises together. There is also an overview of the 12 steps of the deliverance process in Appendix C (pg 293).

Let me also remind you not to let <u>anything</u> stop you from reading the rest of this book. You are half way through so don't abort the journey now. Reading just about nine pages per day, you will be done in about 2 weeks! As always, I am here to encourage you and cheer you on. I know that you can do this! OK, let's get ready to embark on the second half of this exciting journey into victorious freedom and newness of life!!!

Chapter 7:
≈≈≈≈≈≈≈≈≈≈
Laying the foundation for deliverance

Deliverance is not a "1, 2, 3, I'm done!" thing. It is going to take study, time and diligence. Let us lay a solid foundation by examining our existence as human beings.

For years I kept getting "delivered" from things only to find myself in bondage once again some time afterward. I would find myself back at the altar for the same struggles over and over again. At times, I was so beat down and discouraged that I just wanted to quit. It really seemed like I was never going to win the battle. Unbeknownst to me at that time, I had not been getting *total* deliverance. I failed to understand the dynamics of an absolute deliverance.

Man is a triune being. We consist of spirit (heart), soul (mind, will, and emotions) and body (flesh, earthly, physical vessel). I was getting delivered in only one or two parts of my being at a time. For example, I would work on my spirit only or my body and soul only or my soul only, etcetera. The problem was that without a triune deliverance there was always a part of me that was yet in bondage. This would eventually lead to overall bondage once again and a total sense of failure. Because I was receiving a *partial* deliverance, I would see a difference for a time, but it never lasted. Then the Holy Spirit revealed to me that in order to really be totally and completely delivered from something, I must work on all three aspects of my person – spirit, soul and body – simultaneously.

The soul man

Since we are talking about receiving a triune deliverance, let us take a more in-depth look at the trinity of man. We now know that the trinity of man is made up of the spirit, the soul and the body. But what does each person of the trinity consist of and represent? Let us examine the soul first.

Commonly, the soul is defined as the mind, will and emotions. The soul is the medium between our bodies and our spirits and is the bridge between the physical and spiritual worlds. This is the part of us where our thoughts, personality and feelings exist. The soul is what really defines the *person* that other people interact with. It reflects who we are in both spirit and in flesh and really gives a person that definitive make up as an individual. The soul is also the realm in which we have the most potential for successfully controlling who we are. This is because the soul is the dwelling place of the mind. By utilizing our minds as an asset we can lay a foundation for totally restructuring who we have come to be. Of course, this means that we will have to allow our <u>minds</u> to be the dictating influence in our souls.

It has to be the mind that dominates. It cannot be the will or the emotions. If we allow ourselves to be dominated by our emotions, we will be double-minded and unstable persons *(James 1:8)*. Emotions are very temporal and are so easily affected by what goes on around us. An emotion is nothing more than a feeling. Those feelings are based solely upon our own personal interpretation and perception of the worlds (both physical and spiritual) and happenings around us. There is no truth to be found in emotions because they are totally subjective – subject to the personal views of the person experiencing them. No one experiences your emotions but you. Your emotional experience is relative to you only and no one else. That is why we always say, *"You don't understand how I feel!"* And we are right when we say this. Emotions are nothing more than dramatic, intrinsic expressions of our own opinions and personality make-up.

What makes one person happy can make someone else sad. Take for instance the 9/11 attacks. They made citizens of America cry and citizens of Baghdad rejoice. There was no truth to be found in the emotions of either group of people. The facts were plain but the absolute truth behind those attacks still eludes us to this day. So what credit can we give our emotions that years later have changed or revealed nothing? In a 24-hour period we can experience such a vast array of emotions that it can be dizzying. Walking out of the door to a beautiful, sunny day can make us feel exuberantly happy. Then five minutes later we get stuck in traffic or we miss the bus and we are totally frustrated. Twenty minutes later we arrive to work on time after we thought we would be late, and we are overwhelmingly relieved. A co-worker compliments our outfit and we feel proud as a peacock and then we have to deal with a nasty client that rubs us the wrong way and we are consumed with fury. All of these emotional changes and it is only nine o'clock AM. Phew! I'm tired just thinking about it. There can be no stability in a soul that is ruled by its emotions.

Well, why can't we let the will dictate? We often hear the term "will power". Will power is no good, because will power can only hold up for a period of time. Besides God Himself, **there is a definitive limit to every power that exists**. Will power is no exception and can only progress a person to the point of its limitations. Truly, will power is no more than the drive of our passions. Our <u>will</u> to do something is founded in our desire to do it, either for the pleasure of the act itself or the outcome that it will yield. To "will" is the same as to "want"; to want means to desire. As we go through life, our desires and passions are greatly affected by our experiences, associations and growth. Therefore, what we will to do today, we may no longer will to do next year. Think back to all of the hobbies that you were so passionate about as a kid. You willed yourself to pursue certain things because you had a passion for those things at that time. Once you lost the desire, you did not will to do them any longer because you had completely lost interest in something that had once stirred you. Without the desire, there was no passion; without the passion, your will lost its power; without the power to will, you ceased the pursuit.

I can remember being pregnant at the age of 18. I had been smoking cigarettes and marijuana for a number of years at the time that I found out that I was pregnant. I had been trying to get pregnant for almost three years. Thus, I was absolutely elated when I found out about the baby that was growing inside of me. However, because I had been diagnosed with lupus as a child, I was told that there was a great chance that I would miscarry. I had a great desire and passion to be a mother. I wanted to be the best mother ever and did not want to do anything to hurt my baby or increase the risk of a miscarriage. By the power of my own will, I stopped smoking immediately for the desired outcome of a healthy baby. But after I gave birth, that desire had been met and I no longer had any underlying passion to motivate my will to not smoke. So I started smoking again and did so for years afterward. The point that I am making is that will has no power without desire. The more passionate we are about something, the more empowered our will is to accomplish that thing. However, desires although not as fleeting as emotions are still temporal. Therefore, we cannot let our will be the dominating force of our souls because its power is limited to the passion of our desires. *(Will power also teeters very dangerously on the borderline of witchcraft and must be carefully guarded. No power should control us or the circumstances in our lives except the power of the Holy Spirit!)*

Neither emotion nor will can give us long, lasting change within our souls due to their instability, but our minds are different. The mind represents our mentality, our intellect, our philosophy and our ideals. The mind is where our thoughts are born and where the universal facts that are consistent and true are retained, maintained, nurtured and potentially transformed into greatness. The mind is strong and consistent in whatever knowledge it acquires and retains. Just consider this – once your mind learned how to count, did you ever forget? Don't you still know how to recite your ABC's, although your mind acquired this information decades ago as a child? How about your name, your address and other pieces of information?

Through this we learn that unlike emotional feelings and will power, knowledge is preserved in our minds and lends empowerment to our endeavors enabling us to achieve. Furthermore, whereas emotional feelings and the passions of the will are subjective and exclusive to the individual experiencing them, knowledge, once proven or accepted, is objective and widespread. The key to a successful soul is allowing a strong and well-informed mind to be in control. In a healthy mind there is stability. Through the input of truthful information we can change our entire lives and enjoy long-lasting results. Although we must work on all parts of our being simultaneously, we have to start somewhere. The soul is a good place to begin as long as we allow the focus to be on the renewing and strengthening of the mind. (*That mind must of course first be renewed and subjected to the mind of Christ, before we allow it to be in control because the carnal mind is death! [Rom 8:6]*)

The spirit man

It is a little difficult to clarify the difference between the soul and the spirit. This is because they are very closely related and do not function apart from one another. The Bible even notes the close relation between the soul and spirit in Hebrews 4:12, *"For the Word of God is quick, and powerful, and sharper than any two-edged sword,* **piercing even to the dividing asunder of soul and spirit***, and of the joints and marrow, and is a discerner of the thoughts and intents of the heart."* However, even though the close relation is noted, a clear distinction is made.

One of the main differences between the soul and the spirit is that the spirit functions only in the spiritual realm while the soul functions in both the spiritual and physical realms. The spirit is the essence of who we are. Although it has no direct functioning in the physical world, everything that we are and do here on earth is a derivative of our spiritual existence. Who we are in spirit will eventually be manifested through our physical beings. So even though we have the most potential for control in our soul man, the soul simply acts as a bridge of transition; transferring what exists in our spirits to existence in our physical bodies.

The spirit is often thought of as the heart of man and is the reality and strength of who we are. We are not primarily beings of flesh or of soul. We are spirit beings that live in a body and possess a soul. If it is the case that we are primarily beings of flesh, then how is it that The Lord said to Jeremiah, *"I knew you before I formed you in your mother's womb. Before you were born I set you apart and appointed you as my spokesman to the world. (Jer 1:5)"*? You see, before Jeremiah ever had a body of flesh or a soul, he already existed as a spiritual being. So is the case with us all. Our spiritual existence is primordial. Our physical existence is an after effect and result of our primordial spiritual existence. We are only given bodies and souls so that we can operate here in the earth realm for a season of time. God had an assignment for Jeremiah to fulfill on the earth. He appointed Jeremiah to be His spokesman, a prophet to the world. In order for Jeremiah to carry that assignment out, he needed an earthen vessel to house his spirit.

Another major difference between the soul and the spirit is the amount of control that we as human beings have in our spirit man. We have a great deal of control in our soul man, but we have very little control in our spirit man, which is the heart of us. Matters of the heart are God's business. Only Jesus can cleanse us of the evil that exists within our hearts. Only He can cause us to be born again in spirit. That is why David cried out in *Psalm 51:10, "Create in me a clean heart, O God. Renew a right spirit within me"* and why God said through the Prophet Ezekiel in 11:19, *"And I will give them singleness of heart and put a new spirit within them. I will take away their hearts of stone and give them tender hearts instead."*

The significance of the word "tender" in that text is the implication of pliability – in other words, a heart that is soft, receptive and easy to work with. This is an indication that the Holy Spirit needs to mold our hearts. We must allow God to control our hearts. If we do not allow Him to control our hearts, evil will most certainly consume and oppress us. In fundamental nature, the spirit realm consists of only two things – the Light of God's Holiness and the darkness of satan's evil. Given that the existence of the spirit man is primarily in the spirit realm, one of these two powers will control our spirit man.

Have you ever seen a room that has neither light nor dark in it? Of course not! Perhaps you have seen a room that has different degrees of either light or dark, but you have never seen a room that has neither because that is not possible, nor is it possible for a human spirit to have neither light nor darkness within it. The person that you are and the works that you accomplish are not just due to your personality. Whatever fruit you produce is a direct derivative of the unseen forces of either the darkness of satan or the Light of The King of all creation that is at work in your spirit.

This lack of control that we have over the spirit man is the reason that I do not suggest making your heart a starting point for deliverance. We can influence the condition of the heart but cannot concisely guarantee a change or an outcome. *"If only you would **prepare your heart** and lift up your hands to Him in prayer! (Job 11:13)"* "Listen to His instructions, *and **store them in your heart** (Job 22:22)"* These two scriptures in Job teach us that we can influence the condition of our hearts by preparing them with the teachings of the Bible and by doing things that will edify our spirits. However, even when we do these things, there is no immediate effect on the heart. The immediate effect is in the soul.

For example, we usually leave a good church service in a certain emotional state and mindset. That emotional state and mindset exists within our souls. Yet it does create an atmosphere within our hearts that is conducive to receiving Jesus' changing power. If we live an evil and sinful life rejecting the truth, then we prepare our hearts to receive a negative change, as in the case with Pharaoh in his dealings with the Children of Israel. *"So **The Lord hardened Pharaoh's heart** once more, and he would not let them go (Ex 10:20)"*. Whether for the worse or for the better, once we make the preparation, it is God who causes an actual manifested change to take place. This is shown to us again by the Apostle Paul, *"My job was to plant the seed in your hearts, and Apollos watered it, **but it was** God**, not we, who made it grow.** (1 Cor. 3:6)"*

Another major problem that we have when dealing with the heart is the fact that we know so little about it. Remember, the heart exists in the spirit realm and most of us are so out of touch with that world. Why is it that we have so little control and know so little about our spirit beings? After all, aren't we spirit more than anything else? Yes, but sin caused a separation of man from God. Once sin entered into the world, we became separated from God and His Kingdom. God's Kingdom is not of this earth. Thus, our separation from Him also separated us from our awareness of the things of the spirit realm. Because we live here on earth, our focus tends to be on the temporal and passing things of the earth.

We know much more about our bodies of flesh than we do our spirits. As a result, there are many hidden areas of sin and darkness in our hearts that we know nothing of. Thus, even if we could change our own hearts, we would never change everything that we need to because we would fail to know all that needs to be changed. The Bible tells us that, *"[9]The heart is deceitful above all things, and desperately wicked: who can know it? [10] I The Lord search the heart, I try the reins... (Jer 17:9-10)"* *"The Lord would surely have known it, for he knows the secrets of every heart (Ps 44:21)"*.

Only God alone can truly reveal to us all of the evil that is lurking within our hearts. Surely we must address our spiritual beings when seeking deliverance, but it is crucial that we understand that without the power of Jesus we will see no change in our hearts. The best and most important thing that we can do is to prepare our hearts to receive the Holy Spirit's changing power.

The flesh man

The last part of our being is our bodies of flesh. Our bodies are weak and fragile and the least formidable part of our beings. They are literally nothing more than containers made of dirt. Without our spirit and soul, our bodies would be only limp and lifeless figures awaiting a purpose to be assigned to them. The body is the part that returns to dust when our time on earth expires. It has no life or power in and of itself. As I mentioned earlier, the body simply serves as a vessel that allows us to operate on the earth for a season of time.

So why does it seem that we are so helpless in our flesh at times then? Why does it seem that our bodies tell us what to do and dictate our actions? This is the case because we do not understand who God created us to be. We fail to realize that we are primarily and foremost spiritual beings. We are caught up in what we can interact with here on earth with our five senses. This is what is *real* to us. We have been spiritually dead for so long that we do not realize that what we see in the physical is nothing more than a manifestation of what exists spiritually. Without that spiritual existence, there would be no physical world.

Our separation from God and entanglement with sin has blinded us from this truth. The Bible tells us in Romans 5:12 in the KJV, "*...**Sin entered into the world...***" Sin entered into the earth, the world and everything that is a part of the world. Our flesh is a part of the world and sin (the spirit of satan) literally entered into mankind. As a matter of fact, in the NLT version of the Bible, that same scripture reads, "*...**Sin entered the entire human race**... (Rom 5:12)*" After entering into us, satan made us slaves to himself, forcing us to take on his evil nature. This is indicated in Romans Chapter 6:6, "*Our old sinful selves were crucified with Christ so that sin might lose its power in our lives.* ***We are no longer slaves to*** *sin."* Without the power of Christ working in our lives, we remain slaves to sin.

Part of that enslavement is the impeding of our ability to discern the spirit realm. Satan aims to keep us focused on this temporal world hoping that we will never understand God's Kingdom or our purpose within that Kingdom. The Bible tells us that we died once sin entered the world. *"When Adam sinned, sin entered the entire human race.* **Adam's sin brought death***, so death spread to everyone, for everyone sinned." (Rom 5:12)* Adam did not die physically when he sinned in the garden. His death was a spiritual death.

Satan knew that disobedience would cause separation from God. He knew that separation would bring on a spiritual death because God is the very source of life and satan knew that once death was accomplished he could enslave us in the flesh to employ our bodies as instruments of evil. Just like a rotten corpse that lies in darkness and is devoured by the creatures of the dark that take residence in it, so our dead spirits became a place for all types of evil and wickedness to dwell and devour. Remember, the soul is the bridge of transition in our trinity. God's intention was for the spirit and soul to cause our earthen vessels to manifest the glory of Him, but once we were disconnected from Him it left us to the devices of the enemy. Darkness consumed our spirits and that is what we began to manifest.

Yet, sin did not enter our spirits. The spirit was consumed by darkness because it no longer had accessibility to the Light, but sin by definition is lawlessness and that is what entered the flesh. Since sin is the controlling force within our flesh through the power of satan, and since our spirits are dead (if we have not been born again), we are enslaved by our flesh. So in a sense, the flesh does control us, but not the earthen vessel itself. It is the sin nature of the vessel, it is the power of satan that is really dominating and oppressing us. That is why it seems that our flesh is in control although it truly is lifeless and powerless in and of itself.

However, sin is only in control until we have accepted Jesus the Messiah as our Lord and Savior, thus becoming alive in spirit once again – reconciled with God who is the life source! Yet, even once we become born again, satan will work overtime to keep us from gaining knowledge of the spirit realm. If we ever really understand who we truly are as spiritual beings and the power that we have in our spirits as children of God, satan would have no opportunity to operate through us ever again. He wants us to continue to operate as if we are spiritually dead so that we will feel powerless and helpless over the impulses and desires of the sin nature of our flesh.

Even though darkness no longer consumes us spiritually because we have been brought into the Light through the work of the cross, satan is still left with the potential to bind us. He does not need our spirits because he himself is a spirit and operates liberally in the spirit realm. All he needs are earthen vessels. All he needs is this sin-natured flesh of ours, which will not change even after spiritual newness is worked in us, through which to work his evil here on the earth. If we remain ignorant to the fact that we are empowered with Righteousness through Jesus and the fact that our flesh is not able to control us, we will continue to live like slaves even though we are royalty. Thus, deliverance in the flesh is no less important than deliverance in the spirit or the soul. However, due to the weakness of our bodies and the perpetual sin nature of the flesh, it is never a good place to start.

Summary of the foundation

It is very important that you understand the fundamental make-up of humanity before we talk about deliverance. Now that we have explored the trinity of mankind, let's put it all into perspective. We must get deliverance in all three parts of our being: deliverance in the spirit man, deliverance in the soul man and deliverance in the flesh man. Because the soul is the connector between the spirit and the flesh, we should begin with the soul man. In this way, we can most efficiently affect our entire being in a triune sense. After initially seeking deliverance in the soul man, we must not neglect to turn our attention to our spirit man and our flesh man as well.

You cannot get total deliverance in any one part of your being without addressing the other parts as well. It becomes a cycle. As one part of your being is strengthened, it will enable another part to be strengthened, which will enable another part to be strengthened, which will then enable another part to be strengthened even further, and so on and so forth. It is a cycle that will never end. Therefore, *total* deliverance is going to be totally dependent upon how well you balance out the cycle of the deliverance process within the trinity of your being.

Now that we understand that we must approach deliverance as the triune beings that we are, we can explore some practical steps that can be taken in the quest for total deliverance. First, let me say this though; some people do not understand that **deliverance is a process**. The word 'process' is defined as *"a series of actions or operations conducing to an end;"* (www.Merriam-WebsterCollegiate.com 12/05/2004). You do not just go to an anointed church service and come home delivered or recite a scripture everyday for 30 days and get delivered. **Deliverance is a process, not an event**. It is a progressive work that once accomplished, must be maintained daily for the rest of your life. For this reason, as you read this part of the book and begin to go through the process that will be discussed, I do not want you to have any unrealistic expectations. Deliverance should definitely be approached with a sense of urgency but should not be put on a timetable.

Do not go into this thinking that you must accomplish your goal within a certain amount of time. Instead, grasp hold of and understand the fact that in order for this to work, it has to be approached as a total lifestyle change. **Do not focus on how fast or slow you are seeing results. Let your focus be on living a new life for the rest of your life and eternally changing who you are**. Furthermore, let your focus be toward the restoration of the *you* that God created you to be. It may seem discouraging at first and as if nothing is really changing, but there are changes occurring that you cannot yet discern. If you persevere and continue to pursue the Righteousness that is yours through Christ; one day suddenly you will realize that you are no longer the same. You probably will not be able to pinpoint the exact day or hour that it happened, but you will know that you are a new person in Jesus!

Now we are about to go into the next chapter where we will begin delving into the 12 steps of deliverance. Since we have already discussed approaching deliverance from a triune perspective, I will categorize the process in this way as well. There are 12 points that I want to bring out concerning true and complete deliverance. I do believe that the Holy Spirit has revealed the divine order of these 12 steps and that is why I have numbered them. Ultimately though, you have to follow the course that the Holy Spirit sets for you specifically – allowing yourself to freely flow in Him, and work on all parts of your being simultaneously.

Each individual's needs are different. Their struggles are different. There are different levels of bondage and different degrees of relationship with God and knowledge of Jesus. All of these factors and some others as well will have an affect on how you go about your process. That is the wonderful thing about the Holy Spirit. He can customize a deliverance plan especially for you! **<u>These steps that I am going to outline should only serve as a guideline and not a rigid regimen</u>**. You never want to limit what the Father can do in your life. The Bible says that we only know in part *(1 Cor 13:9)* and thus I can only share with you the *part* that I know. The Holy Spirit may want to reveal to you some things that He did not reveal to me, so it is important that you remain flexible and receptive to Him.

As you read, I want you to know that even though this book's primary focus is sexual sin, this deliverance process will work for any vice or sin that has you bound. I have specified it to sexual perversion, but it can be generalized to deal with any type of stronghold you may be struggling with. Do you have a spirit of drug, alcohol or nicotine addiction? Are you struggling with hatred, unforgiveness or depression? Whatever it is, you can apply this deliverance process to your struggle. So just be mindful of that as you are reading.

Before we go into the steps, I want to make you aware of the fact that I will be using the life of King David as an example of the deliverance process quite often. Most of us are familiar with this great man's terrible fall into adultery, but I also found when studying his life that he really exemplified this deliverance process that I am about to outline. I suggest that you read the account of King David's sin of adultery which can be found in 2 Samuel chapters 11 and 12. I will be referring to this story for several of the upcoming steps. **Now – it is time for Deliverance; IT'S TIME FOR ANOTHER LEVEL!**

Chapter 8:
Deliverance for the soul man

Since we have already established that the best place to start in the deliverance process is your soul man, we will talk about this first.

Step 1 – Confession/Acknowledgement

There are three steps that I want to share with you concerning deliverance for the soul man. The first of these steps is confession. Even most non-Christians know that change cannot even begin until confession has taken place, but did you know that there are actually three different aspects of confession? Only one of these aspects deals with deliverance in the soul man. We will take a look at that one now. It is the first aspect of confession, which is *'acknowledgement'*. The acknowledgement aspect of confession is all about admitting within yourself that you have a problem. It is about you being honest with you.

We can see an example of this in Psalm 51, which was written by King David in response to his sin of adultery. It was written as a prayer of compunction to God. In the very first verse of Psalm 51, David cries out to The Lord for mercy. However, David, initially after committing adultery had gone on for months not seeking God's mercy or forgiveness. Why? This is because he had not acknowledged his sin up until that point. David did not acknowledge that he had sinned until the Prophet Nathan came and confronted him. After listening to the Prophet Nathan, in 2 Samuel 12:13 David said, *"I have sinned against The Lord."* Finally, he was consciously aware of the fact that he was in sin. That is why in verse 3 of Psalm 51 *(AMP)* he says, *"For **I am conscious of my transgressions and I acknowledge them**: my sin is ever before me."*

You too must acknowledge that spirits of sexual perversion are operating in your life before deliverance can become even a possibility. The Bible says seek and ye shall find *(Mat 7:7),* but no one that is unaware of their need for help is going to bother to seek for it. David was not seeking God's help initially because he was unaware of or in denial about his need for it. That is why it was critical that **Part I** of this book be written truthfully poignant, regardless of how painful or uncomfortable the words may have made you at times. You needed to see yourself in the Light of Jesus' truth and become unequivocally aware of and totally conscious of your need for His deliverance.

Once confession/acknowledgment has taken place, the door for deliverance is open. By now, after everything that you have read in **Part I**, you should have already implemented this step of the deliverance process because as I said earlier, this step is about admitting within yourself that you need deliverance. I do not believe you would have read this far if you wanted to continue to be in denial. This is certainly not a book that promotes denial! Yet at the same time, I did warn you earlier, this process works in a cycle and you may find that more acknowledgements need to be made as you progress further along. The more of God's truth you get, the more you are going to be aware of your need for His intervention.

Please do not forget about what I discussed with you in Chapter 4. If you are a Christian who is not physically involved in acts of sexual perversion at this time of your life, do not be deceived about the possibility of your need to be delivered from these spirits. Even if you committed these acts before you were in Christ, they may still be oppressing you. You should consider your lifestyle in the past and whether or not any of these acts of sexual perversion were ever committed by you. Consider if any of your family members or past sexual partners (even ex-spouses) have ever indulged in these acts, also consider your current spouse's sexual behaviors, past and present. Consider if you were ever involuntarily exposed to any of these acts. *(You will learn more about how to do this in the next step and the "Tracing Your Past" Appendix B, pg 289.)* Satan is such a deceiver. He thrives on ignorance and deception and these become his greatest weapons against us.

The other two aspects of confession deal more with spiritual deliverance, so we will discuss those aspects in the next chapter.

Step 2 – Discovery

The second thing that needs to happen in this process is the discovery of how these spirits entered into your life. This is a **very important** part of the deliverance process. Discovery helps you to pray more efficiently because it enables you to not only pray for forgiveness for the act itself but also to pray against the weakness that enabled it to become a part of your life in the first place. You need to trace back over your life until you discover when and how these spirits entered in.

Think of it as an infestation of rats in someone's home. When the exterminator comes, one of the first things he wants to know is how long the rats have been in the home. Knowing this will help him to assess the severity of the problem. He can do some calculations and determine how many rats have possibly been bred in the time period in which they have been in the home. Having an idea of how many rats exist enables him to properly equip himself for the job.

Then the next thing that he wants to know is how they got in. You see, it is not enough for him to just wait around for a rat to appear and then kill it. Knowing where they entered in permits him to go back to the initial opening and track all of their hiding places. He can then kill all of the rats that are in the house, destroy their nesting places and seal off the place that they entered in through. This is necessary because even if he successfully kills all of the rats in the house, if he does not seal off the openings, new rats will enter in. Just as there are an abundance of rats in the world, there are an abundance of demons seeking to devour you. If the entrance site is not sealed, new demons will continuously enter into your life even after the old ones have been evicted!

King David understood the importance of discovery. In Psalm 51 and verse 5 he writes, *"Behold, I was brought forth in [a state of] iniquity; my mother was sinful who conceived me [and I too am sinful].(AMP)"* In the book of 1 Samuel 16, you can read the story of how it came to be that David was anointed to be the king. God had rejected the current king and then told his prophet, Samuel, to find a man named Jessie and anoint one of his sons to be the new king. God did not tell Samuel which son to anoint. He let Samuel know that He would show him whom to anoint when Jessie's sons were presented to him. Jessie was told to come to a dinner and to bring his sons with him. Jessie showed seven of his sons to

Samuel and none of them was God's chosen. Samuel then asked Jessie, *"Are all your sons here?"*

You see, Jessie had neglected to invite his son David to the dinner. Prophet Samuel, when he found this out, instructed that David be invited to the dinner as well. When David arrived, the Bible made a point to describe his physical features. None of Jessie's other sons were described, which seems to make it apparent that David was not a full-blooded brother of the other sons. He obviously must have looked much differently than the rest of them, due to the fact that he had a different mother.

David makes a point of saying in Psalm 51:5 that it was *his mother* that was sinful. In the culture that David lived in, it was legal for a man to take as many wives and concubines as he desired. This was not however the case for women. A woman could belong to only one man. David specifying that *his mother* was sinful is an indication that she was already married to another man or that she was a prostitute when David was conceived between she and his father Jessie.

That is why David was not invited to the dinner. He was not an honorable son. He was a son of shame. The KJV version of psalm 51:5 reads *"Behold, I was **shapen in iniquity**; and in sin did my mother conceive me."* This scripture lets us know that not only was David conceived as a result of sexual perversion but also that he was raised in an environment of such. He was shaped, molded and taught to live a sinful life. The Bible does not say for sure, but the fact that David was still in his father's life could mean that his mother and father stayed in contact with one another and more than likely continued on in their sinful relationship. The Bible also makes no mention of Jessie's relationship with The Lord. He more than likely had an unrepentant heart and did not impart to his sons the knowledge that what he had done was wrong. This is just a theory however, what I really want to emphasize is that King David took the time to trace back over his life and discover when and how spirits of sexual perversion entered in.

All throughout chapter six of this book, where each demon was assessed, I took you on a journey back in time with me to reveal when and how those spirits of sexual perversion entered into my life. This was such a critical part of my deliverance process. All of the effort that I put into trying to get delivered, while neglecting to implement this step, turned out to be in vain. Without discovery, I was like a person indoors during the summer trying to shoo all of the flies out of the house through a window but neglecting to close the door to keep them from coming back in!

You can avoid making this mistake by learning of these four main ways that spirits enter into your life. Before we continue, I want you to now go to Appendix B (pg 289). If you can, print out the pages of Appendix B and keep them with you as you read about these four entranceways. If you cannot print them out, you can do the exercises right within the book. After you read about an entranceway (A, B, C, or D) stop before going on to the next and complete the exercise in Appendix B that coincides with that entranceway. *(Complete the exercise to the best of your ability because some of them you will be working on for quite a while.)*

A. **Generational curses**: One way that demons can enter in is through a generational curse. A generational curse is a demonic stronghold that is manifested in more than one generation of the same genealogical bloodline. There is a lot that can be said concerning generational curses, but I do not want to get off course. The basic understanding is that if your grandmother was a lesbian and your mother was a lesbian there is good possibility that you will be one too. Generational curses can come in all forms. It does not have to be a curse of sexual perversion. It can be a stronghold of poverty, murder, lying, suicide, deformed children and etcetera. Commonly people say, *"Such and such runs in my family"*. But, the truth of the matter is that when something *'runs in a family'* such as cancer, mental illness, alcoholism or crime, it is not just a coincidence or due to DNA and genes. There are spiritual forces at work behind the scenes carrying out the assignment of a generational curse.

You can find evidence of generational curses all throughout the Bible. One quick example is Abraham, Isaac and Jacob. If you read the history of these Patriarchs in the book of Genesis, you will find that they all showed favoritism toward one of their sons in particular. True to form when it comes to generational curses, the manifestation of this behavior grew stronger and more blatant with each generation. Abraham showed only slight favoritism toward Isaac. Isaac showed even more favoritism toward Esau, and Jacob (Israel) showed unrestrained favoritism toward his son Joseph.

The point is that the longer a generational curse is operative in your family, the greater that stronghold is going to be. That is because generational curses are carried out by a collective body of demons that are all assigned to a particular task. That collective body increases in number with each generation and thus gains strength. It is important for you to know how strong the generational curse operating in your life is because this will give you insight into how much of a **strong**hold this particular act of sexual perversion really is. With this insight, you can properly prepare yourself to close this entranceway.

I also want to warn you, especially those of you that I addressed in Chapter 4, that not physically committing acts of sin any longer (or even if you have never committed a particular act of sin) does not mean a generational curse has been broken. That is why so many times you will see a curse *'skip'* a generation, or it will seem that a particular generation has overcome a certain stronghold and yet it will rear its ugly head once again in the next generation. When you do not get TOTAL deliverance, it leaves the door wide open for generational demons to afflict the generations that come behind you. These demons are familiar spirits that are familiar with your bloodline and they will hang around as long as they can, looking for an opportunity to operate.

Each of the four demonic entranceways has to be dealt with differently. To close the entranceway of a generational curse you must renounce those demons. Technically, the demons had no right to afflict you in the first place because you had no say so in the matter, but you know what they say, *"You can't choose your family."* So you got your mother's brown eyes and her demon of masturbation too. What you have to realize now is that you had a DNA transplant once you became part of God's family. You no longer carry the blood of your father or the genes of your mother. You now have the Blood of Jesus running through your spiritual veins and the genes of your Heavenly Father.

Every curse was automatically canceled when you accepted Jesus, Yeshua the Messiah as your Lord and Savior. The problem is that no one told those generational demons this. They are like apartment tenants whose lease has expired; if you do not evict them, they will gladly continue to reside on your premises. You have to let these demons know, that you know, that they no longer have a right to dwell with you. You do not have to just defenselessly accept the curses of your ancestors any longer. Just like Jesus said in the book of Matthew, *"⁴⁸...'Who is my mother? Who are my brothers?'...⁵⁰Anyone who does the will of my Father in heaven is my brother and sister and mother!'(12:48, 50)"*

You are part of a new family. That family is the Body of Christ and no demon in hell can penetrate His Bloodline! Stand strong against these demons. Take authority over them in the power given to you by Jesus, The Lord of lords Yeshua; *"And I have given you authority over all the power of the enemy...(Luke 10:19a)"* In Step 9 you will learn how to use your mighty spiritual weapons to defeat these and other demons in your life. Just like tenants that do not want to move, you may have to fight with them for a while, it may even be a long and intense battle. This is especially true if you are dealing with a particularly strong generational curse. Yet in the end, if you do not back down, truth will prevail. What is that truth? That truth is that Jesus is the rightful owner of your life and your body, He has appointed you as the superintendent and no demon can live in your life without your permission! Just tell the devil to 'Gets to steppin'!

B. Involuntary exposure: Another way that spirits of sexual perversion can enter in is through involuntary exposure, which is sexual abuse or exposure to these acts when it is beyond your control. What you see and hear greatly affects how you think and grow. How your parents and other influential adults live their lives in front of you has a terribly significant and profound impact on your life and who you eventually become. If you have ever been sexually abused or raped; if you were raised in a home where sexual perversion was a part of your upbringing; if you have ever lived with a spouse or others that practice sexual perversion, then you have been a victim of involuntary exposure. This type of exposure even takes place in school, on the job or just in the environment that you live in.

In my own childhood, I cannot really remember a time when sexual perversion was not a part of my life. All of the adults in my life were either homosexuals, fornicators, prostitutes, adulterers, masturbators, pedophiles, involved in incest, pornography or beastiality, were full of sexual lust – and even in some cases all of the above! I was constantly exposed to pornography and all other types of sexual perversion. I was destined to become a victim of these spirits because the seeds had already been planted and were being watered daily.

Generational curses are really the most indirect of all entranceways simply because, as we already discussed, they come without permission or full rights. But what generational demons do, is they attach themselves to your life (however many there may be). They then wait for opportunities to plant seeds of their kind in you and opportunities to water those seeds that are successfully planted. Therefore, where there is a generational curse, you will usually find involuntary exposure as well. Involuntary exposure is one of the main ways these generational seeds of evil are watered and nurtured.

For example, if you have a generational curse of molestation in your family, demons of pedophilia will follow you around until you come in contact with a person that has an opening in their life for those demons of pedophilia to work through. Once the demons find someone who is willing to take the bait, they will work through that individual to see to it that you are molested. If there is a generational curse of pornography in your family, then demons of pornography will influence the adults around you to make sure they leave pornography around the house in places where you will find it. Those demons will then whisper into your mind, *"Look at this. Aren't you curious? Go ahead look at it!"*

Involuntary exposure does not always happen as a result of generational curses, but regardless of how the exposure takes place these demons are able to plant seeds in you through their works. The more involuntary exposure you are subjected to, the more those seeds are nurtured, fertilized and likely to grow into something big. We can see an example of involuntary exposure in the Bible in Genesis chapter 19:30-38 in the lives of Lot's two daughters. These girls were raised in the wicked and lascivious vicinity of Sodom and Gomorrah. Their mother carried the nature of the environment she lived in, as well as did their fiancées. The daughters did not choose to live in this environment, but yet they were constantly being involuntarily exposed to sexual sin.

Before long, the seeds that had been planted and nurtured over the years finally sprouted and blossomed. As a result, they eventually committed incest with their very own father. Reality check ya'll – these girls were not virgins! No virgin female is going to know how to get on top of an unassisting man; do all of the necessary maneuvering on her own; and then work it until a drunk man, I said a <u>drunk man</u>, has an ejaculation; **hello**! This tag team duo of devilish daughters knew just what they were doing! They were skilled and experienced. My point is that involuntary exposure took its toll on them after a while and what they had been exposed to eventually manifested itself in their own lives in a very major way.

Entranceways of involuntary exposure are a little stronger than entranceways of generational curses. This is not to minimize generational curses because they are still a formidable entranceway. However, involuntary exposure allows demons an opportunity to literally *train you*. With each instance of involuntary exposure, you are being molded into what you are being exposed to. That is why David says, *"I was **shapen** in iniquity."* To close the entranceway of involuntary exposure, you are going to need to renounce every demon that entered into your life in this way. They are just like generational demons in the respect that they are intruders. They are in your life without your permission and through no choosing of your own.

Unfortunately though, the damage has already been done. The training has already taken place. That is why renewing your mind, which we will talk about in Step 3, is going to be very important. You are going to have to reprogram yourself with the truth. You are going to have to undo all of the works that these demons have already begun in your life. You are really going to need the Word of God in order to expose the works of these demons in your life because since their influence was actually a part of your training, you may not even realize that what you are doing is wrong. Yet the Bible says, "***All Scripture is inspired by God and is useful to teach us what is true and to make us realize what is wrong in our lives. It straightens us out and teaches us to do what is right.*** *(2 Tim 3:16)"*

We are all subject to involuntary exposure in this day and age. You can close the entranceway but none of us can escape, by virtue of the society we live in, being subjected to involuntary exposure. However, you can protect yourself from the influences thereof. Cover yourself in the Blood of Jesus, and implement Step 8 which will teach you how to use God's spiritual armor to protect yourself from the enemy's attacks. As in the case with generational curses, just bind and stand strong against these intrusive demons using your spiritual weapons (Step 9). It may take some time for you to see the results, but you are already the victor in this situation because God is going to see to it that you are vindicated! He already knows that it was not your fault!

C. Spiritual wounds: The third way that demons can enter into your life is when spiritual wounds are created, often times through some sort of abuse or emotional trauma. A wound is a cut; a laceration, an opening or weak place in the flesh – or in this case an opening or weak place in the spirit. It is an opening that should not be there. Where ever there is a wound things that would not normally be able to enter in do get in; things such as germs, bacteria and demonic influences into your spirit. The devil's purpose in wounding you is not just so you can hurt. You need to understand something about the devil. He could care less if you are giddy with laughter or burdened down with sorrow, as long as he causes your destruction in the end.

His purpose for wounding you is to create an opening in your heart in which he can enter in and abide! Throughout your life, he sets you up to be wounded. Generational demons attempt to cause wounds in your life for this purpose as well. This is another way in which they plant and water because once you are wounded, if you do not respond the right way, you *"…give place to the devil (Eph 4:27)"*. Demons enter into your life at the site of spiritual wounds and just wait for the opportunity to work their evil doings through you. This is what Jesus was referring to when He said that He had been anointed *"…to set at liberty them that are bruised. (Luke 4:18) "*. He did not say that He had come to *heal* them that are bruised. He said He came to liberate them. What did Jesus come to liberate the bruised from? The bondage of satan and all of his demons!!! The bruised are bound by satan because those wounds leave openings through which demons enter in.

The types of things that can wound you in spirit include rejection, betrayal, loss of a loved one or cherished possession, being teased, neglected or not being able to fit in. There are too many ways to name them all but just know that once you feel hurt inside a wound has been made. When your heart aches and moans, you have been wounded. Different kinds of wounds will make an entranceway for different types of demons. Not every demon can fit into every wound. How demons accomplish using wounds as an entranceway into your life is that they present themselves as the remedy for your pain. As an example, a wound of rejection will cause you to seek out acceptance. It allows all types of demons that come with the promise of acceptance to enter into your life. A wound of neglect will cause you to over indulge yourself in things that bring comfort to try and fill that void of neglect. Thus, whatever demon presents itself as a thing of comfort (for example, masturbation or alcoholism) will be able to enter into that opening of neglect. A wound of abandonment will cause you to seek out companionship. This was the case with King David.

King David was wounded because he was abandoned and neglected by his mother and rejected by his father. In Psalm 27:10 it says, *"Although my father and my mother have forsaken me, yet The Lord will take me up [adopt me as His child]. (AMP)"* David sought out companionship everywhere he could. He had many wives and concubines, yet his harem still was not enough. King David failed to understand the wound of abandonment that he was dealing with. In this respect, David was not dealing primarily with a spirit of lust when he slept with Bathsheba. Instead, it was the spirit of adultery. Adultery presented itself as the remedy (companionship), for the pain in David's heart that had been caused by the wound and opening of abandonment. This is made apparent because he did not just have sex with Bathsheba and throw her away. He made her his wife. The demon of adultery promised him companionship because there was an opening available and David took the bait!

In my own life rejection was a huge wound in my spirit. Demons of sexual perversion presented themselves to me as a remedy for rejection with the false promises of acceptance, popularity and love. If only I had understood back then that what I needed was not to self-medicate the pain with sexual perversion but instead to allow The Healer to cure me. You see, the only way you are going to be able to close the entranceway of a spiritual wound is to get healing.

If you do not allow Jesus to heal you, you will never be able to walk uprightly before God. *"[5]Why should you be stricken and punished any more [since it brings no correction]? You will revolt more and more. The whole head is sick, and the whole heart is faint (feeble, sick, and nauseated). [6]From the sole of the foot even to the head there is no soundness or health ...but wounds and bruises and fresh and bleeding stripes; they have not been pressed out and closed up or bound up or softened with oil. ...[No one has troubled to seek a remedy.] (Isa 1:5-6, AMP)"* This scripture helps us understand that without spiritual healing, we will continue on in sin.

There are three keys to experiencing spiritual healing in your life. First and foremost you must grieve. Jesus teaches in **"The Sermon on the Mount"** that *"God blesses those who mourn for they will be comforted. (Mat 5:4)"* We also learn in Isaiah 61:2-3, *"To all who mourn.... he will give beauty for ashes, joy instead of mourning, praise instead of despair..."* God is all prepared to heal your wounded spirit, but too many of us feel that mourning is a sign of weakness. We feel like we have to be strong all of the time, but if you never mourn then the Father can never comfort you. If you do not pay the price of mourning, then you will not receive the merchandise of joy. Grieving is critically important. You have to allow yourself to grieve. I do not care how long ago something happened to you, you need to grieve about it if you have not yet. Cry, scream, yell, wail – whatever you have to do to get it out – do it! God is waiting to give you joy and comfort in exchange for your tears.

The next very important part of healing is forgiveness. You must forgive the people and circumstances that inflicted those wounds. You may blame a person, God, yourself or maybe just life in general, but regardless of whom it is you find to be at fault for your wounds, you have to forgive them. We discuss this more in Step 7. Finally, you need to learn how to be refreshed in the presence of God. This is really about worship, which is discussed in Step 10 in more detail. For now though, think of it in terms of natural tears. Have you ever cried really hard and long about something? Doesn't it make your face hot and puffy? Doesn't it leave tear and mucus stains all over your face? Where is the first place you go after crying like this? You go to the bathroom to get <u>refreshed</u>, and this is what you must do when you have been wounded and mourning in spirit. You need to get refreshed in the presence of the Father through worship.

Once you have received healing, you will finally be able to stop sinning in those areas of your life because the demons that entered in through those wounds will no longer have a place of residence within you. You can find evidence of this in John 5:14 when Jesus says to a man that he has just healed, *"...Now you are well; so stop sinning..."* However, after you have been healed, you need to protect yourself from future demonic strongholds entering into your life through wounds. It is a truth that wounds will be inflicted continually as long as we live. Yet, you do not have to *"give place to the devil"* just because you are wounded. If you respond correctly to spiritual wounds, they can actually cause you to be elevated instead of denigrated.

*"You will be accepted **if you respond in the right way**. But if you refuse to respond correctly, then watch out! Sin is waiting to attack and destroy you, and you must subdue it (Gen 4:7)."* You see, spiritual wounds in your life serve a very important purpose. The Bible lets us know in Isaiah 66:2, *"...But this is the man to whom I will look and have regard: he who is humble and of a broken or **wounded spirit**...(AMP)"* And in Isaiah 57:15 it tells us, *"I dwell in the high and Holy place, **with him also that is of a contrite and humble spirit**...(AMP)"*. Spiritual wounds will occur in the lives of us all until the day we die, but what we must understand is that although the devil has a purpose for wounding us spiritually, God has a purpose for allowing it. The devil's aim is to take us lower, but God's aim is to take us higher. It all comes down to how you respond to your pain. Use this powerful knowledge to walk victoriously from now on even when you are wounded!

D. <u>Voluntary exposure</u>: The last entranceway that we are going to discuss that demons of sexual perversion enter in through is voluntary exposure. Voluntary exposure happens when **<u>you choose</u>** to involve yourself with people, places and things that are associated with sexual perversion. Exposure, whether voluntary or involuntary, opens doors in the spirit realm and creates an opportunity for the demons that you have been exposed to, to enter into your life. In most cases though, voluntary exposure occurs as a result of generational curses, involuntary exposure, and/or spiritual wounding in the past. It is seldom that a person is going to, without any other influences, voluntarily expose themselves to demons. The only instance that I can think of for this is if a person is raised in a completely God-less environment, but even this is a type of passive involuntary exposure.

The reality of the matter is that when you have been exposed to any of the three prior entranceways that we have already discussed, you have a predisposition to voluntarily make the choice to involve yourself with sexual perversion because it has already become a part of who you are. The spirits of sexual perversion that are already present in your life take advantage of every opportunity to increase in strength and number and cause you to open the door to even more of these demons. However, you do not necessarily have to have any familiarity with spirits of sexual perversion per say in order to voluntarily expose yourself to them. Other demons such as rebellion, lust or ignorance can cause you to make the choice to associate yourself with spirits of sexual perversion too. ***Any demonic oppression creates an opportunity for* every *demonic oppression***, simply because all demons are linked to the kingdom of darkness and its ruler.

    Voluntary exposure is one the main workings of the spirit of promiscuity that we discussed earlier and is often incited by this spirit. Regardless of how voluntary exposure is incited in your life, there is a greater strength of oppression that comes with this particular entranceway. This is because you give these demons so much more liberty and authority when the exposure is voluntary. In the case of a generational curse, involuntary exposure or a spiritual wound, they have to fight, connive or force their way in. However, in the case of voluntary exposure, the door is opened wide and invitingly. These demons are invited in like welcomed guests and given the liberty to do as they please. It is like the difference between being an expected and honored visitor coming in from out of town, as opposed to an unwelcome burglar who trespasses and intrudes.

    We can once again refer back to King David. We have already established that he was a victim of generational curses, involuntary exposure and spiritual wounding, but he voluntarily exposed himself to sexual perversion as well. When you read the story, you learn that before falling into adultery with Bathsheba, David was watching her take a bath. He did not have to watch her, but he *chose* to indulge in sexual fantasy and lust when he could have just walked away. That voluntary exposure opened the door wide for the spirit of adultery to rise up in him. David had many women before Bathsheba, but he had never before done something so wicked. It was through making the choice to *voluntarily* expose himself to sexual perversion, that the demons that already had access to him were able to gain that much stronger hold in his life.

I too, made a conscious decision to let sexual perversion into my life at some point. I had struggled with sexual perversion from early on in childhood, but that was all due to circumstances beyond my control. When I struggled with these demons as a child, they had very limited power in my life for a very long time. Once I made that *choice* to open the door to these spirits, the bondage that I experienced far exceeded what I had suffered as just a victim of my environment. Believe it or not, voluntary exposure is a form of witchcraft. The Bible teaches us that rebellion is equated to witchcraft *(1 Sam 15:23)* and voluntary exposure in its truest essence is <u>willful rebellion against Righteousness – It is sin</u>. Therefore **any type of willful exposure to sinfulness** can, and most often does, lead you directly into satanism, occultism and witchcraft even if in just very subtle ways. That is what makes these voluntary exposure strongholds so powerful. You are dealing not only with the demon of the sin act itself but also the powerful ruler of the darkness named witchcraft that is at work in the world.

To overcome the entranceway of voluntary exposure Steps, 4, 5 and 6 (confession admittance, penitence and confession exposure) are going to be very important. You cannot do anything about the things that happen to you in life, but this wise saying is true, *"Life is only 10% what happens to you but 90% how you respond to it."* You do not have to make the choice to voluntarily expose yourself to sexual perversion just because some unfortunate events have occurred in your past. That is why for voluntary exposure, you need to take full responsibility for your actions. You have to open up your mouth and confess to The Lord that you have done what you know is evil and ask Him to forgive and cleanse you. *"If we [freely] admit that we have sinned and confess our sins, He is faithful and just (true to His own nature and promises) and will forgive our sins [dismiss our lawlessness]* **<u>and [continuously] cleanse us from all unrighteousness</u>** *[everything not in conformity to His will in purpose, thought, and action]. (1 John 1:9, AMP)"* After doing this, you have to determine in your heart and mind that you are committed to not voluntarily exposing yourself again (refer to Step 12 to learn more about this).

This is the only way to close the entranceway of voluntary exposure. This entranceway is the most powerful entranceway and is going to take the most commitment and sacrifice to close, but once God cleanses you, no demon can decide to keep you dirty! However, if you have been involved in satanism, occultism or witchcraft (even to any minor degree) and/or if you are demon possessed, you will probably experience a great degree of difficulty in getting freed. Sexual perversion is a very integral part of occultism, witchcraft and satanic worship. The door for <u>new demons</u> to enter in will be closed by confession as we just read in the above scripture and by you being committed to not re-exposing yourself, but expelling the powerful demons that have already taken residence within you could be an arduous task for a novice. Furthermore, as long as the demons are still present they will continually drag you back into sin and voluntary exposure. You should, in this case, seek the help of a skilled deliverance minister to bind and cast out the devils and you should also give careful attention to Steps 9 and 10.

Please do not delay on dealing with this opening of voluntary exposure. If you do, you are playing Russian Roulette with your spiritual life! This is the entranceway that can take you all the way to the point of no return! Voluntary exposure also causes you to reap greater consequences, but it is never too late for Jesus to turn your life around. I do not care if your marriage has been destroyed, your reputation ruined or even if your body is being ravished by AIDS. You can still live the rest of your days victoriously free in spirit and avail yourself to the Mercies of God that can even revoke consequences. He can heal every part of your heart, life and body. I know that He can because He did it for me (I once had two medically incurable STDs, but am now healed)! Just wholeheartedly repent and turn to God and watch how He moves in your life!!!

To summarize Step 2, these are four of the ways that demons of sexual perversion can enter into your life. Discovery is a very important step because it informs the mind by making you consciously aware of what you are dealing with. That information that is acquired can then be used to help strategize a plan and give direction as how to "close doors" in the spirit realm. Discovery can also help you determine which demon is the strongman and how that demon got into that position. It will furthermore help you protect yourself from being oppressed in the same way again in the future. Part of this protection is discussed in Step 6 (confession exposure), which is actually one of the necessary steps to close each one of these four entranceways that have been discussed. Please bear this in mind when reading that step.

Even though discovery deals primarily with the mind and the soul man, deliverance in the spirit is going to rely heavily on this step. There are different and specific ways that certain entranceways must be sealed and all of those ways are outlined in each one of the seven steps that we will discuss coming up in the next chapter on deliverance in the spirit man. So please take the time to do the exercises in Appendix B (pg 289), and discover how these spirits entered into your life. You will need to continue to work on these exercises throughout the next chapter because you probably will not remember everything all at once. Sometimes you will need the Holy Spirit's help in order to remember certain things, but He will reveal it to you if your spirit is open to receive from Him. It is usually the case that these demons have entered into your life in more than one way. But regardless of how or when they came in, The Lord of lords has already signed their eviction notice!

Step 3 - Renewing the mind

The Bible tells us *"to be ye transformed by the renewing of the mind (Rom 12:2, KJV)"* and that is why Step 3 is *"Renewing the mind"*. We have already clarified that the mind is a good point of beginnings for the deliverance process. You learned in Chapter 7 that by utilizing your mind as an asset you can lay a foundation for totally restructuring who you have come to be. However, in order for the mind to become an asset, it has to be empowered with the proper information. I cannot read comic strips and expect that to result in me becoming a mathematician. If I want to be a mathematician, I have to put factual information about mathematics into my mind. So is the case concerning deliverance from spirits of sexual perversion. You need to inform your mind concerning God's truth about your deliverance. "The Truth" that can set you free is available, but in order for it to benefit you in any way, it must be acquired – it must be put *into* your mind.

Your mind consists of a collection of information. It is what we learn that structures and molds the mind. Thus, if you are going to re*new* your mind, you have to learn something *new*. You have to put new information into your mind. David emphasizes the importance of renewing the mind in Psalm 119:33-34 where he says, **"Teach me, O Lord, to follow every one of your principles. Give me understanding** *and I will obey your law; I will put it into practice with all my heart."* I believe that David realized here the same truth that one day enlightened me. He realized that a lack of God's Word being in his mind had afforded him the opportunity to sin. His mind needed to be renewed concerning God's Righteousness. David understood that he needed to learn more about His ways in order to remain upright in His sight.

Like David, if you are going to change, you will have to change your mind. If you are going to live as a new creature in Christ and walk in newness of life according to 2 Corinthians 5:17 and Romans 6:4, you must put newness into your mind. Over the years, you have allowed the devil to fill your mind up with deceptions and false information. You have come to believe that you are weak and powerless and unable to change. These are all lies. Within the pages of the Bible is the truth about your ability to be free from sin in Jesus Christ. The truth of the Word of God will bring about that newness of mind that you need and that newness of mind will give you the empowerment that you seek to become a new person all together.

Obviously, we cannot neglect the fact that if the Word of God is what is going to renew your mind then you will have to get as much of that Word into your mind as is possible. Get it in anyway that you can – read the Bible, go to church, listen to teaching tapes, converse with those knowledgeable in the teachings of the Bible and read Christian books. Because your mind is already structured on deception, renewal is not going to happen through just reading a few scriptures randomly, every once in a blue moon. You have to aggressively and divisively plan the restructuring of your mind. Every opportunity that is available, you need to be getting the truth, God's Word into your mind.

You should also have certain scriptures that you memorize and meditate on everyday. For example, if your weakness is fornication then find scriptures in the Bible that speak against fornication – like, " *Run away from sexual sin! No other sin so clearly affects the body as this one does. (1 Cor 6:18)*". In conjunction, find scriptures that reveal who you really are in Christ such as, *"Know ye not that ye are the temple of God and that the Spirit of God dwelleth in you? (1 Cor 3:16, KJV)"* Then personalize them when you recite them like this, *"I know that I am the temple of God and His Spirit lives in me!"*

In light of all of this, it is important that you understand that it takes more than just *knowing* the Word. You cannot just have knowledge of the Word, you must apprehend and understand it as well. You can acquire knowledge yet never gain understanding of that acquired knowledge and thus never be able to apply it. I will give you a prime example. I have had knowledge of Einstein's physic's formula, $E=MC^2$, for as long as I can remember. However, I have absolutely no idea what it means so it is of no use to me. It does not empower me in any way. It is said that "knowledge is power", but I would have to add to that to say that *acquired, apprehended,* and *applied* knowledge is power. That is why the Bible says, *"Wisdom is the principal thing; therefore get wisdom:* **and with all thy getting get understanding.** *(Proverbs 4:7, KJV)"*

Tantamount in importance to putting truth into your mind is keeping lies out! If you are truly going to renew your mind, you cannot continue to put the same old lies and deception into it. It is not enough to just put new information into your mind. You also have to completely eradicate all of the lies, deception and perversity that have been the foundation for so long, just as we are taught to do in this scripture; *"Casting down imaginations, **and every high thing that exalteth itself against the knowledge of God**, and bringing into captivity every thought to the obedience of Christ; (2 Cor 10:5, KJV)"*

This means that you have to remove from your life **every** influence that is inclined toward sexual perversion. Maybe you are wondering how you can do that. Well, how does information get into the mind? You learn through the use of your five senses. That means that every one of your five senses is a gateway to your mind. Everything that you see, hear, taste, touch or smell is going to make a deposit in your mind. Anything that you involve yourself in that is not inclined toward Righteousness is going to work against your progress and ability to be delivered. When we talk about the five senses, we are talking about deliverance in the flesh man so I will not say any more about that right now. I will discuss this more in Step 12. *(This is just another example though of the necessity of working on the trinity of your being simultaneously.)*

Let me just leave you with this thought concerning renewing the mind. Remember, you learned that your emotions are just feelings based on your own personal perception and interpretation of things, which has everything to do with how you think. Therefore, once your thinking changes, your emotions and how you feel will naturally change as well. Your emotions have everything to do with your desires, which stir passion, which in turn motivates your will. Consequently, your will is going to change as well. You see, by renewing your mind you are going to renew your entire soul man. Just as the scripture says, you will **be transformed by the renewing of your mind**. So constantly take in the Word of God and be encouraged to know that you are already implementing this step in the deliverance process just by reading this book – 124,071 words of mind-renewing truth!

Chapter 9:
Deliverance for the spirit man

With deliverance in the soul man under your belt you are well on your way to liberation, but we cannot stop there. Now you need to learn what must be done to prepare your heart for God's changing power.

Step 4 – Confession/Admittance

Now that we have outlined a plan for deliverance in the soul man, I want to talk about deliverance in the spirit man. Let us start by talking about the second aspect of confession, which is admittance. After acknowledging within yourself that you have a problem, you need to be honest with your Lord. We learn this in Psalm 51:6. It says, *"Behold You desire **truth in the inner being**, make me therefore to know wisdom in my inmost heart. (AMP)"*

Sometimes when you consider the Father's Holiness, you cannot come to grips with admitting to Him your many faults especially those most heinous. You must remember though that God is not only Holy, He is also Omniscient. He already knows everything about you anyway. You cannot hide from God or hide anything about yourself from Him. The Lord despises deception and hypocrisy, but that is what so many of us give Him. We get in His face (or at least we think we are in His face) talking about any and everything. *"Lord please bless me with this and bless me with that. God, help my neighbor Sally. Help the nations to turn from their sins and blah, blah, blah, blah, blah..."* – all of this praying without ever admitting to God the truth concerning our own sinful nature.

Truly, it is really showing a total lack of reverence for God because it is indicating that you think you can fool Him the same way that you are able to fool some people. Not only is this type of deception disrespectful to God, but it is insulting as well. Just think of how you would feel if someone who claimed to care for you knowingly treated you badly and terribly offended you. Then that person came to you and began to talk to you, attempting to interact with you as if they had done nothing wrong. Wouldn't that make you angry? It would add insult to injury?

Then, a lot of times when we do finally pray to God concerning our own faults, we will try to minimize and downplay them. We will say something basic and unrevealing like, *"Lord please forgive me for my sins."* You need to really talk about it with God. You need to get down to the nitty gritty so to speak and give Him all of the details. He desires truth. The more you admit to Him, the more He will be able to help you. Confession to God is not to make Him aware of something that He is not already aware of. Instead, admittance is extending to the Holy Spirit an invitation to come into your life and execute Righteousness.

If you recall, I shared with you how I used to have sexual images of my children when the spirit of pedophilia was still operative in my life. I believe the thing that prevented this spirit from causing me to actually molest my children or someone else's child was the fact that I implemented the three aspects of confession. I acknowledged within myself that I had a problem and I admitted to God that I had a problem. I also implemented the third aspect which you will read about shortly. My point is though that through confession, I invited Jesus into my heart to heal those wounds and bring about newness. I did not operate in denial by trying to pretend that everything was alright. I was open and I was therefore cleansed.

Jesus is not intrusive. He is not going to bombard your spirit with a deliverance that you do not desire. The Holy Spirit is not a brute. He is a gentleman. God wants you to extend an invitation to Him through admittance. Of course, you will not be aware of everything that needs to be confessed in the beginning. That is why the scripture says in the second clause of Psalm 51:6, *"make me therefore to know wisdom in my inmost heart."* In other words, David was telling God that he needed Him to teach him what he should admit. As I said previously, the process works in a cycle. So you will just have to start by admitting all that is obvious to you and as God cleans you up, you will be enlightened to more of what in your heart needs to be confessed.

Step 5 – Penitence/Humility

Penitence is defined as, *"feeling or expressing humble or regretful pain or sorrow for sins or offenses."* (www.Merriam-WebsterCollegiate.com 12/05/2004) Admittance and Penitence kind of go hand in hand, but there is somewhat of a difference. You can accomplish admittance without penitence, but you cannot experience penitence without first executing admittance. Admittance is when you talk things over with God. You just lay it all on the line and say, *"Father, I know I shouldn't be having sex with my boyfriend, but I like it and I don't want to stop."*

Penitence is that next step though, when after discussing it with Yah, you experience brokenness and remorse over your sins. That is why admittance is so important. Just think about it: How can you express remorse to God for something you have not yet admitted to Him? A criminal cannot express remorse to a judge for a crime that he has not yet admitted to. In this respect, the difference between admittance and penitence is like the difference between a criminal simply confessing to a crime, or the criminal confessing and then breaking down in tears due to his sorrow for committing it. Admittance is important, but without going on to penitence you will not get very far in the deliverance process.

In the very first verse of Psalm 51, King David cries out for mercy. *"Have mercy upon me, O God, according to your steadfast love: according unto the multitude of Your tender mercy and loving-kindness blot out my transgressions. (AMP)"* Here, David was experiencing the brokenness that leads to repentance. By understanding and common definition, repentance means to turn away from sin, to amend your ways, to utterly disgust your past lifestyle. It means that you come to hate the sin that you once so loved and refuse to partake of it any longer. Repentance is the goal that you are now pursuing. You want to change your ways, but that can truly only happen by the hand of God. It is going to take a renovation of the heart to get to the level of deliverance that is necessary for you to never commit the sin again.

It was highlighted earlier in Chapter 7 that only God can change the heart but that we can prepare our hearts for that change. Penitence is part of the preparation. It is the condition of the heart that is necessary to cause repentance to come to past. If you do not feel sorry for the sins you have committed, what is to stop you from committing the same acts of sexual perversion over and over again? We learned also in Chapter 7 that God can only mold a soft and pliable heart. Humility and brokenness is what softens a heart and makes it fit for God to mend and to mold into newness. *"For thus saith the high and lofty One...I...revive the spirit of the humble, and...revive the heart of the contrite ones. (Isa. 57:15)"*

Penitence is the proof that there has been brokenness in your spirit. In verse 17 of Psalm 51 *(AMP)* it reads, *"My sacrifice [the sacrifice acceptable] to God is a broken spirit; a broken and a contrite heart [broken down with sorrow for sin and humbly and thoroughly penitent], such O God, You will not despise."* In that verse, we see once again that humility is the key. In Isaiah 66:2*(AMP)* it says, *"...But this is the man to whom I will look and have regard: he who **is humble and of a broken or wounded spirit**..."* What I am trying to make clear is that penitence is a product of humility. If you are unable or unwilling to experience remorse over your sins, it is due to the fact that you are full of pride. Pride is one of the seven things that the Bible tells us the God of Holiness hates *(Prov 6:16-17, AMP)*. God desires no dealings with a prideful heart.

The same principle even holds true in our courts of law. Just think about it. A defendant who is going to be sentenced for murder is much more likely to get the stiffest penalty if he shows no remorse. Such pride and arrogance is an offense to all who see him, and without remorse and brokenness over the crime committed, there is very little hope or assurance that he will not go out and commit the same crime again. However, a defendant who shows remorse and brokenness often times wins the compassion of the jury and the judge. If it is at all possible, they will let such a criminal go free or give him a very light sentence. Mercy will be extended to him, and those involved will do all that is within their power to help him rebuild his life.

All of this being true, I want you to be aware that penitence in and of itself is a process. It is not always an instantaneous thing. As you grow closer to God and are able to see yourself more and more in the Light of His Holiness, you are going to experience more sorrow over the wickedness of your heart and your actions. As you go through this deliverance process at this season in your life, you are going to experience a certain degree of penitence. Due to that, God will be able to bring about a certain degree of cleansing and newness in your spirit. Yet, I guarantee you that if you stay on the path of Righteousness that you are on today, a year from now you are going to be much more broken over your sins than you are presently. Two years from now, you will be even more broken.

It is part of the cycle of deliverance that we spoke of in Chapter 7, and penitence is going to come over you in waves during different phases of the cycle. You will think that you are all cried out over a sin. Then suddenly, months after you have dealt with it, you will encounter a greater revelation of God's Holiness, which will reveal a deeper depth of your wickedness, and you will find yourself on your knees seeking mercy all over again. This will continue to happen until you experience **complete** brokenness in that area of your spirit and in turn God thoroughly cleanses and renews you in that area.

Please do not fail to realize the importance of this part of the deliverance process. The scripture says, *"a broken and a contrite heart [broken down with sorrow for sin and humbly and thoroughly penitent], such O God, You will not despise."* The Bible is letting us know here, that God despises any approach to His throne other than an approach of penitence and humility. Dealing honestly with God through admittance is only one step, but what will really allow and motivate Him to come into your life and give you that clean heart that you desire is the brokenness and humility of penitence. It is only then that you will see your desire of total repentance come to pass. Only then can you be truly and totally set free and delivered.

Step 6 – Confession/Exposure

Now, I want to discuss the third and final aspect of confession, which is exposure. This might be one of the hardest aspects of confession to execute because it will leave you the most vulnerable. Why, you ask? The reason is that this aspect of confession is about exposing your sins to other people. *"Gasp! Screech! Oh no! You mean I actually have to tell other people what I've done?!!!"* Yes you do!

This is a part of the deliverance process that most people "conveniently" overlook. They fail to see the necessity of it. Then even when people do understand its necessity, cowering fear of the possible consequences of others knowing and the pride of wanting to always be well thought of by others will prevent them from actually following through with it. Yet you **must** carry out this step. For the Word of God tells us in Proverbs 28:13, *"He that covereth his sins shall not prosper: but whoso **confesseth** and forsaketh them shall have mercy."*

I am sure you are wondering why you have to tell others what is going on or has gone on in your private life. I am sure you want to know how exposure is going to progress your deliverance process. Well first of all, exposure is another product of humility. If you are operating in pride, you will never be willing to let anyone else know that you are struggling with sexual perversion. Pride means always having to appear wonderful in the eyes of others. The humility that it takes to expose your faults to other people is pleasing to God and lends to the preparation of your heart for His power of renewal. Yet, even besides humility, there are two other very important reasons that you need to fulfill the exposure aspect of confession: 1) The protection of accountability and 2) The power of intercession.

A. Accountability: First and foremost, when we are talking about accountability, we are talking about responsibility. We are talking about you standing up tall and taking responsibility for your own actions. When King David was confronted by the prophet concerning his sin of adultery, he did not say, *"Bathsheba has sinned"* or *"A terrible sin has been committed."* He plainly said, *"**I** have sinned against The Lord."*, and in doing so implemented this step of confession/exposure.

The most powerful thing about the accountability that is brought on through exposure of your sins is how it empowers you to overcome the "victim mentality". As long as you continue to perceive yourself as a victim, you are bound to wallow in defeat. As a victim, you have no choice concerning what occurs in your life. You have no choice but to helplessly stand by as your life plummets into the depths of barrenness. Having no control over your life or your actions will mean having no control over your deliverance as well. On the other hand, taking responsibility for your actions puts you in the driver's seat. It empowers you to be in control.

When you can honestly confess to someone that you are involved in sexual perversion, and then take responsibility for that involvement and your need to be delivered, you win a major battle in the spirit. Once you stand flatfooted and say, *"This is my struggle, I have the power to change it and I choose to exercise that power starting today!"*, no devil in hell will be able to stop you! But this cannot happen as long as you are still cowering in fear not wanting anyone to know about your secret shame, afraid to boldly step out and profess that you will be delivered. Destroying the shroud of secrecy affords you the opportunity to approach your deliverance with a great liberty because you are no longer afraid of what others may think and will more boldly do whatever The Spirit tells you to do in order to receive your newness.

Secondly, when we talk about the accountability that comes along with exposure, we are dealing not only with responsibility but also with obligation. When you openly confess your faults to others, when you confide in them and say that you desire to change, they begin to weigh your behavior to measure whether or not you are living up to your professed penitence. Once King David exposed his sins, he made himself accountable to everyone who knew about it. He was then obligated to make amends for his actions because his followers had been made aware of his error. Even though you may already have a desire to change for the better, knowing that you are being surveyed challenges you even further to meet that desired goal.

Every human being wants to achieve and know that others are going to celebrate their accomplishments. That is just a part of our nature. Of course, your flesh is more comfortable with the idea of confessing <u>privately</u> to God, but secret confession leaves you unaccountable and without obligation. Knowing that others are aware of your struggle and your desire to be delivered and that they are rooting for you, lends a sense of obligation to your quest for deliverance. There is a protection in this sense of obligation that exposure yields because it decreases the chances of you secretly slipping away to indulge in the pleasures of your sinful nature.

We all do things in secrecy that we would never do if we knew we were being watched or would be accountable to report to someone at a later time. Just consider your behavior when you are at home alone, relaxing. You may do things like neglect to brush your teeth all day, dig in your toes and smell the jam or pick your nose and wipe the residue in unsanitary places (*laugh*). You probably would not do these things if you knew that you were being watched or that you were going to have to give a report about it when it was all over! Therefore, regardless of how uncomfortable the idea may make you feel, the accountability and obligation that comes along with exposure is an asset. It rescues you from the "victim mentality" and helps protect you from falling into sin again.

B. The power of intercession: OK, I will admit that confession to others is intimidating. I mean, if it were at all possible some people, once they find out something like this about you, would sign, seal and deliver you to hell in a hand basket without a second thought! You do have to be very careful about to whom you confess your faults. When the Bible tells you to confess your faults to others that does not mean that you have to stand on a street corner with a large sign hanging around your neck. It does not mean that you need to carry around a bullhorn and announce it to all whom you encounter. As a matter of fact, the Bible lets you know exactly whom it is that you should be confessing to because not everyone's heart has been prepared for them to be an instrument of healing.

You can find out who you need to confess to in James 5:16, *"Confess your faults one to another, and pray one for another, that ye may be healed. The effectual fervent prayer of __a righteous man__ availeth much."* This scripture reveals to you the second reason that the exposure aspect of confession is so important and also reveals whom it is that you should expose yourself to. Who you should be confessing to is a righteous man or woman of the anointing because it is all about the power of intercession and who can get a prayer through. In this text of James you also learn that the purpose for exposure is for others to learn what to pray for you about. *"Confess your faults one to another,* ***and pray one for another*** *..."*

Even though you can pray for yourself, you cannot do so effectively in this area of your fault or sin. Remember what we discussed earlier? We talked about how spiritual wounds allow the enemy to enter into your life, bind you and bring about sin. The very fact that you commit a sin is indicative of the fact that you are wounded inside. You know that someone who is bruised or wounded is not strong but instead is weak. Therefore because you are wounded, you are going to need some assistance breaking free from the bondage of satan and getting healed. That is why James said, *"Confess your faults one to another, and pray one for another,* ***that ye may be healed****..."*

There are two things that you need to understand about this clause of James 5:16, *"...The effectual **fervent** prayer of a **righteous** man availeth much."* First of all, the word "fervent" in this scripture means, "to show forth one's power". You now know that you being in sin is an indication that you are wounded. You can also easily deduce that because you are wounded, you are not strong. Considering that you are not strong, how then will you show forth power in prayer? How can you show forth power if your spirit is already weakened in that area? Secondly concerning this clause, the word "righteous" means "to be in right standing with God". If you are not in right standing with God, which you already know at this point you are not, your prayers are hindered *(John 9:31, 1 Pet 3:12).* That means that even if you can muster up the strength to pray showing forth power, your prayers are still ineffective because you are not yet in right standing with God in this area.

It is the prayers of the righteous, those that are in right standing with God that availeth much. I believe that this is why David wrote Psalm 51 (the prayer written in response to his sin of adultery) and gave it to the chief musician. Every time the choir sang that song they were interceding on the king's behalf. David realized that he was going to need someone beside himself to pray for him. As long as you are still bruised, spotted and blemished, you are not yet fit to come before our Almighty, Holy, Righteous and Perfect God in certain aspects. Your relationship with Him will always be obstructed.

This does not mean that all of your prayers will be ineffective. What it means is that in this particular aspect or dimension of your spirit, you are not in right standing with God; although you very well may be in right standing in other aspects. Understand that the spirit realm is the realm of unlimited dimensions. In effect, it is possible that you are able to come before God in one dimension but not in another. For example, you can always go to the Throne of Mercy to seek forgiveness. As soon as you ask the Father for forgiveness in Jesus' name, it will be granted to you (as long as you are not harboring unforgiveness toward anyone else). But, we are not talking about simply being *forgiven* for your sins. We are talking about being **healed** spiritually and sinning no more.

The Word of God teaches you that your prayers have to be a sweet smelling savor to His nostrils *(Rev 5:8)* and any prayer sent up that is weak, blemished or defective is a stench to Him. It will not be accepted by Him. Just think of it this way – you have a festering, rotting, stinking wound in your spirit, which is the place through which the sin was committed. Now you are attempting to offer up a sweet smelling prayer to God from the place of that stinking wound! The wound is sodden with stench, so how do you think your prayers smell? It just cannot be done and you need to realize that it is not enough to just receive God's forgiveness. It is so important that you experience His total spiritual healing. If you don't, then the devil will forever be able to operate through the wound in your spirit and you will never be free in that area or whole in your relationship with God.

Does this mean though, that the persons that you are confessing to are faultless? No, it does not. They do not have to be perfect or faultless. They just need to be able to pray for you in the area in which you are weak and wounded. The only requirement is that they are fit to offer up a fervent prayer, that is a sweet smelling savor to The Lord, from a place of right standing in that particular dimension of the spirit realm. We all have wounds, weaknesses and faults. That is why the scripture tells us to confess <u>one to another</u> and pray for <u>one another</u>.

It is a simple principle. Pray and confess <u>to God yourself</u> for forgiveness and cleansing *(1 John 1:9)*. But, when it comes to healing – you pray for me in the areas in which you are strong but I am weak, and I will pray for you in the areas in which I am strong but you are weak. In this way, we all continue to need each other and can strengthen and uphold one another. The bottom line is that without the spiritual healing that is accomplished through the intercessory prayer of other believers, you will never experience total deliverance. *Exposure* = humility, accountability, obligation and intercession. Do not forget to implement this very important step, which is going to be elemental in closing the demonic entranceways that we talked about in Step 2.

Step 7 - Forgiveness and letting go

There is another very elemental act that needs to take place in order for you to experience healing and wholeness in your heart. It is called forgiveness. There is not a person on this earth that has not been hurt by someone at some point in time – you included. You may look back over your life and cringe at the thought of the abuse you have suffered at someone else's hand. It may even be the case that you have terribly abused yourself in times past. No matter who it is that has hurt you; mother, father, aunt, uncle, teacher, child or even you yourself, forgiveness is an essential part of your deliverance process.

The Bible plainly tells you in Matthew 6:14 -15, *"¹⁴If you forgive those who sin against you, your heavenly Father will forgive you. ¹⁵But if you refuse to forgive others, your Father will not forgive your sins."* This scripture literally means exactly what it says. If you do not forgive others their offenses against you, the Father will not forgive your offenses against Him. If you do not partake of God's forgiveness, then right standing with Him is not even a possibility. As it has already been stated, without right standing with God your relationship with Him will always be obstructed. If that is going to be the case, you may as well forget about this whole process because this entire deliverance process is not only about being free from the bondage of the enemy but also being fully restored in your relationship with your Heavenly Father. After all, that is what Jesus ultimately died for *(2 Cor 5:18-20, Col 1:19-22)*.

Forgiveness does not always come easily though, especially when something really devastating or traumatic has taken place in your life. I can remember a time in my life when I truly thought it would be impossible for me to forgive some of the people that had hurt me. I knew that I should forgive them. I understood that it is God's requirement for me to forgive others, but I still seemed unable to extend forgiveness toward certain people. It was very frustrating because it was as if I would try but it wouldn't work. And I'm not talking about experiencing this as a baby in Christ either. I am talking about being a mature Christian, walking in the power and anointing of Jesus and yet feeling unable to forgive some people. Then I received a breakthrough. It was one little phrase that set me free. On a particular morning, as I was watching Joyce Myers, who is one of my favorite teachers of the Bible, she simply said this, *"Forgiveness is not a feeling; it's an action."*

I was instantaneously set free. Just being made aware of this truth was all that I needed to overcome unforgiveness in my life. You see, all the while I had been using my feelings to measure whether or not I had forgiven people. I believed that if I was still feeling angry or upset, I had not forgiven, but if I no longer felt emotional concerning an offense, that I had forgiven. When Joyce Myers said that forgiveness is an action, I finally realized that how I feel has nothing to do with forgiveness. It is not how you feel; it is what you do. You may not always be able to *feel* differently toward a person right away and that is ok. Emotions are hard to control but even when you cannot control your emotions, you still do not have to let your emotions control you. What I am trying to help you understand is that you can feel an emotion without allowing it to dictate your actions.

A. The act of forgiveness: So now that you understand that forgiveness is an action, all you need to know is how to carry out that action. In order to exercise the action of forgiveness, there are four main things that you need to do. *"But I say unto you,* **Love your enemies, bless them that curse you, do good to them that hate you,** *and* **pray for them which despitefully use you, and persecute you;** *(Mat 5:44, KJV)"* Doesn't that just say it all? Instead of focusing on trying to change how you feel about people who have hurt you, let your focus be on carrying out these instructions given to you by Jesus Himself.

He starts out by telling you to **love your enemies**. People who oppose you and are hostile toward you are the enemies that Jesus is talking about in this text, and the word love is used as a term of endearment. It means being willing to express your affection. It means not giving people the cold shoulder but instead treating them warmly. When people are against you, you be for them. If they frown at you, you smile at them. If they speak in a loud, harsh voice, you speak in a soft, kind voice. If it is at all possible, make yourself available to bring joy into their life. In this way, you are walking in love and demonstrating your forgiveness toward them.

Next Jesus tells you to **bless them that curse you**. There have probably been people in your life that have constantly spoken negativity over you. Maybe your relatives, a teacher or a spouse said things to you to put you down such as, *"You're a worthless piece of trash. You ain't never gonna be nuthin'. You're stupid just like your father!"* If you have heard things like this in your life time, the ones who said it are the people Jesus is talking about in this clause of the scripture. To curse someone means to speak or wish evil against the person. To bless them, means the opposite. Speak well of these people that curse you and hope for blessings in their lives. Even the worse people have some good qualities. Speak of the good of people that have cursed you and at the very least, if you do not know what a person's good quality is, then decree a good quality over them. Ask God to send His favor upon them. This is how you can bless them that curse you.

Jesus then goes on to tell you to **do good to them that hate you**. When a person hates you, it stirs up within you a strong temptation to hate them back and to display that hatred by doing evil to them. Jesus is telling you here to resist that temptation. Do not do evil to people that do evil to you. People who have hated you in your lifetime have not only cursed you but have made every attempt to carry out those curses against you. They do all that they can to cause calamity and misery in your life. You will not be able to show affection toward these people or be a part of their lives to bless them because they hate you. Hatred is a murderous spirit and any wise person is not going to fellowship with a person that desires to murder them. But, you can determine within yourself not to hate them back or perform any acts of evil against them. That is what Jesus is trying to teach you here. Do not pursue them to cause bad things to happen in their life. No matter what they do to you, govern yourself with integrity, honesty and moral goodness. Let your actions always be pleasing in the sight of God.

Then, the last thing Jesus instructs you to do is **pray for them that despitefully use you and persecute you**. There is no greater act of love that you can display toward a person than to pray for them. Those people that have just evilly taken advantage of you; the ones who have slandered your name; the betrayers and backbiters; these are they who are being spoken of here. One important thing that I learned about forgiveness is that *my* forgiveness toward a person does not do much for them at all. Some people could really care less whether or not you forgive them. For you to forgive someone helps you more than it helps the person that you are forgiving. What is really going to help the person is not when *you* forgive them but when God forgives them. So when you pray for someone who has hurt you, your prayer should be what Jesus prayed on the cross, *"Father forgive them for they know not what they do. (Luke 23:34, KJV)"* Once God forgives them, it is then that healing can begin in that person's life.

If you can implement these four acts of forgiveness – 1. Love your enemies, 2. Bless them that curse you, 3. Do good to them that hate you, 4. Pray for them that despitefully use you and persecute you – then you have adequately met the requirement. Again, this has nothing to do with your feelings. You can still feel hurt and angry inside and yet implement forgiveness by adhering to these instructions. Maybe you are in a situation where the person who has hurt you is no longer a part of your life for you to act out forgiveness toward them, but you can still pray that God touch them wherever they are. If the person is dead, pray for their living relatives. There is always a way for you to walk in forgiveness. You may not – **probably definitely <u>will not</u>** – experience any emotional relief in the beginning of the act of forgiveness, but you will be amazed to discover what an emotional healing will take place as time passes. The way you feel toward them will change. The anger and the hurt will continually subside until it no longer exists.

B. Bitterness and letting go: If you have been unable to forgive in the past because you failed to understand how to carry out forgiveness, you now know what you must do. However, what if your problem is that you do not want to forgive? The question would be "why?" and the answer is, "bitterness". Sometimes you can hurt so long and walk in unforgiveness for so long that you become bitter inside. You must realize that holding on to all of that unforgiveness is only going to hurt you. You are the one that is really going to suffer the most because of it. Bitterness will eat away at you inside. It will destroy your heart and bring misery upon you for your entire life.

If this is your case, then you really need to ask Jesus to help you. You will be unable to implement forgiveness without Him first touching your heart and enabling you to release the bitterness that is within you. It will also help a great deal for you to get as much of the Word of God into you as possible. This is because the Bible says that the Word is sweeter than honey *(Ps 119:103)*. Bitter is the opposite of sweet, so if you allow the Word of God to sweeten you up it will overtake the bitterness that is in your heart. Someone that *fills their heart* with God's Word cannot be bitter.

It takes so much energy to hold on to hatred and bitterness. It takes so much energy to curse and hate and persecute people. If you are always tired, always exhausted, sleepy and lacking energy, forget about the doctor's diagnosis of Chronic Fatigue Syndrome and Anxiety Disorder. What you really have is CBB – "Chronic Bitterness Burnout"! What's more, for all of the energy you expel you don't even receive a reward. There is no positive return or profit for all of your effort. As a matter of fact, you put yourself in a position for even more bad things to come to pass in your life. Jesus teaches us that what you do to others will be done back to you even more so *(Luke 6:38)*! If you hate people, people will hate you. If you will not forgive people, then people will not forgive you. I am not just talking about the people that you are bitter toward either. I am talking about people that you like unexpectedly turning on you; people that you have treated well suddenly turning their backs on you over some insignificant offense and not being willing to forgive you. You will be cut off from favor and close the door to so many blessings that could otherwise come your way.

I know that it is not easy to let go sometimes, but it will help you to understand that the people who have hurt you have themselves been hurt. They are in need of deliverance and healing just as you are. Just think of how many people you have hurt in your life. You probably do not even know why you hurt some people the way that you did, but I know why. You did it because you were so wounded inside and all of those wounds allowed so many places for demonic spirits to enter in and operate through you. It is the same case for the people who have hurt you. If you are willing to allow the Father to touch your heart and implement the act of forgiveness, you will be able to see these people through the eyes of Jesus. You will see the hurt, pain and desperation inside of them and understand why they hurt you the way that they did. I know it is hard to imagine right now but you will even have compassion for them one day.

I know a lot of people that claim they have forgiven others, but it is so obvious to everyone except them that they have not! So let me also clarify this. If you claim that you have forgiven people and a significant amount of time has passed since your claimed forgiveness, your emotional state should have changed by now. I did say that you will probably not feel better at the beginning of the forgiveness process, but there does come a point in time after forgiveness has been implemented that you no longer feel hurt and angry. When forgiveness is mature in you, all you will feel toward that person is love and compassion. I cannot put it on an exact timetable, but I am going to say that within one year's time at the very most, you should <u>feel</u> better.

If after a while, you still feel something stirring in you every time you think of them; if you get a subtle little incline of pleasure at the thought or mention of them suffering; if you cannot picture yourself stretching your arms wide to them to hug them and to kiss them with sincerity if they came to you in such a way, then you have not matured in forgiveness. You may be carrying out some of the acts of forgiveness but not all four steps, or perhaps you are just doing it in the flesh and out of formality. This is not truly walking in forgiveness. What this really is, is a way for the devil to deceive you into thinking that you have forgiven people so that he can keep you bound by a spirit of bitterness. Do not let him fool you. Get delivered and get delivered for real!

The truth of the matter is that in spite of all of the evil things you have done in your lifetime, God is still willing to forgive you because He understands the 'why' behind your actions. All that He wants is for you to extend the same grace toward others. Therefore, confess to bitterness, let Jesus clean you and in His name move forward with your life. Take your peace and your joy back and use your energy to achieve happiness instead of to harbor bitterness. It is time to let go of the past and embrace your future.

Finally and probably most importantly as far as forgiveness is concerned, I want to remind you not to forget about yourself. Sometimes the hardest person to forgive can be you. If you cannot forgive yourself, it is indicative of you not being able to receive God's forgiveness. Furthermore, if you are unwilling to forgive yourself, you will not be able to truly forgive anyone else either. You cannot do anything to someone else that you cannot first do to yourself *(Mat 22:39)*. Remember, to forgive means to love, to bless, to do good to and to pray for. If you do not forgive yourself, you will not be able to treat yourself in this way. You will continually be bound by self-condemnation, self-hatred and self-destructive behavior. It is not at all possible for you to move on in this process if you will not forgive yourself!

Forgiving yourself and others is probably the greatest investment you can make in your spiritual healing. Unforgiveness will keep you trapped in the past but forgiveness will enable you to say what the Apostle Paul said in Philippians 3:13, *"... I am still not all I should be, but I'm focusing all my energies on this one thing:* **Forgetting the past and looking forward to what lies ahead***"*. It truly is time for letting go!

Step 8 - Spiritual Warfare:
Putting on your spiritual armor

The last thing that I want to discuss concerning deliverance in the spirit man is "spiritual warfare". So far, every step that we have covered in this process has dealt directly with either you as a person or you in your relationship with The Lord. The one thing we have not talked about dealing with directly is the demons in your life. That is what spiritual warfare is all about. It is a direct assault on satan and his cohorts. The other steps in the process definitely rain on the devil's parade but this is the ambush; this is the drive of the attack; this is where you declare all out war against the spirits of sexual perversion in your life! I know that may sound a little intimidating to some because every step we have discussed so far has been so practical. Do not let the terminology shake you though. Although it is called *spiritual* warfare, it can still be approached in a very natural and practical way. There are actually three different aspects of spiritual warfare, so I am going to break it down into three different steps. The first aspect that we are going to discuss in this step will cover how to defend yourself in the spirit by putting on your spiritual armor.

A. The battle is not yours: Before we go any further let me make absolutely clear that the battle is not yours. It is The Lord's *(2 Chron 20:15)*. I do not want to give you the wrong impression. You are no match for the devil. Your *natural* against his *supernatural* will fail every time, but Jesus' omnipotence against the devil's supernatural – now that is a different story. As long as you operate in the power of the Holy Spirit of Jesus, you cannot lose. That is why the Word says, *"...the Spirit who lives in you is greater than the spirit who lives in the world" (1 John 4:4 b)*. As a matter of fact in another scripture, The Bible tells you that you are already more than a conqueror *(Rom 8:37)*.

Well if that be the case, why do you even need to battle with satan at all, right? The reason is because the victory that you have exists in the spirit realm. If you want to experience that victory here on earth, a transfer has to take place and satan will do everything that is within his power to stop that transfer. You are going to have to allow yourself to be a warrior vessel of the Holy Spirit in order to bring it to past. Satan certainly knows that every child of God already has the victory but even though he is aware of this, he will still try to defeat you. He even tried to defeat Jesus, The very Son of Yahweh God, so do not think that he will not do his best to make a failure out of you *(Rev 12:17)!*

So now, let's read the following text that teaches us about spiritual warfare and about the armor of God and then examine it more closely. *"¹²For **we are not fighting against people made of flesh and blood**, but against the evil rulers and authorities of the unseen world, against those mighty powers of darkness who rule this world, and against wicked spirits in the heavenly realms. ¹³Use every piece of God's armor to resist the enemy in the time of evil, so that after the battle you will still be standing firm. ¹⁴Stand your ground, **putting on the sturdy belt of truth** and **the body armor of God's Righteousness**. ¹⁵**For shoes, put on the peace that comes from the Good News**, so that you will be fully prepared. ¹⁶In every battle **you will need faith as your shield** to stop the fiery arrows aimed at you by satan. ¹⁷Put on **salvation as your helmet**, and take the sword of the Spirit, which is the Word of God. (Eph 6:12-17)"*

B. Your fight is not with people: In verse 12 we learn that the first key to being fully equipped for this battle is understanding that **your battle is not with people**. You have to know who your enemy is. Your enemy is not the person who raped, molested or abused you. Your enemy is not your mother, father or spouse. Your enemy is not you. Your enemy is satan and all of his evil demons. Do not ever waste your energy fighting against people because you can defeat the person without defeating the spirit. Demons are not stationary creatures. They have the ability to move in the spirit realm, so even if you stop a demon from operating in your life through a particular person, it will just find another person to operate through. You need to defeat the evil spirits that operate through people and not the people themselves!

C. The belt of truth: Next, we learn that we must wear the belt of truth. A belt is used to hold up whatever you are wearing on the lower part of your body, which is where your "indecent" body parts are located. Even if you have on a pair of pants, without the belt to hold them up, you would still be exposed. For most people, these parts of the body being exposed bring on a sense of shame or guilt. Thus, having the belt on protects them from being exposed, from being made vulnerable and ashamed. The belt of truth protects you from spiritual shame. It protects you from guilt and condemnation. The Bible says, *"...the truth shall make you free (John*

8:32 KJV)." The belt of truth is the first piece of armor that is listed because without the truth to make you free from condemnation, guilt and shame, you will not be able to go any further.

Jesus said, *"I am the way,* **The Truth***, and the life (John 14:6 KJV)."* He is also the Living Word *(John 1:1).* In this respect, we understand that without the truth of God's Word concerning His forgiveness and redemption, you will be full of condemnation. A person who is condemned is guilty and someone who is guilty is imprisoned. Therefore, you will not be free to do any of what God requires of you if you do not know the truth; that you are loved by your Heavenly Father, purified by the Blood of Jesus and made clean through the Word of God. You will be protected from the guilt and condemnation of shame and exposure of your indecencies and sins when you have on the belt of truth.

D. The body armor of Righteousness: Then you have to put on the body armor of Righteousness. You have already learned that Righteousness is right standing with God. In other words, Righteousness is to be acceptable to God or to be received by Him. The only way that can be achieved is by accepting the sacrifice of Jesus as recompense for your sins. There is nothing that you can do in and of yourself to be made Righteous. Doing good deeds or being a nice person is not going to make you acceptable in the sight of God. Even in light of your commendable qualities, your heart is still filthy with sin. It is like using a dirty rag to wipe crumbs off of a table. Just because the rag successfully removes the crumbs from the table, does not make the rag clean nor do your good deeds make your dirty heart clean. That is why the Bible tells us that even our so-called Righteousness is like filthy rags *(Isa 64:6).* There is no one who is Righteous in the sight of God due to his or her good works *(Rom 3:10-12).*

In order to make a dirty rag clean, a cleansing agent must be applied. In order for a cleansing from sin to take place, there has to be a blood sacrifice. The Blood of Jesus is the cleansing agent that must be applied to our dirty hearts, in order to make them clean with Righteousness. In His sovereignty, this is the requirement that The Lord set. That is why He sent His Son Jesus to die for the sins of the world. God set the requirement and then sent the provision for the requirement to be met. Not every person will be made righteous, but every person has the same opportunity to be made righteous by choosing to accept Jesus as Lord and Savior. The way you put on the body armor of Righteousness is by choosing to believe that Jesus is the Son of God that died for your sins; that He was raised from the dead and lives even today; and accepting him as your personal Lord and Savior so that you can have a right relationship with God. The reason that Righteousness is called the body armor is because the Blood of Jesus, which brings about Righteousness, covers you entirely once you accept Him in your heart! (You can read more about the process of Righteousness and accepting Jesus as your Savior on pages 277-281.)

E. The shoes of peace: You are then instructed in this way, *"For shoes, put on the peace that comes from the Good News, so that you will be fully prepared."* In bible times the most common means of transportation was by foot. The people wore what we would call today, sandals. The purpose of the sandals was to protect the bottom of the foot as they walked. If your feet get damaged in any way, it will impede your ability to walk, which will in turn slow down or completely suspend your ability to mobilize yourself. Therefore, what you use to protect your feet is very important. What is on your feet will determine how, when and where you walk.

The text tells you to wear the peace that comes from the Good News, the gospel of Jesus, on your feet in order to be fully prepared. The peace of the gospel is that assurance that comes from knowing and acknowledging that you have a proper relationship with God. It's that tranquil state of spirit and soul that you have when you know and accept that you are protected in life and in life after death. It is the peace of knowing and wholeheartedly embracing the fact that you have a reliable hope and that there is a way for you to be delivered, set free and to live an abundant life through obeying the commands of God.

If your natural feet are hurting badly, you may skip the walk in the park or the extra stop to the store and go straight home instead. If they feel good, you may decide to walk to your destination as opposed to taking the bus. Your spiritual feet have the same effect on you. Having the peace of the gospel on your feet is going to cause you to walk in the way of peace and to travel where that peace leads you. When you are at peace with your Creator, you will be at peace within yourself. When you are at peace within yourself, you will walk in that peace regardless of what is going on in the world around you. When you do not have that inner peace, you will be at war with everything and everyone.

When you know that no matter what, you win in the end; no amount of warfare will be able to shake you or move you from your place in Yah's Kingdom. That is why Paul tells you in verse 14 to, *"Stand your ground"*, but it will be difficult to stand for long on the ground of the battlefield without the proper shoes on. A soldier that is preparing to go to battle may have on his or her entire uniform. The soldier may have on a protective hat, belt, pants, bullet proof vest, army decorations and even a rifle, but if that soldier has no shoes on or even the wrong shoes on, he or she is not fully prepared.

One little blister on the bottom of your foot or a corn on your pinky toe can completely immobilize you and ruin your entire day. That is why you must protect your feet. Although you may have all of the other pieces of your spiritual armor on, you will not be *fully* prepared if you are not wearing the shoes of the peace of the gospel. Having inner peace prevents you from becoming weary and thus, without those shoes on you will not be able to stand and fight!

F. The shield of faith: Now it is time for you to pick up your shield of faith. What is faith? There is a scripture that says, *"Now faith is the substance of things hoped for, the evidence of things not seen. (Heb 11:1 KJV)"* Faith is that assurance that allows you to hope for something that you desire because you just know that somehow, somewhere what you hope for does exist and can be manifested in your life. It is that knowing in your heart that is evidence enough for you to keep believing in something, even when there is no natural evidence to support your belief. It is faith that allows you to be able to even believe that God is real. You would not be able to believe that Christ Jesus died for your sins and lives today so that you can be forgiven for your sins, if not for faith. That is why the Bible says that *"without faith it is impossible to please God (Heb 11:6)."*

First and foremost, faith's purpose is to make Jesus your Lord and Savior. Yet, many people are deceived. They are convinced that they do not have faith. That is a lie from satan himself. The Bible says that God has given **every man** a measure of faith *(Rom 12:3)*. You have lived by faith from the moment you were born. It took faith to believe that when you opened your mouth to suck milk would fill your belly. It takes faith everyday to sit in a chair or to believe that when you pick up the phone, you will hear a dial tone that signifies you can make a call to talk to someone that you cannot see, who hundreds of miles away from you is. Every person alive on this earth has faith, including you. You would not be able to function without it!

You learn in Ephesians 6:16 that the shield of faith is used to protect you from the fiery arrows of the enemy. The enemy can attack us in many different ways, but an arrow is a specific kind of attack. An arrow is a small, pointy weapon that is designed to inflict a very specific part of your body. Sometimes the enemy will drop a bomb on you, but other times he will shoot an arrow at you. Whenever he shoots arrows, he is aiming for your weak areas, but faith in God's Word will protect you in these attacks.

Regardless of what your weakness is, faith in God's Word will assure you that His strength is made perfect in your weakness and that His grace is sufficient for you *(2 Cor 12:9)*. Faith will remind you to be strong in the Power of His might and not your own might *(Eph 6:10)*. Faith can be defined very simply as "believing that God's Word is true." the Word of God addresses every area of your life. There is no weakness or struggle that you face neither is there any attack of the enemy that the Father has not equipped you for in His Word *(2 Tim 3:16-17, AMP)*. Those fiery arrows will not be able to penetrate you as long as you believe in the Word of truth. Yet of course, in order to believe it you must first know it. So do not forget what we discussed in Chapter 8 about renewing your mind with the Word!

G. The helmet of salvation: Finally, the Apostle Paul instructs you to put on the helmet of salvation. He could not talk about the helmet of salvation without first addressing faith because you cannot be saved without faith. But after you exercise your faith to believe in Jesus, you will need to put on the helmet of salvation. A natural helmet is worn on the head and therefore the helmet of salvation will be used to protect your mind. The helmet of salvation is really about understanding. We talked about getting understanding earlier in the *"Renewing the Mind"* section of the book. Understanding this warfare and the strategy that is being used to win it will greatly empower you. What it is that you need to understand about salvation is that, like so many other things concerning this walk with

God, it is a process.

You may have often heard the term "get saved", but you do not just go to the altar and repeat a prayer after someone and "get saved". Salvation is something that is happening to you everyday once you give your life to Christ, but it is only those who endure until the end that will truly be saved *(Mat 10:22, 24:13)*. When you first give your heart to Jesus you have become born again *(1 Pet 1:3, 23)*. Your formerly dead spirit is reborn because it is once again alive to its Creator, but nobody is really **saved** until they are safe. When a person says, *"I'm saved."* that phrase is really symbolic terminology. It represents their faith to believe that Jesus is going to finish the work that He began in them; causing them to endure until the end so that they will one day be safe in His Bosom, with a new body that is incorruptible.

In several different places in the New Testament of the Bible the Apostle Paul talks about **"being saved"**. One such verse can be found in 1 Corinthians 1:18, *"I know very well how foolish the message of the cross sounds to those who are on the road to destruction. But we who are **being saved** recognize this message as the very power of God."* Paul makes clear in this text here that he himself, and other followers of Jesus, are in the process of "being saved". Once you understand that salvation is a process and that only those who endure to see this process through to the end will be saved, you then have your helmet of salvation on. That helmet will protect you from the disappointment that comes from having unrealistic expectations. It will protect you from giving up when you fall and from getting too relaxed when you are doing well. The helmet is the understanding that this war is one that you must fight until the day you meet Jesus face to face and then using that understanding to set your mind to endure until that day arrives!

These are the five pieces of your spiritual armor. God has given you everything you need to protect yourself from the snares of the enemy!

Step 9 - Spiritual Warfare:
Using your spiritual weapons

Let us now discuss the second aspect of spiritual warfare. We already know that the armor of God is for <u>defending</u> yourself in the spirit realm, but no good war can be fought unless both sides have weapons that enable them to launch attacks against one another. So in this step, we are going to discuss some spiritual weapons and how to use them. This is a spiritual battle that we are fighting. You are going to have to learn how to stop fighting horizontally (on this earthly plane) and start fighting vertically (on the spiritual plane)!

Satan does have weapons. We have already read about his fiery arrows. Certainly, God did not leave us shorthanded when it comes to spiritual weapons. In 2 Corinthians 10, verses 3 and 4, in the Amplified version of the Bible it reads, *"³For though we walk (live) in the flesh, we are not carrying on our warfare according to the flesh and using mere human weapons. ⁴For the weapons of our warfare are not physical [weapons of flesh and blood], but they are mighty before God for the overthrow and destruction of strongholds."* God has given us an arsenal of mighty weapons infused with His very power that are guaranteed to defeat satan and tear down his strongholds!

A. The Sword of the Word: You have already read about one of our weapons in Ephesians 6:17, *"and take the sword of the Spirit, which is the Word of God."* In this scripture, the Word of God is likened to a sword. A sword is used for close combat. Thus, you can use the Sword of the Word to cut the devil when he gets in your face! This is what Jesus did in the book of Luke chapter 4:2-13, when the devil came to tempt Him after He had been fasting in the wilderness for 40 days.

Satan came to Jesus and tried to find opportunity in the weakness of Jesus' flesh, that was due to the fast, to make Him sin against the Father. Yet, every time the devil made his attempts, Jesus boldly proclaimed *"It is written"*. This was not a sneak attack that the devil launched. Neither was it an attack that was launched from afar off. The devil got up close and personal with Jesus and for that reason Jesus needed a weapon that could be used in close combat. He used the Sword of the Word.

The Bible teaches that *"Death and life are in the power of the tongue (Prov 18:21 KJV)"* and also that *"The words you say now reflect your fate then; either you will be justified by them or you will be condemned (Matt 12:37)."* It is not that red, flappy piece of flesh in your mouth that the Bible is talking about when it speaks of the tongue. The power is not in the flesh of your tongue but instead in the words that roll off of your tongue. There is awesome power in what you speak – power to produce life or power to produce death; power to justify or power to condemn. Jesus told his disciples that he is *"...the Way the Truth and the Life...(John 14:6a)"* You can also read in the Gospel of John that Jesus is the Living Word *(John 1:14)*. Therefore, the power of Life that is in the tongue is released when it is used to speak the Word of God. By speaking the Word, you are speaking Jesus Himself – you are speaking Life into your situation and wielding a sharp Sword in the face of the father of all lies!

By speaking anything other than God's Word, you are choosing to speak death into your situation. Everything contrary to God's Word represents sin and separation from Him – the wrong way, deception and death. Words contrary to Jesus' truth represent darkness and the sinful nature of the flesh, which brings about condemnation. That condemnation is what makes you guilty and gives the enemy the right to keep you imprisoned. The Word of God, which is Jesus Himself, is what justifies you, sets you free from bondage and produces life in your dead spirit. Thus, by speaking against His Word you are producing death. There is no such thing as being neutral either. By choosing to not speak at all, you are silently killing yourself.

You must **speak** the Word in order for it to have any damaging effects on the enemy. You can have a sword, but it will never destroy your enemy if you do not actually use it. The way you use the Sword of God's Word is by speaking it, and you can rest assured that it will cut the enemy and force him to back off! Yet, how are you going to speak the Word of God if you do not know the Word? You cannot talk about what you do not know about. It is very, very important that you read the Bible every day, as much as you possibly can. Read Christian literature such as this book and listen to anointed preaching and teachings about the truth of the gospel. The more well-versed you are with the Word, the more skillfully you are going to be able to use it as a Sword! Read scriptures daily, read the Bible out loud everyday and talk about the gospel as often as you have the opportunity.

I know that many new or undeveloped believers complain that they do not understand the Bible. I admit that it can be quite difficult to comprehend due to the fact that it cannot be comprehended using your human intellect. The Word of God can not be mentally unpeeled, it must Holy Spirit revealed, but do not allow lack of understanding of the Word to dissuade you from reading it. Just pray for understanding before you read the Bible and know that you will get that understanding eventually.

I recall my days as a new believer. the Bible made very little sense to me, but I knew that the Bible was the most powerful link that I had to God at that time. I wanted to be connected to my Savior and so I just kept on reading in spite of the puzzlement that I was caused. One of the best moves I made for myself was getting a more modern translation of the Bible. The Amplified was the version that I was reading. I read the entire Bible in a matter of months. Yet, even with the more modern translation, I honestly did not understand even half of what I read. However, I read it anyway.

The thing that amazed me though, was to learn that as time went on and I matured in my relationship with God, scriptures that I had read months and even years prior were spontaneously being revealed to me at moments when I really needed Father's wisdom concerning situations. I was really glad about this because soon after reading the Bible in its entirety, I got married and had a baby every year. I never had time to read the entire Bible like that again, although I have always wanted to. (I am actually reading the Bible from cover to cover with my children right now, but after 2½ years we are only up to 1 Samuel. It will probably be quite some time before we finish! *smile*.)

Now-a-days, I can only manage to read a few chapters at a time, but because the Word has already been planted in me, the Holy Spirit is able to bring scriptures to my remembrance and give me the revelation when I need it *(John 14:26)*. I always have the sharp two-edged Sword of the Word ready to cut the devil when he gets in my face! The Word of God is the most reliable weapon that you can have in your arsenal. *"Heaven and earth will disappear but **my words will remain forever** (Matt 24:35)."* Get to know it and learn to use it skillfully!

"I have hidden your Word in my heart, that I might not sin against you. (Ps 119:11)"

B. The power of praise: We also have praise as a weapon. Praise is a powerful weapon because it renders the enemy's attacks powerless against you! When we praise the Great I AM, it angers the devil because it reminds him of everything that the True God is and what he himself is not. Have you ever heard the term "blind fury"? Intense anger blinds you to all else and confuses your thinking. No one thinks straight when they are enraged. This is the type of anger that is stirred up in the enemy when you praise The Lord, and it causes satan to engage in self-destructive behavior. He will set himself to be at war with you and will not even realize that the trap that he has set for you is going to self-destruct and backfire. He makes desperate moves out of intense anger and confusion, moves that are incapable of accomplishing what they were meant to accomplish. You will barely have to lift a hand toward the enemy when you know how to really praise The King. Your enemy will destroy himself.

We see evidence of this in several places in the Old Testament of the Bible *(Josh 6:20, Jud 7:19-23)*. In the book of 2 Chronicles chapter 20, there is an account of King Jehoshaphat going out to face several armies that had risen up against him. Read what happened: *"^{21}After consulting the leaders of the people, the king appointed singers to walk ahead of the army, singing to The Lord and praising him for his Holy splendor. This is what they sang: 'Give thanks to The Lord; his faithful love endures forever!' ^{22}At the moment they began to sing and give praise, The Lord caused the armies of Ammon, Moab, and Mount Seir to start fighting among themselves. ^{23}The armies of Moab and Ammon turned against their allies from Mount Seir and killed every one of them. After they had finished off the army of Seir, they turned on each other. ^{24}So when the army of Judah arrived at the lookout point in the wilderness, there were dead bodies lying on the ground for as far as they could see. Not a single one of the enemy had escaped."*

What an awesome account of God's deliverance power! King Jehoshaphat and his army never had to lift a finger to fight against the enemy, all they had to do was to lift their voices in praise. The scripture goes on to tell us that after Judah arrived on the battlefield, the dead armies left so many possessions behind that it took three days to gather it all! Not only were the lives of God's people spared, but they also walked away from the situation with more blessings than they had gone into it with – all because they knew how to praise God. Note that in verse 21 of the scripture exactly what the singers were saying is expressed *"Give thanks to The Lord."*

The key to being a praiser is giving God thanks and having a grateful attitude. They could have murmured and complained about God not giving them peace with their enemies, but instead they chose to praise Him for His Greatness. They chose to thank Him for all that He had already done in their lives. Everyone enjoys blessing people that are thankful, just as God enjoys blessing you when you are thankful. Because of the thankful spirits of the people of Judah, God not only delivered them, but He also gave them even more blessings because He knew that they would be grateful for all He had done for them. Open up your mouth and sing and shout praises to The King. Have a grateful heart toward Him and watch how He will confuse and destroy your enemies and cause every adverse situation to work in your favor!

"I will come in the strength and with the mighty acts of The Lord; I will mention and praise Your Righteousness, even Yours alone. (Ps 71:16 AMP)"

C. Christian fellowship: It says in Ecclesiastes 4:12, *"A person standing alone can be attacked and defeated, but two can stand back-to-back and conquer. Three are even better, for a triple-braided cord is not easily broken."* Christian fellowship is one of the most effortless weapons that you can take advantage of. There are three benefits that you can reap from the use of this weapon: 1) The power of agreement; 2) The casting out of devils in Jesus, Yeshua's name and/or the laying on of hands for healing, and impartation; 3) Absorbing strength from the strong. Let us explore these three advantages a bit more.

One of the main benefits of Christian fellowship is the power of agreement. We learn this in Matthew 18:19, *"I also tell you this: If two of you agree down here on earth concerning anything you ask, my Father in heaven will do it for you."* Agreement can be used as a weapon against satan because it enables God to more readily answer your prayers, which are in part purposed to defeat satan. It is a biblical principal that everything should be established in the mouths of at least two witnesses *(Mat 18:16)*.

Therefore, when more than one of God's saints believe Him for an answer to prayer, it confirms spiritually that the need is legitimate. Home Bible studies with other believers, small support groups or prayer on the phone with an anointed servant of God are all great ways to use this weapon of agreement. Church services can offer this benefit as well, although perhaps not as efficiently in some instances since you may not always be able to voice your prayers specifically in such a large group setting.

The second benefit that I mentioned concerns the casting out of devils and the laying on of hands. In the book of Mark you learn about the power that Jesus has given His true followers, *"These signs will accompany those who believe: They will cast out demons in my name... They will be able to place their hands on the sick and heal them (Mark 16:17a, 18a)."* Whenever Jesus confronted evil spirits, they had to submit to the Holy Spirit that was within Him. Often times, Jesus did not even have to address a demon for it to bow to Him. Likewise, when a believer is really walking in the Holy Spirit, demons will recognize Jesus' Spirit in that person. As much as the demons do not like it, they have no choice in the matter – demons must submit to the authority of Jesus Christ! An anointed man or woman servant of God can personally address you to cast out a demon (like in a prayer line or such), but they can also rebuke demons in your life just through the Words they speak or preach – even their very presence.

You may want more information on demon possession. However, as I mentioned earlier, the question of "demon possessed or not" is not a critical issue. The very fact that sexual perversion is a part of someone's life is evidence enough of some sort of demonic stronghold; and this knowledge is sufficient for one to proceed in deliverance successfully. As to how to evaluate whether or not you are dealing with a demonic stronghold or just the habits of your sin nature, here is a simple test: If you have done everything within your power naturally and applied every Word principle that you know; if you have confessed and prayed and prayed and confessed and yet still cannot get the victory in a certain area, then you are certainly dealing with a demonic stronghold. Demonic deliverance is a necessity in such a case in order for you to be victorious in that area.

Then you might wonder what level of demonic deliverance is warranted: *"Can I just pray about this calmly in my home, or do I need to call in an exorcist team?"* Some demonic strongholds are very apparent with obvious physical manifestations, while others can be very subtle and inconspicuous. Still, in either case it can be difficult to tell the necessary degree of intensity in deliverance, and each instance should be determined on a case-by-case basis. But do not let the knowledge of demonic strongholds in your life drive you crazy, and if you know that you are plagued by a demon do not become obsessed about it being cast out. I am not saying that you should not care. Definitely be proactive and aggressive, but don't be *anxious*. Be calmly and peacefully led by the Holy Spirit as to what course of action you need to take.

Believe me, demons can be like tumors. Some tumors can be removed immediately after they are discovered. Yet there are others that have become such a part of a patient's body that it would kill the person to remove it too quickly, especially in a weaker patient. In such a case, special precautions must be taken and preparations made to ensure that the patient survives the removal of the tumor. The same is often true concerning demonic infestation and strongholds. I have often observed preachers ignorantly casting demons out of people to the person's detriment. Why? Because a person needs almost immediate healing and fulfillment of the void left behind when a demon is cast out. If a preacher is unable to do this, or the person being delivered is not prepared to receive such healing and fulfillment, the demon that has been cast out soon returns with other more powerful spirits. The person ends up in an even worse condition than before *(Mat 12:45, Luke 11:26)*.

So I say again, just proceed at the unction of the Holy Spirit concerning demons in your life. I have personally found that the most effective way to deal with demonic infestations and strongholds in my own life is to just consistently and steadily walk out Yah's call on my life. When I live an obedient life, serving God in every way that I know how to and answer my call to the best of my ability, it is a natural subsequent result that demons have to detach and disassociate themselves from me. How can two walk together unless they agree *(Amos 3:3)*? Diligently and consistently implementing these 12 deliverance steps in my life has been the most powerful and effective exorcism I could have ever received. At times when more specific and straightforward demonic deliverance was necessary, the Holy Spirit always led me, and He will lead you too. But for now, attending Christian fellowships out of the pure joy of coming together to worship God corporately, and the desire to be more fully equipped to serve Him, will suffice in establishing the foundation for deliverance from every demonic infestation and stronghold.

But remember, casting out demons is only part of the second benefit of Christian fellowship. The scripture also said that, *"...They will be able to place their hands on the sick and heal them..."* As far as healing is concerned, we tend to think only of the physical body. We definitely can receive healing in our physical bodies – you may even need healing from a sexually transmitted disease and that can be done – but an anointed vessel of God can also, by laying hands on you, heal wounds in your spirit. The spiritual healing is just as important, if not more so, as the physical healing. As I just mentioned, once demons are cast out of you, you need to immediately be healed and filled: the open wound in your spirit must be closed and the void that is left behind must be satisfied, in order to keep those demons from entering back in. The laying on of hands can often times accomplish this. *(That is of course **If** you are willing to receive healing – some people love their wounds!)* Not only will the laying on of hands heal the open wound, but it will also fill the void by stirring up the gifts that God has placed inside of you *(2 Tim 1:6)*. There are some gifts that you will never give birth to until an Anointed Vessel lays hands on you and makes an impartation into your spirit.

Now onto the third benefit that you can reap from Christian fellowship, absorbing strength from the strong. Being in the presence of an anointed Christian brother or sister can really boost your spirit. There are times when we get weak and need to feed off of the anointing that is on other believers. At times, I feel ready to conquer the world and as if the Power of the Holy Spirit in me is so strong that I will never need another jumpstart in my life! But, then there are other times that I feel too weak to fight off even a teeny tiny demon (*smile*). In those weak times, I know that what I need is to fellowship with other strong believers in order to absorb some of their strength. When strong anointed believers gather together to praise, worship and study the Word, the atmosphere becomes rich with anointing and spiritual strength. Just by being present in such an atmosphere, I am absorbing the sweet residue of the anointing and glorious power of the Holy Spirit. This is truly a great benefit.

However, absorbing strength from other strong believers should be thought of as getting a boost for your car. You do not need a jump every time you start your car. If you did, you probably would not drive often because there is not always going to be someone around to give you a jump. Furthermore, having to rely on others to get your car started every time you drive would be frustrating, time consuming and disheartening. Once you get that boost, you have to keep your engine running and take care of your car so that you can drive safely, consistently and with the liberty of not having to depend on others. Being in the presence of other strong believers is the same way: it will definitely boost you ahead in the deliverance process and benefit you spiritually, but relying totally upon this will hinder you tremendously.

When you do feel the necessity and leading to be in the presence of an anointed man or woman servant of God, you may immediately think about a preacher. Ministers, Evangelists, Pastors and other titled and/or well-known Christian leaders can certainly fit into the category of an anointed believer, and you certainly do not want to fellowship with weak believers that are going to pull on you, if you yourself are not strong. However, recognized spiritual leaders are not God's only anointed vessels on earth. Fellowshipping with other believers of all kind is so important. Church is one way that fellowship can take place and attending anointed church services can definitely be advantageous, but do not become a church junky or leader leech.

What I mean by that is this; you can reap the three benefits of Christian fellowship when you are in the presence of *any* strong and anointed believer. Therefore, you should not limit God's ability to work in your life by thinking it can only happen in the presence of a preacher or at a traditional church service. Many times we become leader leeches by trying to latch on to particular preachers that are known to us. We then attempt to suck all of the anointing out of them. We also sometimes develop the mindset that we can only be delivered in church and so we become church service junkies. We wear ourselves out by attending service, after service, after service.

The truth of the matter is, your specific deliverance needs cannot always be met in a large church setting, and there is only so much that a busy preacher or spiritual leader can do for you in way of personal attention. So be careful not to seek after the big names and large conferences only. If you cause your deliverance to become dependent on these things, you are setting yourself up for a disappointing downfall. Honestly, there cannot be anointed services going on 24/7 and big name preachers are not always going to be in town. I just want you to understand that the power is not in the large numbers or the popularity of the preacher. You should go to church as often as the Holy Spirit leads you to, but do not limit your definition of fellowship to *church*.

This summarizes the three ways that you can use Christian fellowship as a weapon. These three benefits gained from Christian fellowship are certainly powerful and are to be regarded. Yet, I must admonish you with a warning. I did mention earlier that Christian fellowship is one of the most *effortless* weapons you can take advantage of and that is why it can be so very addictive. You must use this weapon with caution. This deliverance process is going to take work and you cannot try to look for the easy way out. There is no easy way out. After the request has been agreed upon, the devils have been cast out, some healing has taken place, the gifts have been stirred and you have gotten your boost, there is nothing more that fellowshipping can accomplish for you.

You should fellowship with other believers as often as you are led to, especially as a new believer, but what you need more than anything else is that personal devotional time with your Heavenly Father. Do not let group fellowship rob you of all of your intimate time with the Lover of Your Soul. You cannot spend all of your time seeking out fellowship. People will not always be available and will not always be walking in the Spirit and therefore will let you down. And remember, other believers are fighting in this warfare too. They need to be strengthened just as you do and cannot always be expected to give out to you. Besides by being in constant fellowship, you are avoiding the real battlefield where this war is fought. Without fighting the battles you cannot win the war.

None-the-less, I encourage you to fellowship with other believers. You will definitely be doing yourself a disservice and putting yourself at a disadvantage if you don't.

"^{24}And let us consider and give attentive, continuous care to watching over one another, studying how we may stir up (stimulate and incite) ... ^{25}Not forsaking or neglecting to assemble together [as believers], ...but

admonishing (warning, urging, and encouraging) one another... (Heb 10: 24-25, AMP)"

D. Praying and fasting: You have not even begun to do serious warfare until you have implemented praying and fasting! The combination of prayer and fasting is a one, two knock out punch right in the devil's face! Yet, you have to have a proper understanding of what prayer is and why fasting improves the effectiveness of prayer. Fasting alone would really belong in the chapter dealing with deliverance for the flesh man. This is because fasting in and of itself merely takes physical discipline. Therefore, I will discuss the specifics of fasting in more detail in the next chapter, but we will talk about fasting as it relates to prayer right now.

The simplest definition that I can give you for prayer is to say that it means to communicate with God. However, to leave it there would really be over-simplifying the issue. There are so many different types of prayer and so many different ways to communicate those prayers. The number of different types of prayers and ways to communicate those prayers would be equivalent to the number of different dimensions of God and the different roles that He plays in your life. Think of it this way; if your spouse were a judge you would not call him or her *'Honey'* while he or she was officially sitting on the bench nor would you normally call your spouse *'Your Honor'* at home. There may be times when you address your spouse as 'Mister' or 'Misses', other times by their first name and yet other times with a term of endearment such as 'Sweetie'. It all depends on in which aspect you are interacting with them at the time.

On the other hand, you may address them using the same title, but with a different tone and volume for different occasions. For example, if your husband has left his socks on the floor for the fourth time in a week, you may say *"HOOONEEEYHHH!"* in a very loud and annoyed tone. Yet, if it is 2:00am and you want him to get out of bed to get you a glass of juice, you may say, *"Hooooneeey."*, in a very soft, sweet sounding voice. Prayer, or communication with God, is the same way. He has to be addressed and approached differently according to the interaction. Yet, the truth of the matter is, it is hard for any of us to know exactly how we should pray. The Bible proves this in Romans 8:26, *"...For we don't even know what we should pray for, nor how we should pray..."*

If we go on to read verse 26 in its entirety and also the verse that follows it we learn the key to prayer. *"And the Holy Spirit helps us in our distress. For we don't even know what we should pray for, nor how we should pray.* **But the Holy Spirit prays for us with groanings that cannot be expressed in words.** *²⁷And the Father who knows all hearts knows what the Spirit is saying,* **for the Spirit pleads for us believers in harmony with God's own will***."* Again, we can look at another insightful scripture in the epistle of 1 John, chapter 5, verses 14 and 15 to confirm this point, *"¹⁴And we can be confident that he will listen to us whenever we ask Him for anything* **in line with his will.** *¹⁵And if we know he is listening when we make our requests, we can be sure that he will give us what we ask for."*

In these scriptures, it is made apparent that the only way you can pray with the assurance that God is going to hear you and grant your request is when your prayers are presented with the correct approach and are precisely in line with His will. As far as I am concerned, that is a tall order to fill. I do not personally know a single person that always knows exactly what God's will is, concerning all things in life. There are times when God will reveal His plans to us, but even what He does reveal to us, we still only know in part *(1 Cor 13:9)*. Our finite minds and limited intellect cannot even begin to conceive the awesome plans of the Great I AM. Thus, we really need the Holy Spirit to pray on our behalves.

This brings me back around to my initial aim, which is to help you understand the important link between prayer and fasting. So often times the reason you are met with frustration and disappointment concerning your prayers is because they fail to line up with God's will. Now you understand that the problem is that you do not know how to pray or what to pray for. You also understand now that the solution is that the Holy Spirit must pray through you on your behalf, in order for your prayers to be in line with God's will. There is still one thing missing though – submission. The Holy Spirit can only work through a submitted and yielded vessel, and this is where the breakdown in the solution usually takes place. This is when you can reap the benefits of fasting as a supplement to your praying.

There is a constant power struggle going on in every human being, between the flesh (our sinful nature) and the Spirit of God that lives in we who are born again *(Gal 5:17)*. In your spirit, you often times want to do the right thing. However, the nature of the flesh, if not subdued, will prevent you from doing what you know you should do and what you do desire to do. This is because the flesh is too weak to do what is Righteous in the Father's sight. That is why Jesus said to His disciples, *"...the spirit is willing but the flesh is weak (Mat 26:41, KJV)"*. This power struggle that is constantly going on between your flesh and your spirit can prevent the Holy Spirit from being able to work through you. Thus, the Bible tells us in 1 Thessalonians 5:19, *"Don't stifle the Holy Spirit."* According to Merriam-Webster's On-line Dictionary, the word stifle means *"to cut off (as the voice or breath) b :* **to withhold from** *circulation or* **expression** *: REPRESS c :* **deter, DISCOURAGE**" (www.Merriam-WebsterCollegiate.com 12/05/2004). That means that when the scripture tells you not to stifle the Holy Spirit, God is warning you not to withhold His Spirit from having expression in your life; and to not deter or discourage the Holy Spirit from operating through you.

It is made plain in the Bible *(Rom chap 8)* that stifling of the Holy Spirit in your life is caused when you are still controlled and dominated by your sinful nature. You have to subdue the nature of your flesh and allow the Holy Spirit to control your life. It says in Romans 8:14 that those that are **LED** by the Spirit of God are His children. The Holy Spirit is not in the business of <u>forcing</u> or <u>dominating</u>. He is no taskmaster. He will only lead; you must follow. Because The Spirit and the flesh are hostile to one another, the only way you are going to be able to follow the leading of the Holy Spirit is if your flesh is under submission. That is why you must fast. Fasting is one of the most effective ways to accomplish submission of the flesh. We will talk about fasting more in the next chapter. Here, I just wanted to make clear to you the essential link between prayer and fasting.

Having established an understanding about prayer and fasting, let me address this question: Is there any particular style of prayer that you should use? Should you walk, should you kneel, should you yell, should you cry, etcetera? Initially, you should pray in whatever fashion you are comfortable with, but I warn you not to get locked in to any one particular style. Even in this, you should be led by the Holy Spirit. The Holy Spirit may move on you in different ways at different times and it is very important that you be liberal in your prayer life, not limiting how the Holy Spirit intercedes through you. Be open to pray in whatever way you are led to, even if it is in a way you are unfamiliar with or in a way that seems strange to you. Remember, this is warfare and the fight might get ugly sometimes. The battlefield is not the place to be comfortable or to look cute. It is a place to engage in bloody warfare!

One type of prayer that I do want to highlight before I conclude this step is that of praying in tongues; also sometimes referred to in the Bible as *unknown, new* or *other tongues* or *languages (Mark 16:17, Acts 2:4, 1 Cor 12:10, 13:1)*. Have you been baptized in the Holy Spirit and endowed with the gift of speaking in tongues? If not, I am sorry to say that you are at a great disadvantage. Praying in tongues is critically important in this warfare and this Christian walk. Praying in tongues is one of the most effective ways to allow the Holy Spirit to intercede through you. Often times, the distractibility of your mind will interfere with the Holy Spirit's liberty to pray through you. As you hear yourself praying, your intellect wants to add and modify God's will to fit your desires and/or understanding. That is why praying in that Heavenly language that your mind cannot comprehend is so powerful. There is no way for you to interject your own will when you are praying in tongues. You are completely submitted to the Holy Spirit and allowing Him to use your mouth however He needs to. *"[2]For if your gift is the ability to speak in tongues, **you will be talking to God** but not to people, since they will not be able to understand you. **You will be speaking by the power of the Spirit, but it will all be mysterious**. (1 Cor 14:2)"*

You see, by praying in tongues you are able to speak directly to God and pray according to the *mysteries* of His will about things that you might not be able to handle if your mind comprehended what you were praying about. For example, you may be praying for strength because a close relative is soon to die or something of that nature. Or, something good may be about to happen to you and you may get so excited or anxious about what is revealed to you in prayer that you abort the preparation process due to the excitement and completely miss the blessing that was in store. Also, do not forget what we discussed earlier; you do not even know all that needs to be said and confessed concerning the wounds and evils in your heart. This too is a mystery to you but still needs to be prayed about. There are things about yourself that you are just not mentally and emotionally ready to deal with. The Holy Spirit can make intercession for you in all of these instances in tongues, while still preserving the mystery of God's will until He is ready to reveal it to you. In doing this, the Holy Spirit is guarding your peace of mind.

    I do not want to go into too much more detail about it here, but just know that the scriptures say that a person who speaks in tongues is personally strengthened and edified *(1 Cor 14:4, Jude 1:20)*. Don't you need to be strengthened and edified? Of course you do. Thus, if you are a believer and you have not yet been endowed with the gift of speaking in tongues, you can ask The Lord for it right there, right now where you are. You can also go to a church that believes in the speaking of tongues and ask one of the leaders of the church to pray with you that you may receive the gift. However you choose to do it, just do it. (Please don't be discouraged if it does not happen right away though. You can still be filled with the Holy Spirit even f you don't speak in tongues.) You need to be able to pray in tongues if your prayer life is ever going to be elevated beyond the elementary level of your own human understanding!

    In conclusion, you can find an account in the book of Mark chapter 9, of Jesus instructing His disciples on how to be victorious over demons. He says to them, *"²⁹...This kind cannot be driven out by anything but **<u>prayer and fasting</u>**. (Mark 9:29)"* Jesus was trying to teach us here that the combination of prayer and fasting is the most powerful weapon that we have in our spiritual arsenal. Through prayer and fasting you can even expel demons from yourself, not having to rely on another person. Notice that Jesus did not instruct His disciples to speak the Word, give thanks and praise or fellowship with other saints. He told them to pray and fast! The reason that prayer is so powerful is that it is not based on our ability as human beings to do something spiritual. It is based on the unlimited power and knowledge of the Holy Spirit. God knows what His will is, prays a prayer according to His own will by His own Spirit and then executes the answer to that prayer! Now that is one awesome weapon. No demon nor satan himself will be able to withstand such a weapon!!!

"But in my distress I cried out to The Lord; yes, I prayed to my God for help. He heard me from his sanctuary; my cry reached his ears. (Ps 18:6)"

"...I afflicted myself with fasting, and I prayed with head bowed on my breast. (Ps 35:13, AMP)"

Step 10 – Spiritual Warfare: Retreat and replenish

There is one more thing we need to discuss concerning spiritual warfare. You have already learned how to protect and defend yourself. You have also learned about some spiritual weapons that you can use to launch attacks. Yet, in every long war the warriors must retreat and replenish themselves frequently. You will never make it if you attempt to remain engaged in battle 24 hours a day and seven days a week! This is a deadly mistake that most believers make at some point in their Christian walk. If you do not learn how to pace yourself, you will be burnt out and defeated before you ever get a glimpse of the victory that is already yours.

Zeal for deliverance is an excellent thing. Having that spiritual zeal to be set free, delivered and walking in the power of Jesus gives you the spiritual energy that is needed to go forth with momentum and tenacity. However, there is a down side to zeal. Zeal can create a sense of anxiousness when it is not coupled with wisdom and experience. The Word of God tells us that we should not be anxious *(Phil 4:6)*, but even still we often times find ourselves ***anxious*** concerning deliverance. Anxiousness will cause you to push yourself beyond your limitations, leaving you exhausted and unable to fight. So here is what you need to do – **retreat and replenish!**

Retreating and getting replenished is really quite simple. You only need to do one thing – worship the Father. However, you cannot forget that the devil's main purpose in introducing sexual perversion into the earth was to pervert man's ability to effectively worship God. Therefore, considering that the enemy has already been successful in perverting your spirit, you will not at this time have full liberty when worshiping God. You should not let that deter you from pursuing to worship Him though because there are many levels of worship. You can still worship Him at the level that you are currently on because it is going to be detrimental to your deliverance that you worship God and worship Him often. It is when you retreat into God's presence that your spirit is going to be refreshed and strengthened to go back out on the battlefield of deliverance. It is there in His presence that you will receive the greatest healing.

Remember how we discussed earlier in the book the correlation between human sexual relations and spiritual worship relations with God?

Bearing this in mind, when you worship God you should be pursuing intimacy with Him. To help you understand this correlation I want to speak from my own personal experience as a married woman that is blessed with a very fulfilling intimate relationship my husband. There are so many things that my husband and I do together. We parent together, we minister together, we run our business together, we fight our enemies together and we talk, laugh and play together as well. Yet, even in the midst of all of this togetherness, nothing can compare to our intimate time together; not even the time we spend together as friends.

When it seems that life is really wearing me down, I reach for the comforts of intimacy that I find in my husband. Nevertheless balancing out my life, especially in light of the challenge of raising six small children, finding opportunities for intimacy with my husband can at times be an elusive goal. Furthermore, just being a woman means that there are times when physically I cannot be intimate with my husband. *(I am sure you understand what I mean by that, smile.)* I find that at these times of my life, when my husband and I are not able to be intimate for extended days regardless of what the reason may be, I become so tense. That tension creates fatigue and sometimes weariness. I begin to feel as if I just cannot do *it* – everyday life – anymore.

When I get like this there is nothing that refreshes me more than intimacy with my husband. A good church service, hanging out with my girls, a trip to the salon, not even a nice warm, Calgon bath will do the trick – nothing refreshes me like intimacy with my husband does. It is like with that first kiss, with that first touch – stress literally begins to melt away. Tension eases, frustration gives way to relaxation and fatigue is consumed by the energizing passions of intimacy. It soothes, it comforts, it fulfills and it satisfies. By the time the intimate experience has come to an end I feel renewed and *ready* – ready to go change another stinky diaper, cook another meal and fruitfully tolerate yet another telemarketing call!

Now, I do not want to make anyone who is not married feel slighted. God's Love is more than adequate to meet every need in your life. I cannot honestly say that sexual desires will ever leave you, but I can assure you that you are able to move beyond the point where you feel that sexual intimacy is a *need*. As a married woman, sexual intimacy has to be a _need_ for me. If it were not, my marriage would be in trouble! But, as a single person I did not _need_ sexual intimacy to refresh me because there was a different grace of God upon me. My goal in sharing with you the refreshing that I experience when being intimate with my husband is to paint a picture for you, of your intimate relationship with God and to illustrate to you the importance of that intimacy with Him. Just as the menial tasks and obligations of marriage, family and everyday life often times leave me tense, weary and in need of replenishing; so do the menial tasks and obligations of the deliverance process leave you weary and in need of replenishing. You need to just get into the presence of your Spiritual Husband and Lover and be refreshed. Lay prostrate before Him and let Him touch you. Let Him comfort, soothe and fulfill you. Allow Him to ease away your tensions and re-energize your spirit.

I know that sounds good, but perhaps you are having difficulty understanding what it means to be intimate with God. When I am in sexual intimacy with my husband we do not function in any other aspect of our relationship other than the capacity of two intimate beings coming together to adore and pleasure one another, bringing about oneness in soul, spirit and body. You have to understand this when you are worshiping your King. When you are being intimate with Him you should interact with Him as your Lover only and nothing else. Worship is not a time to petition God, it is not a time to bind satan, it is not a time to intercede for the nations. Worship is a time to prostrate yourself in the presence of The Lord, make Him feel wonderful and let Him do the same for you. Remember also, _"...they that worship Him must worship Him in spirit and in truth (John 4:24, KJV)."_ – truth is nakedness. Just get naked in spirit before God and be at ease in who you are. Touch His Spirit and allow Him to touch yours.

No one can really _teach_ you how to worship. The only way to learn how to be successful at sexual intimacy is to practice it and learning how to worship God is the same. However, I can teach you the basic principles of worship. The most important thing you must remember about worship is that true intimacy with God has to begin with thanksgiving and praise. _"Enter into His gates with thanksgiving and a thank offering and into His courts with praise! Be thankful and say so to Him, bless and affectionately praise His name! (Ps 100:4, AMP)."_ You cannot enter into that most Holy and Sacred Place without first offering thanks and praise. I know for me, nothing stirs my passions like when my husband begins to praise and adore me, and often times when I want to be sexually intimate with him, I begin by just affirming and admiring him.

Prayer is sometimes the best way to proceed in worship after praising. There are times when demonic strongholds in the atmosphere will prevent you from entering into God's presence or sometimes just the failure to be truthful with Him about your sinfulness will hinder you as well. Prayer will help you break through these strongholds. Another thing you should know about worship is that it needs to be affectionate. I am sure you well know that sex and intimacy do not always go hand in hand. To be "intimate", means to be "in-to-your-mate". It takes more than just the physical act of intercourse in and of itself to create intimacy. There has to be affection and oneness; a spiritual connection is necessary in order for it to really be intimate. Likewise, when you are worshiping God, there has to be a spiritual connection. Bowing before Him is very important, but you can't just lay your body on the floor and expect something to happen. You need to be affectionate with Him. As the text says, *"bless and **affectionately** praise His name!"*

Be romantic with God. Fill the room with the sweet aroma of prayer and incense, have a candlelit feast of the Word, play some soft praise and worship music and set yourself up for a night of passion with The King. The Holy Spirit can help with this as well by speaking through you in tongues. Often times when I worship, I notice that I speak in a particular type of tongues that I do not use at any other time. It sounds very sweet and tender. Another effective way to stir your affection toward God is by reading, reciting or listening to His Word. In this way you are reminded of how wonderful He truly is and the so many reasons there are to adore Him: *"As pressure and stress bear down on me, I find joy in your commands. (Ps 119:143)"* By partaking of the Word, you can easily change the tone of your praise from phlegmatic and mundane to affectionate, tender and passionate unto His Majesty: *"How sweet are your words to my taste; they are sweeter than honey. (Ps 119:103)"* You can romance your Lover with your praise and woo Him into intimacy by speaking to Him His own Word concerning His greatness and worth.

As I said, I cannot really teach you how to worship God *functionally*, but I can assure you that the key elements of thanksgiving, praise, being affectionately prostrated before Him and speaking His Word will get you started on the path to an intimate experience with Him, the Lover of Your Soul. At any rate, it is paramount for you to understand that this deliverance process and daily warfare between The Spirit and the flesh can really wear you out! One of the most powerful messages I ever preached was out of the book of Genesis, 25:27-34. It tells the story of how Esau sells his birthright to his brother Jacob. Esau was anointed by God to be a hunter and one day, while out hunting, he allowed himself to become over exhausted and weary with hunger and fatigue. What really enlightened me was the revelation that Esau became tired and hungry from doing what he was called and anointed to do. He was supposed to hunt. He had great favor with his natural father Isaac because of the game that he hunted. Yet, doing the thing that he was supposed to do caused him great exhaustion and fatigue. Why? Because, he did not stop to retreat and replenish soon and often enough.

By the time Esau realized that he needed to be replenished, he felt too weak to make it back into the presence of his father Isaac. He then made the foolish, desperate decision to sell his birthright in order to be replenished. You see, this Christian walk is arduous at times and can cause you great weariness if you are not careful. Let refreshing in The Lord's presence become a regular part of your daily Christian walk and deliverance process. Do not make the mistake that Esau made by waiting until you are so exhausted and depleted that you just do anything out of the desperation to replenish yourself. Go into that secret place with God, lay down your weapons, take off your armor and get naked in the presence of your Lord. Let Him kiss away the pain and send you back out onto the battlefield with a renewed energy and strength!

Again we can learn from King David in his implementation of this important step. He says, *"One thing have I asked of The Lord, that will I seek, inquire for, and [insistently] require: that I may dwell in the house of The Lord [in His presence] all the days of my life, to behold and gaze upon the beauty [the sweet attractiveness and the delightful loveliness] of The Lord and to meditate, consider, and inquire in His temple. (Ps 27:4, AMP)"*

"You are a garden fountain, a well of living water, as refreshing as the streams from the Lebanon mountains. (Song of Sol. 4:15)"

Chapter 10:
Deliverance for the flesh man

We have covered a great deal so far. Now at last you are going to learn how to deal with that stinking flesh of yours! You may be surprised by the simplicity of this part of the process!

Step 11 – Discipline of the flesh

Finally, it is time to talk about deliverance in the flesh, and what is the first word you see? Yeah, that's right, good, ol' fashion **discipline**!!! I know you are probably thinking, *"Aww maaan! Discipline?"* Trust me, I know how you feel, but it is probably not as bad as you're thinking (*smile*). There is some good news and some bad news concerning discipline. OK, let me give you the bad news first. The bad news is that you have probably already "tried" discipline in the past and failed at it. You may have said to yourself in times past, *"Self, this is it. You're not going to _____ anymore. I mean it this time. This is it!"* But before you knew it, lo and behold your flesh was doing _____ again. So your attempt to discipline yourself did not work. Am I right about this, or am I right about this? I guess you can figure how I know this – been there, done that!

But here is the good news. The good news is that disciplining your flesh now is not going to be as hard as it was in the past. Why you ask? It is because of what we discussed earlier. Do you remember that we learned earlier that deliverance must be approached from a triune – soul, spirit, body – perspective? Well, the reason that your past attempts to discipline your flesh have failed is that you did not understand the truth about approaching your deliverance as a triune being. You tried to deliver your flesh without working on your soul and your spirit! Not only were you denying yourself a full deliverance experience, but you were also ignorantly trying to execute deliverance through the weakest link in your trinity! No wonder you failed miserably! It is going to be different this time.

A. Understanding why your body sins: You need to fully understand why you commit sins before we get into more about discipline. I asked two prevalent questions earlier. I noted that the flesh is the weakest part of our trinity and has no power in and of itself, and then went on to ask, *"So why does it seem that we are so helpless in our flesh at times? Why does it seem that our bodies tell us what to do and dictate our actions?"* I answered these questions earlier, but now I would like to elaborate further. We can find the best answer to these questions in the book of Romans. Let us look at this very insightful and powerful passage of Romans, chapter 7, verses 15-25:

*"^{15}I do not understand myself at all, for …^{19}When I want to do good, I do not. And when I try not to do wrong, I do it anyway. ^{20}**But if I am doing what I do not want to do, I am not really the one doing it; the sin within me is doing it**. ^{21}It seems to be a fact of life that when I want to do what is right, I inevitably do what is wrong. ^{22}I love God's law with all my heart. ^{23}But there is another law at work within me that is at war with my mind. This law wins the fight and makes me a slave to **the sin that is still within me.** ^{24}Oh, what a miserable person I am! Who will free me from this life that is dominated by sin? ^{25}Thank God! The answer is in Jesus Christ our Lord. So you see how it is: In my mind I really want to obey God's law, **but because of my sinful nature I am a slave to sin.**"*

This passage in Romans makes it painfully obvious that what causes us, who are born again believers in Jesus, to lose the battle of temptation time and time again is the sin nature. We know that it is not the spirit because the Apostle Paul said, *"^{22}I love God's law with all my heart [spirit]."* Nor is it the soul because he said also, *"^{23}But there is another law at work within me that is at war with my mind [soul]…"* Then he concluded that since it was neither the spirit nor the soul that caused him to do evil, it had to be the flesh. *"^{23}…the sin that is still within me [my flesh]."* But he then goes on to make it clear that it is not the clay vessel that we call our bodies that causes us to break God's law of Righteousness when he writes, *"…but because of my **sinful nature** I am a slave to sin."*

So in essence, it is not the flesh itself that dictates your evil behaviors but instead is the sin nature of your flesh.

Now the Apostle Paul had already made it absolutely clear that we are *"no longer slaves to sin"*, in Romans chapter 6:6. So then why would he turn around and say in the next chapter that he is a slave to sin? He was a very illustrative and dramatic writer and so I believe he wrote this clause to help us understand the power of sin and what a formidable foe our adversary the devil is. *"Be careful! Watch out for attacks from the devil,* **your great enemy**. *He prowls around like a roaring lion, looking for some victim to devour. (1 Pet 5:8)"* In this text, *the Bible* refers to satan as a "great enemy" so we know for sure that Paul was warning us about the power of this great enemy when he said that he was a slave to sin! We know this also because scripture teaches us that sin comes from the devil: *"[But] he who commits sin [who practices evil doing] is of the devil [takes his character from the evil one], for the devil has sinned (violated the divine law) from the beginning... (1 Jn 3:8a, AMP)"*

With Paul issuing us this warning and satan being referred to as a "great enemy", it almost seems like there is no hope for us! Yet, that is only because you have not seen the rest of the text yet. You see, verse 25 of Romans 7 is the end of that chapter. The very last clause of chapter 7 is, *"...but because of my sinful nature I am a slave to sin."* However, with the beginning of chapter 8 Paul finally brings clarity to the revelation, *"^{1}So now there is no condemnation for those who belong to Christ Jesus. ^{2}For the power of the life-giving Spirit has freed you through Christ Jesus from the power of sin that leads to death. (Rom 8:1-2)"* And again we read in 1 John, *"...because the Spirit who lives in you is greater than the spirit who lives in the world. (I Jn 4:4b)"*

So you see, you have the power! It is true that the sin nature of the flesh will never change. It is also true as well that the devil will never stop trying to use you as an instrument of evil on the earth. But he is already a defeated foe and you do not have to fear him or his power. You have the power of the Almighty and Omnipotent God of all creation working in you through His Spirit. Truthfully, you should not take the devil lightly and fail to consider him a threat, but neither should you make him out to be more powerful in your life than he is. The devil is only mentioned just a little over 100 times in the New Testament of the Bible, where as Jesus (in different forms of His name) is mentioned over 4,000 times! This proves that the significance and power of the enemy greatly pales in comparison to the power and significance of Jesus the Savior.

It is important for you to understand most positively that when you do not want to sin but still do it anyway, **it is not because your body is making you do it**. You must understand that sin takes place in your life because of the evil workings of satan. Once you understand that sin takes place because of the evil workings of satan and **not because your body controls you**, you then need to know most assuredly that you are not a slave to satan or to sin. You are in no way obligated to fulfill the evil desires of your flesh that are prompted by satan, who has been stripped of all power in your spirit and soul. Your flesh cannot *make* you do anything, the devil does not control your life, and sin is not your master!

Nonetheless, in light of all of this truth, you still sin. So where is the victory hidden? The victory is hidden in this one fundamental element that has not yet been factored into the equation. When we are talking about the flesh, it all comes down to that one little word I said earlier – **d-i-s-c-i-p-l-i-n-e**!!! You may be thinking something along the lines of, *"Well if the Holy Spirit has so much power why is discipline such a big deal?"* Discipline is a big deal because consistently throughout scripture, God makes it clear that His reward is for those that of their own accord *choose* to obey His commands *(Duet 30:19, 2 Kings 18:32, Jer 38:20)*. This is just another part of His sovereign plan. He decided that this is the way it is going to be and we have the obligation to comply. We have to *choose* to serve The Lord. He does not want mindless zombies that are in some comatose state of servitude.

God will do His part. He will cleanse your spirit and give you a new heart by the power of the Blood of Jesus. He will even help you in the deliverance of the soul man by giving you the mind of Christ *(1 Cor 2:16)*. However, the scriptures make it plain that you alone are responsible for controlling your flesh! Your flesh, your old sinful nature, has been buried with the death and burial of Jesus and **you** must keep it in the grave *(Rom 6:1-12)*. Let's look at these scriptures found throughout the New Testament of the Bible to verify this point. (I have added the pronoun "**YOU**" where it fits, when you see it capitalized and in bold print.)

"So **YOU** *put to death the sinful, earthly things lurking within you.* **YOU**

have nothing to do with sexual sin, impurity, lust, and shameful desires. **YOU** don't be greedy for the good things of this life, for that is idolatry. (Col 3:5)"

"**YOU** don't let any part of your body become a tool of wickedness, to be used for sinning. Instead, **YOU** give yourselves completely to God since you have been given new life. And **YOU** use your whole body as a tool to do what is right for the glory of God. (Rom 6:13)"

"And so, dear brothers and sisters, I plead with <u>you</u> to give your bodies to God. **YOU** let them be a living and Holy sacrifice – the kind he will accept. When you think of what he has done for you, is this too much to ask? (Rom 12:1)"

"So **YOU** humble yourselves before God. **YOU** Resist the Devil, and he will flee from you. (James 4:7)"

"...**YOU** die daily [**YOU** face death every day and die to self]. (1 Cor 15:31b AMP)"

After reading these poignantly revealing scriptures, **you** cannot escape the truth that the burden of responsibility to keep your flesh yielded to the Holy Spirit and God's Righteousness is on **you**. The Holy Spirit will assist you when you seek His help, but the truth in its simplest form is revealed in this phrase that Paul says in 1 Corinthians 9:27: "*^{27}I discipline my body like an athlete, training it to do what it should. Otherwise, I fear that after preaching to others I myself might be disqualified.*" What did he say? "*<u>I discipline my body</u>*."

B. More about discipline: Once you accept the fact that it is your responsibility to discipline yourself, you have to understand something else. The flesh is habitual. It has a memory and getting delivered in your flesh is going to be partly about breaking the habits of the flesh. All of the habits of your sin nature are evil. You have a habit of doing certain things with your body. You have a habit of responding a certain way when lust confronts you. After years of being in bondage to something, you are going to have a habitual inclination to continue to do that thing even after your spirit has been cleansed and healed and your mind has been renewed. You are still going to fall back into the same old addictive patterns of habitually evil behavior unless you discipline your body. You have to do what Paul says to do in 1 Cor 9:27 – train your body to do what it should. This is the only way you will ever overcome these demons and especially the spirit of sexual lust.

Please do not be intimidated by the idea of disciplining your flesh. I told you before that it is not going to be as hard as you might think. Not to say that it is going to be easy. It won't be, but neither is it impossible or a grievous task once your soul man and spirit man have been figured into the equation of the deliverance process. Isn't there an old adage that says "the majority rules"? Yes there is, and this holds true in the trinity of your being as well. As long as your spirit and your soul are both lined up with God's Righteousness, your flesh has no choice but to come in line. It is outnumbered!

How do you think it is that people who have been bound by drug, alcohol or nicotine addictions for years, even after having made many failed attempts to kick the habit, suddenly accomplish the impossible? I will tell you how. It is because one day that person's soul and spirit came into agreement to change their life, and finally they were successful. For every failed attempt in the past, some part of that person's trinity was outnumbered. Perhaps the person decided to quit because they were sick in their body, but could not because in their hearts and minds they did not want to quit. Or, maybe using drugs kept landing them in jail, so in their minds they knew they needed to change, but in their bodies and their hearts they did not want to change. Or, perhaps deep in their hearts they wanted to live right, but their body was so addicted that it did not want to comply, and their mind kept telling them all the reasons that they would not be able to succeed. It was not until the majority finally ruled in favor of quitting the bad habit that the person finally did quit. The majority will soon be ruling in you too, in favor of sexual purity and uprightness before God.

I do caution you though that if you are still in the preliminary phases of this deliverance process, you may have little to no success in the area of disciplining your flesh right now. That is why I say that the majority *will soon be* ruling in you. Deliverance in the flesh man is the last chapter before the conclusion because it is unlikely that you are going to have much success in this area until you deal with your soul man and your spirit man. Some people are just naturally anointed or gifted to exercise discipline. If you are one of these people, then you might be able to achieve sexual discipline just because you decide to do it. But for the rest of you, (uhh, um – let me clear my throat – me included) you will only serve to frustrate yourself by placing too much emphasis on discipline or making it a starting point of this deliverance process.

However, even though implementing discipline may be an arduous task in the beginning, you do not want to neglect this step altogether or try to put it off until later. We learned earlier that all parts of your trinity must be worked on *simultaneously* in order for you to see any real and long-lasting results in this process. So what should you do? What are the specifics of discipline and how can you practically implement it into your life? You have to learn how to exercise [3]self-control by yielding to God's grace. Merriam Webster's On-line dictionary defines discipline as, *"5a: control gained by enforcing obedience or order b: orderly or prescribed conduct or pattern of behavior c: self-control"* (www.Merriam-WebsterCollegiate.com 12/05/2004).

Having discipline means that you are able to uphold responsibilities, fulfill obligations and overcome meaningful and challenging goals or obstacles, and that is why it is about self-control. It is important for you to understand that discipline is not just something that you do in one area or another. Discipline is more of a state of being. It is either a part of your personality and character make-up, or it is not. Usually, people who are disciplined in one area of obligation in their life are disciplined in all areas of obligation in their life. (This does not apply when it comes to the pursuit of non-essential desires or hobbies, such as watching soap operas every day at the same time or completing the daily crossword puzzle!)

The point that I am making is that you need to make discipline a part of who you are. Naturally disciplined people are rare. Most of us have to work hard at it and if you want to be able to exercise discipline over your flesh in the area of sexual perversion, you are going to have to be

---

[3] I am not too crazy about the term "self-control". You should only think of SELF control in terms of yourSELF being totally surrendered to the Holy Spirit and under His control! As I mentioned on page 150, any control other than that of The Lord's Spirit, such as will power and mind control, is often times a form of witchcraft and furthermore makes obsolete the Father's wonderful grace. Please be mindful of this where ever I use this term "self-control".

able to exercise discipline over your flesh in other areas of your life as well. Therefore, begin to pursue discipline in some areas of your life where it might be a little easier to accomplish. Start off with one or two very simple disciplinary goals that you have not accomplished in the past. For example, if you are a late riser and have been wanting to get up earlier, try to get up 15 minutes earlier every day for 21 days, then increase it 25 minutes earlier for the next 21 days, and so on. Give yourself these types of simple assignments to help train your flesh to do what you want it to do.

As you successfully accomplish these small goals, increase the difficulty and intensity of the assignments. This is one great method that you can use to begin to acquire self-control in your life. You may not think that getting up earlier in the morning or exercising for five minutes, three times a week will help you overcome sexually perverse habits, but it will. It will help because it will contribute to transforming your character into one of discipline and self-control. Think of it in terms of this analogy; a person may have a goal of being a body builder who is able to bench press 350 pounds. If the person has never lifted weights before, his trainer is going to start him off at only 10 or 20 pounds of weight.

It may not seem like lifting 10 pounds will enable that person to one day lift 350 pounds, but the truth of the matter is that if he cannot lift 10 then he will never be able to lift 350. As that person gets stronger, his trainer will add more weight until he eventually reaches his goal. But lifting the lighter weights is what is going to *train* his body to be able to successfully handle the heavier weights. Discipline in your body over sexually perverse habits is a heavy goal. You need to be able to successfully accomplish some lighter discipline goals before you can handle this one. So, aim high but start low.

C. More about fasting[4]: I mentioned earlier that we were going to talk more about fasting in this chapter because fasting is probably the best way to achieve discipline and self-control in your life. I explained to you

---

[4] I will not list any reference scriptures for fasting in this section. There are so many scriptures that need to be referenced that it would really disrupt the flow of reading and comprehension to list them all here. Instead, you will be able to view all reference scriptures related to fasting at the end of the book in Appendix D (pg 297). There you will find some helpful information about fasting along with the itemized reference scriptures summarizing what we are about to discuss concerning fasting.

earlier that fasting is not a spiritual act. It is a physical act. Literally, fasting means to abstain from eating or to *decisively* eat less than you normally would. There is nothing spiritual about this act. Many non-Christian religions all over the world practice fasting. People who go on hunger strikes for political reasons or other reasons are fasting. People who abstain from eating for the purpose of dieting are fasting. So there is really nothing spiritual about fasting.

Fasting can become part of a spiritual practice or ritual when it is conjoined with other spiritually edifying activities, such as prayer, praise or corporate fellowship. Yet in and of itself, it is merely a physical act. The purpose of fasting is to get the flesh out of the way so your spirit can connect with God. Fasting is a way to discipline the body and exercise self-control, which will in-turn enable you to subdue the sin-nature of the flesh. This is done in order to prevent yourself from engaging in evil behaviors that will separate you from God and hinder your ability to fellowship with Him, seek Him and hear from Him. Why fasting is so effective in accomplishing this is simple. If you can discipline your body to abstain from something (food) that is a vital survival need, how much more will you be able to discipline your body to abstain from those activities that are not essential to survival?

Even though fasting in and of itself is only a physical act and its main purpose is to establish discipline in your life, you should be aiming to make it part of a spiritual experience. You should think of fasting as a means to an end. That end is to achieve oneness with God. The purpose of fasting is to learn self-control; yet, the goal for you in learning that self control is to be able to subdue the sin-nature of the flesh and deem it powerless and inoperative in your life! As this is accomplished, you will yield to the Holy Spirit more; sin less; grow closer in your intimate relationship with the Father; increase in spiritual maturity; and learn how to maintain a **_consistently_** upright and consecrated life before The Lord. But in order for this plan to work accordingly, fasting must be a part of other spiritual pursuits.

In Old Testament times, because people did not have the privilege of the cleansing Blood of Jesus or the precious gift of His Holy Spirit, fasting was an attempt to reap a spiritual benefit by performing a physical act. It often did not work however because the people would frequently lose sight of the purpose for fasting and just perform the physical aspect of not eating. They would fail to implement any change of heart or behavior. This type of fasting is not accepted by God or counted as spiritual in His eyes. Therefore, I want you to understand what they did not understand in those times: *Fasting will not change you spiritually*. It is just one of the many sacrificial acts that you can offer up to God in order to *prepare your heart* for His changing power, but it only yields a spiritual result when it is used appropriately.

People commonly try to use fasting as this 'quick fix for all.' For example, you live a carnal, complacent life that is completely devoid of prayer, study, worship and fellowship. Subsequently you have a weak connection with Jesus, little to no spiritual power and constantly fall into sin. Then some important event comes up that you want to be extra spiritual for, or you are just feeling really lousy and condemned, and you think you can just omit food from your life for a few days and fix your evil heart! That is a preposterous notion that is highly offensive to God. You cannot use fasting as some token bribe to God to have Him come in and fix all of your problems and endow you with His power for some special event! Nor should you try to use fasting to pacify your conscious when you know you are not living right and not giving God your all!

I say to you once again that fasting is a means to an end and is not the end itself! In light of this, I would like to give you some practical instructions on the proper way to fast for not only self-control but also a spiritual benefit. If you want your fasting to be a sweet smelling sacrifice to God that will move Him to come in and work in your heart, you need to implement these 10 things when you fast:

1) **Restricted eating**: Abstaining from all or selected foods and drinks.

2) **Abstinence:** Omitting all activities that are not spiritually edifying in a way that will increase you in your relationship with God. For example: TV, phone calls, secular music or reading, hanging out, having sex (even if you are married) and other such non-spiritual activities. Your time should be *totally* consumed with the pursuit of Righteousness!

3) **Humility:** Recognition of your lowliness and God's Exaltedness.

4) **Repentance:** Mourning and sorrow for sins committed with a desire and willingness to amend your ways.

5) **Prayer:** Seeking God for answers or for help and deliverance from troubles.

6) **Worship**: Intimate adoration of God for His greatness.

7) **Intercession**: Mourning for others, seeking forgiveness and deliverance for other people.

8) **Secrecy**: Making every effort to conceal the fact that you are fasting from those that are not fasting with you – doing it unto God and not for the amazement of men.

9) **Ministry**: Helping others; giving more of yourself when you are not secluded in your secret prayer closet.

10) **Rest**: Abstaining from all non-essential tasks and engagements so that your time and energy can be spent in intimacy with God.

Implementing these 10 practices will spiritualize your fasting.

I must warn you though that fasting is usually very difficult for people that are not accustomed to it. Therefore, start off slow. Set small, realistic goals for yourself, such as fasting from all food until 12:00 noon for seven days. Or, try fasting from only certain foods *(this is called a partial fast)* all day until dinner for seven days, or omit most foods for the entire day for just two or three days. I do not want to tell you specifically how to do it, but just know that you should set a fast that you will be able to adhere to. Do not make the mistake of trying to put yourself on this astronomically strict fast that even The Christ Himself would not go on and then beat yourself up about not being able to stick to it *(laugh)*! Remember what was said earlier, **aim high but start low**.

Nevertheless, your fast should certainly be sacrificial. Give up something that is a challenge. Do not go on a "seven day no-spinach fast" when you know that you do not like spinach *(laugh)*! The best way to handle it is to pray before you fast and seek the Holy Spirit's guidance on how you should go about it. You should continue to go on short discipline fasts until you are strong enough to go without food for longer periods of time. Fasting will become easier as you become accustomed to it. It will also become easier as your spirit and soul grow stronger. Your spirit will be yielded to Jesus' Spirit, and your flesh will no longer be able to resist your spiritual pursuit of Righteousness.

Fasting should be a part of your life for the rest of your life until you leave this earth. Every Christian goes through those phases where they get distracted and begin to slack off in consecration and pick up in carnality. These are great times to fast, even for mature believers, to bring that sin nature and body right back under subjection before it gets out of hand. However, unless you need to lose weight, I suggest that you do not waste your time with non-spiritual fasting! Even though non-spiritual fasting might teach you physical self-control, it will not move God to work in your heart. Only Christ Jesus can break the power of sin in your life and His Spirit can only work through you when you are yielded to Him and not stifling Him. Non-spiritual fasting will not accomplish this and so although you may gain self-control, you will still lack sin-control.

Having this understanding brings us to the close of this step of the deliverance process. *"Now that wasn't so bad, was it?"* – Of course not! Disciplining the flesh is all about understanding why your body sins, acquiring Holy Spirit led self-control and mastering spiritual fasting! Considering all you have to go through for deliverance in the soul man and the spirit man, I would say this step is pretty easy! So go ahead and kill that flesh with discipline because dead flesh cannot sin!!!

Step 12 – Walking after The Spirit

We are still talking about deliverance for the flesh man and may I remind you that when we are talking about the flesh man we are talking about your literal, physical, earthly body. This includes all that it entails, especially your five senses and how they interact with the world around you. I mentioned this earlier in *"Step 3 – Renewing the Mind"*. The process of renewing the mind has to do with what you <u>put into your brain</u>; to initially renew your mind it requires the input of the proper information. However, *keeping* your mind new and free of corruption has to do with what you <u>keep out of your brain</u>. What goes into your brain is based on what you interact with on earth through the use of your five senses (sight, hearing, taste, touch and smell). Your five senses are the gateways to your mind. Therefore, if your five senses are exposed to corrupt and contaminated interactions, you can guess what is going to happen to your mind. It is going to become (or remain) corrupt and contaminated as well.

That is why renewing of the mind is going to depend heavily on how well you adhere to this step – walking after The Spirit. What do I mean by "walking after The Spirit" though? I am talking about what we read in Romans 8:1 earlier, *"THEREFORE, [there is] now no condemnation (no adjudging guilty of wrong) for **those who are in Christ Jesus**, who **live [and] walk** not after the dictates of the flesh, but **after the dictates of the Spirit**. (AMP)."* You have a responsibility to yourself to follow the Holy Spirit where He leads you. When you do this you are not going to involve your body in things that are corrupt and contaminated, causing the gateways to your mind to be flooded with evil. Wearing the shoes of peace that we talked about in Step 8, which are a part of your spiritual armor, will also help you walk after The Spirit. Remember, if you are wearing those shoes you will only walk in places that will bring peace in your life, and corruption and carnality certainly do not bring peace. They bring sorrow, pain, anguish and death.

Let me make a little clearer to you the practical application of what I am saying. First of all, I have used the word carnal (or carnally/carnality) a few times. You also see this word in Romans 8:6-7 *"⁶For to be <u>carnally</u> minded is death; but to be spiritually minded is life and peace. ⁷Because the <u>carnal</u> mind is enmity against God: for it is not subject to the law of God, neither indeed can be (KJV)."* Thus, let me clarify for you what 'carnality' or 'to be carnal' means. Carnal means the things of the flesh or the world (which we know is evil); the nature of man without mindfulness of the God of Creation or spirituality. To be carnal means to be entangled with your humanity and the earthly world around you without regard to your spirit man or your existence within the spirit realm. To be carnally minded is going to cause you to make the deadly mistake of not recognizing the impact that your physical actions and interactions as a human being have on your spiritual existence as a spirit being. Thus practically, "to walk after The Spirit" means to disassociate yourself from carnality.

Carnality is the canvas on which satan portrays his subtle deceptions. Deceptions such as TV programs that make you laugh but contain content of sinfulness; sinful friends that you have fun with but that are subtly weakening your resistance to unrighteousness; or associations that are beneficial in some aspect but cause you to compromise on righteous integrity in some way. There are many others of these deceptions as well. You have to understand that for everything you do in the natural realm, there is an equivalent reaction in the spirit realm. If you listen to secular songs that promote fornication in the natural, a seed is planted or watered in the spirit. If you watch soap operas, which are full of adultery and gossip, a door is now open in the spirit realm for the enemy to oppress you with those spirits. Every move you make in carnality could be completely undermining all of your efforts to be delivered! That is why it is so important to walk after the Holy Spirit.

This verse in Psalm 1:1 is a very popular scripture, but most people who read it fail to realize that in this scripture King David is talking about walking after the Spirit. He is talking about completely disassociating yourself from carnality. It reads, *"¹BLESSED (HAPPY, fortunate, prosperous, and enviable) is the man who walks and lives not in the counsel of the ungodly [following their advice, their plans and purposes], nor stands [submissive and inactive] in the path where sinners walk, nor sits down [to relax and rest] where the scornful [and the mockers] gather. (AMP)"* This scripture shows a picture of carnality and how it progressively draws you into a state of complete depravation and separation from God. Let us look at it more closely.

"...who **walks** and lives...in the counsel of the ungodly [following *their advice, their plans and purposes]...*" In this first clause, the subtle deception of the enemy begins. You are just *'walking through'* carnality minding your own business, and you happen to notice that sinners are seemingly prospering and enjoying the pleasures of sin. The enemy's enticement and temptation has confronted you and you begin take counsel from their words and their lifestyle. You do not understand what God is doing in your life and have not yet learned to trust Him. You are discontent with your own life, and your flesh is not subject to Righteousness. Therefore, you ponder the ways of sinners and meditate on their words of advice.

Whenever someone is convinced that what they do or how they live is right, the counsel that they give you is going to be based on their own experiences and what they feel has worked for them. Therefore, sinners (or even many carnal believers) are going to advise you to do the same carnal things that they do. It may at the time even seem like a good idea since it worked for them but, *"There's a way that looks harmless enough; look again – it leads straight to hell (Prov 16:25, MSG)."* These are some of the deadly words they may speak to you:

"Just put on the tax form that one of your relative's children lives with you. You'll get a bigger refund that way..." *"Girrrl, if you want a man to marry you, you have to show him that you are willing to get your freak on..."* *"Watching pornography keeps me from cheating on my wife. You should try it, it will help keep you from getting bored with sex..."* *"You should take supplies home from the office. Why waste your money? They are underpaying you anyway..."* *"You don't have to confess Jesus in order to go to Heaven. And you don't have to live all weird. All God wants is for people to be nice and to acknowledge that there's a Man Upstairs..."* *"...That's what I do."*

Of course, as they whisper such poisonous words into your soul, they never tell you about the unseen consequences that are taking place in the spirit realm. Openings are being made for the enemy to come in and oppress you with the bondage of sin and the reaping of the negative consequences is in the making!

An actual person can speak these things into your life, but such counsel does not necessarily have to come through a personal encounter with another human being. Remember that ultimately this is the influence of satan in your life because sin comes from him. He will encounter and influence you in any way and through any source that he is able to. In the world that we live in today, technological advances have made it possible for you to receive counsel in carnality through many different sources. Therefore, you can get this same counsel and influence from watching movies, TV shows, listening to music or tapes, reading books, magazines and newspapers, playing video or computer games or visiting websites that encourage these carnal principles and concepts.

All of this media influence is created by people and thus such media influences carry with them the beliefs and lifestyles of those who created them, many of whom are fathered by satan himself. It may seem harmless to you, but the truth of the matter is that as you flood the gateways of your mind with more and more carnality, you become desensitized to wickedness. It becomes no big deal to you anymore. What used to disgust you now makes you laugh. What used to cause you to pray now causes you to shrug your shoulders. Satan's subtle deceptions and tactics are working, and the progression of carnality in your life continues to move forward.

It moves forward like this, "... **stands** *[submissive and inactive] in the path where sinners walk..."* In the first clause of the scripture, you were just walking through carnality and pondering what you had seen, but now you are standing and gazing in the window at sin, longing for what you are beholding. You are no longer an effective witness of the gospel. There used to be a time that you spoke out against certain evil events or behaviors, but now you do not say anything anymore. You do not want to "rub anybody the wrong way". As they say in the world, *"Live and let live."*

There was a time that you used to think adultery (for example) was wrong and speak out against it, but because of ungodly counsel you see it differently now. I mean after all, shouldn't she be able to hold on to her man? Can love ever really be wrong even if it comes in the form of adultery? You see, you cannot speak out about it now because your own words would condemn you. You yourself are considering doing some of these same things, and you do not want to condemn yourself or give up the ungodly associations that you have grown so fond of. Besides, you do not even have a clear sense of right and wrong anymore. Deception gives way to delusion and the progression of sin and carnality moves into the next phase.

*"...**sits down** [to relax and rest] where the scornful [and the mockers] gather."* You have now given up all resistance to sin. You have become so consumed with carnality that you are totally unaware of the spiritual consequences of what you are doing. You no longer have a sense of conviction or bad conscious for your sinful activities. You now sit down to relax in sin. You are comfortable in sin now. You have completely adopted it as your way of life. The last step in the progression of sin and carnality is soon to follow. *"For the wages of sin is death... (Rom 6:23)"* Your sins lead you to total separation from God, death of the spirit, death of your body, and then finally eternal damnation with satan in hell. He has won, and his strategy was simply to entice you with carnality!

Can't you see the importance of walking after the Spirit? Don't you understand the critical nature of disassociating yourself from things that are carnal and sinful?

There are many believers that would refute the notion that they cannot watch what they want to or listen to and read and play what they want to. They will argue, *"Well, we do these things and it has never bothered us. I don't commit adultery or kill or steal just because I watch these things on TV."* And, those that say this are correct. There are many people that do not actually commit the sins that they indulge in through media and other ungodly associations. However, they are blind to the fact that being involved with such carnality to any degree is a grand set up for failure in their assignment in God's Kingdom.

The **Holy** Spirit of Christ Jesus, which dwells in them, does not want to sit on the couch and watch a movie that is full of sin and wickedness! He does not want to hear it, see it, talk about it or fellowship with it! So it may be true that they do not commit sins of the flesh, but stifling the Holy Spirit in this way causes them to be trapped in a tar pit of complacency; giving lukewarm service to God and being prevented from walking in the true power and authority that is promised them as children of the Almighty God! All such believers live defeated lives in the area of the fruit of the Holy Spirit, fail to fulfill their true destiny in Christ and most are involved in secret sin.

What is the fruit of the Spirit? "*²²But the fruit of the [Holy] Spirit [the work which His presence within accomplishes] is love, joy (gladness), peace, patience (an even temper, forbearance), kindness, goodness (benevolence), faithfulness, ²³ Gentleness (meekness, humility), self-control (self-restraint, continence)... (Gal 5:22-23, AMP)"* These are the fruits of the Spirit and you cannot be carnal and walk after the Spirit of Righteousness at the same time! It just is not possible. So people that are carnal believers will lack this fruit. It will not remain constant in them. This is not to say that there are not times when even the most mature believers fail to operate in the fruit of the Spirit. Of course, we all have those moments but those moments should be the exception and not the rule. They should be few and far in between. The less carnality a believer has in their life, the more **consistently** you are going to see them bearing the fruit of Jesus' Spirit.

What good are we as Christians if we do not bear the fruit of the Holy Spirit? It is for this very reason that Jesus has chosen and ordained us. He tells us so in John 15:16, *"You have not chosen Me, but I have chosen you and I have appointed you [I have planted you], **that you might go and bear fruit and keep on bearing, and that your fruit may be lasting [that it may remain, abide]**... (AMP)"* Everything we believers can do the devil and his children can do too. We can pray – they can pray. We can preach – they can preach. We can prosper in life – they can prosper in life. We can get healed supernaturally – they can get healed supernaturally. We can do good deeds and be nice people – they can do good deeds and be nice people. The only thing we as Christians can do that the devil's children cannot do is **_consistently bear all of the fruits_** of Jesus' Spirit. Being able to bear those fruits *(love, joy, peace, patience, gentleness, goodness, faith, meekness & self-control)* is such a detrimental part of this deliverance process – **_hello!_** However, bearing such fruit can only be accomplished when the Holy Spirit is working on the inside of you and **controlling** your life.

The Holy Spirit's control in your life, you walking after the Spirit, is what really makes the difference. No matter what a carnal believer may try to tell you about how spiritual and deep they are, there is something missing in them and you can just sense it. Often times, when you meet really consecrated Christians that walk after the Spirit and are sold out to God and His ways, you can just sense that they are connected to Him even if you know nothing about them. There is a light and a glow about them. You know that they are Holy. Then, you meet some other individual that does not strike you much at all. He boastfully announces that his name is, Prophet Notice Me, and you are thinking, *"Oh, he's a Christian?"*

The Bible says that we will know who people are by the fruit that they bear *(Luke 6:43-45)*, and as far as those that are neither hot nor cold, He said He would spit them out of His mouth *(Rev 3:15-16)*. Remember, the devil's aim is not so much to get you to sin in the flesh but instead to ruin your relationship with God and your chances for fulfillment on earth and eternity in Heaven. That is why the Bible says to know good and not do it is sin *(James 4:17)*. So please, do not follow the example of these carnal believers that ignorantly think they can continue on partaking of the things of carnality in the name of entertainment, not realizing the detriment that it is causing their eternal souls and the negative impact that it is having on those around them! *(I know I just stepped on some toes there, but please forgive me. It just stings a little. You'll be OK – smile and Selah.)*

✦✦

Now that you know what you should not do, let us explore what you should do. If we continue to read on in the first chapter of Psalms, David lets us know in the second and third verses of Psalm 1 exactly what we must do in order to walk after the Spirit and what the results will be. *"²But his delight and desire are in the law of The Lord, and on His law (the precepts, the instructions, the teachings of God) he habitually meditates (ponders and studies) by day and by night. ³And he shall be like a tree firmly planted [and tended] by the streams of water, ready to bring forth its fruit in its season; its leaf also shall not fade or wither; and everything he does shall prosper [and come to maturity]."*

This scripture teaches us that the way to disassociate yourself from carnality and walk after the Spirit is to meditate on The Lord day and night! Think about God all day and all night; read His Word; sing His songs; praise His name; fellowship with His people. **Give attention to**

Righteousness and the things on the earth that bring God glory! The scripture says you must do this day and night, so come on: Let's be real. How can you sincerely and thoroughly fulfill this mandate if you are fondly entangled with the things of the world? I am sorry. It just cannot be done. And notice that when you fulfill the requirements of verses 1 and 2, the result in verse 3 is that you will *"bring forth your fruit in your season."*

Here again we see another example of the interconnectedness of the soul, spirit and body. Separating from carnality takes place in the flesh man, but it enables you to strengthen yourself in the soul man with the renewing and fortification of the mind. If you cannot renew your mind, you are dead on this entire process. Therefore, you must walk after the Spirit. Walking after the Spirit will not come easily because as I said before, the flesh is habitual and you already have a habit of carnality. But you have to, as much as is possible, make every effort to separate yourself from those things detrimental to your spirit.

As you grow stronger in deliverance, you will be able to walk after the Spirit more and more. It will not all happen at once, but the faster you yield in this area, the faster your entire deliverance experience is going to come to pass. This is probably one of the most important steps. This is because not only will implementing this step speed up the entire process, but it is also inherently necessary in order to maintain deliverance once it is accomplished! It is last, but it is not least. I only placed it last because, since disassociating yourself from carnality is going to take discipline in your body you needed to understand discipline of the flesh before you could understand this step.

So, how will you really know what is carnal and what is not? How will you know what needs to be cut out of your life and what does not? Sorry, I am not going to give you a list. I would run out of memory in my computer trying to do so! Besides, I am not trying to control anybody's life. Your best teacher is the Holy Spirit *(John 14:26, 1 John 2:27)*. The Holy Spirit will give you a conviction in your heart about what you need to do. You will know that you have to give up the TV show when you can no longer laugh with the same ease when you watch it. You will know what songs not to listen to because when you listen to them, you will suddenly hear the lyrics like you have never heard them before. God says that He has written His laws in our hearts, and thus in your heart you will know if it is right or wrong *(Rom 2:14-15)*. However, when the Holy Spirit shows you something that you need to cut from your life, you have to exercise the discipline to do it. Disobedience will lead to dire consequences and the more you stifle The Spirit through disobedience, the less He will be able to lead you and the further from deliverance you will be.

Although I will not tell you per say what you should and should not be involved in, I can at least tell you how I live. I do not want to give anyone the wrong impression about myself or else someone will accuse me of being a hypocrite! I love life. I love to laugh. I love to enjoy the blessings that Yah has given me. I am a very light-hearted, fun and comical person. I certainly do not live like the Amish! *(No offense to any of my Amish Brethren – smile)*. How I decide for myself whether or not I will be involved in an activity that the Bible has not specifically told me to do or not do, is with a general litmus test. The litmus test is this question that I ask myself, *"Is this going to edify my spirit, soul or body in a way that will move me closer to the center of Daddy's perfect will for my life?"* If the answer to the question is no, then I try not to do it. If the answer is yes, then I do it and enjoy it.

I know some believers that think all TV is bad. I do not share that view. For me, watching <u>very select</u> cartoon movies with my children for family time every so often passes the litmus test. Sitting down to watch a sporting event or movie of wholesome or informative content with my husband, as a bonding experience, every once in a while, passes the test also. Spending my precious personal time watching talk shows, sitcoms, soap operas and grimy TV dramas does not pass the test. I do not watch much non-Christian TV unless with my family or either when I am *(rarely)* led by the Holy Spirit to watch something specific. Sometimes I do feel at liberty to watch something funny on TV because laughter is good for the soul, but it cannot be full of sin. This is how I conduct myself concerning television.

I have no desire to listen to non-Christian music accept maybe select love songs or jazz when romancing with my husband. Other than this instance, I have no need of it because it does not make me think of God. I like classical music too because it makes me think of a Heavenly

Choir. I know some believers that feel only *traditional* gospel music is 'Holy'. Although I do feel that you need to be careful when it comes to contemporary music that is labeled as 'Christian', I do not agree with those that say only traditional gospel music can edify the spirit. I listen to all different types of gospel music. I am not listening for whether or not the music sounds traditional. I am listening for lyrics that glorify God and a sound from Heaven that invokes praise and worship in my spirit. This is how I conduct myself concerning music, and I adhere to similar such practices concerning all forms of media and writings.

As far as human associations are concerned; although I make myself available to everyone, I do not tie my soul to anyone who is not a born-again believer in Jesus. I am not partial when it comes to kindness, compassion and prayer. Yet, I am very partial about who I fondly and intimately intermingle with. When I fellowship with such people who are not my brethren in Christ, it is not to be a part of them, but instead to be *set apart* from them as a light and example. Even then only when the Holy Spirit leads me to, will I fellowship with such people.

So you see? I cannot give you a recipe for walking after the Spirit. This walk with Jesus is too personal, and the Holy Spirit leads each one of us differently. We each have a unique destiny and calling and have to do those things that will move us forward in what God has called us personally to do. So what is edifying to me may be a distraction to you, and vice versa. That is why the Bible says, *"...work out **your own** salvation with fear and trembling; (Phil 2:12b)"*. Therefore, I cannot tell you exactly how to live, what to wear, what to watch, listen to or where to go: No one can, nor should they try. Yet, I can assure you of this: What the Apostle Paul says in this sixth chapter of 1 Corinthians, verse 12, is powerfully revealing, *"Everything is permissible (allowable and lawful) for me; but not all things are helpful (good for me to do, expedient and profitable when considered with other things). Everything is lawful for me, but I will not become the slave of anything or be brought under its power."*

I will close this last step of the deliverance process by leaving you to meditate on this clause from Ephesians chapter 5, verses 1-20. You read it and then decide for yourself, with the Holy Spirit's guiding, what you must omit from your life in order to walk after The Spirit.

"Follow God's example in everything you do, because you are his dear children. ²Live a life filled with love for others, following the example of Christ, who loved you and gave Himself as a sacrifice to take away your sins. And God was pleased, because that sacrifice was like sweet perfume to Him. ³Let there be no sexual immorality, impurity, or greed among you. Such sins have no place among God's people. ⁴Obscene stories, foolish talk, and coarse jokes – these are not for you. Instead, let there be thankfulness to God. ⁵You can be sure that no immoral, impure, or greedy person will inherit the Kingdom of Christ and of God. For a greedy person is really an idolater who worships the things of this world. ⁶Don't be fooled by those who try to excuse these sins, for the terrible anger of God comes upon all those who disobey Him. ⁷Don't participate in the things these people do. ⁸For though your hearts were once full of darkness, now you are full of light from God, and your behavior should show it! ⁹For this light within you produces only what is good and right and true. ¹⁰Try to find out what is pleasing to God. ¹¹Take no part in the worthless deeds of evil and darkness; instead, rebuke and expose them. ¹²It is shameful even to talk about the things that ungodly people do in secret. ¹³But when the light shines on them, it becomes clear how evil these things are. ¹⁴And where your light shines, it will expose their evil deeds. This is why it is said, 'Awake, O sleeper, rise up from the dead, and Christ will give you light.' ¹⁵ So be careful how you live. Don't live like fools, but like those who are wise. ¹⁶ Make the most of every opportunity in these evil days. ¹⁷ Don't act thoughtlessly, but understand what the Lord wants you to do. ¹⁸ Don't be drunk with wine, because that will ruin your life. Instead, be filled with the Holy Spirit, ¹⁹ singing psalms and hymns and spiritual songs among yourselves, and making music to the Lord in your hearts. ²⁰ And give thanks for everything to God the Father in the name of our Lord Jesus Christ."

Chapter 11:
Staying Victoriously Free Forever!

Now you have learned all 12 steps in the deliverance process. You are almost there! I just want to give you a few more pointers to help ensure your eternal success.

The five greatest enemies to the deliverance process

I know that you are probably brimming with excitement by now. You are reading the last chapter of this book! You are full of the power of knowledge and ready to conquer the enemy of sexual perversion that has been afflicting you for so long. You are closer to victory now than you have ever been before. However, there are just a few more things that I want to let you know before we wrap this up. Just the fact that you have read the book through to this last chapter shows your commitment and determination to get delivered, but there are many enemies to deliverance.

Other demonic spirits are going to try their hardest to prevent you from successfully completing this process. Satan knows how important sexual purity and wholeness is to your spiritual development and enduring intimate relationship with God. Thus when he sees you trying to get free, he is going to work over time, often times sending his most powerful cohorts after you, to stop you from being liberated. I cannot list the name of every demon or vice the enemy might try to use against you, but I do want to at least highlight what I believe are the five most powerful enemies that you will face in the deliverance from sexual perversion. They are as follows.

1. The struggle to be Holy

Is there any such thing as a 'struggle to be Holy'? Do you feel like you are in this struggle? Is struggling to be Holy your assignment? You might be thinking that it is but the answer is, NO! Let me explain. You cannot make yourself Holy, nor will you ever be able to do this. Yahweh God alone is Holy and when Holiness is brought about in your life, it is because His Spirit has accomplished it – not because you struggled to make it happen. You cannot even fully perceive or understand God's Holiness. So why strain your brain to figure something out that you cannot possibly comprehend? Do not be confused by what I am saying. Look at this passage of Ephesians 1:4-11.

"*[4]Long ago, even before he made the world God loved us and chose us in Christ to be Holy and without fault in his eyes. [5]His unchanging plan has always been to adopt us into his own family by bringing us to Himself through Jesus Christ. And this gave Him great pleasure...[7]He is so rich in kindness that he purchased our freedom through the blood of his Son, and our sins are forgiven. ...[9]God's secret plan has now been revealed to us; it is a plan centered on Christ, designed long ago according to his good pleasure. [10]And this is his plan: At the right time he will bring everything together under the authority of Christ – everything in heaven and on earth. [11]Furthermore, because of Christ, we have received an inheritance from God, for he chose us from the beginning, and all things happen just as he decided long ago.*"

You learn in this text that (if you are a born again believer in Christ Jesus) you are already Holy! God chose you to be Holy long ago before He ever created you! Often times in this Christian walk we see areas of our lives that do not line up with The Lord's Righteousness and feel that it is our responsibility to 'become Holy'. We begin to struggle to be Holy. This struggle to be Holy is truly a deceptive tactic of the enemy to distract us from what we should really be focusing on. Struggling to be Holy is like working 10 jobs to pay off a loan that has already been paid. Your sin debt has already been paid by the Blood of The Savior! His finished work on the cross at Calvary purchased your Holiness and so there is no need for you to now struggle to pay for what Jesus has already purchased and freely relinquished to you.

You should not constantly be *struggling* to do anything. Any type of on-going struggle is going to weaken you and bring about weariness, especially a vain struggle such as this one. And it truly is a vain struggle because no amount of works on your behalf is ever going to achieve Holiness in your life. If you could attain Holiness without Jesus then He would have never come and died on your behalf. If you could attain Holiness on your own that would mean that you have Holiness within you and if that be the case why should you exalt God so highly above yourself?

The Bible teaches us that no man is Righteous or Holy in and of himself, and that we only attain Righteousness through faith in Jesus *(Rom 3:10; Gal 2:16).* The belief that praying, fasting, going to church a lot, wearing long skirts, reading and memorizing scriptures or doing whatever other type of works you can perform will cause you to be Holy, is a dangerous belief. If you hold on to this belief then you will be haughty, high-minded and self-righteous – thinking that you are better than others. You will be full of pride, feeling as if you have accomplished a God-like essence. Oh what a deadly mindset to have!

On the other hand, when you have this mindset that you must work to be Holy it also sets you up to walk in defeat when you miss the mark. You feel condemned and disappointed. You start beating yourself up and putting yourself down. You behave as if you have been bad and must punish yourself. That is why instead of believing the lie that you must remain in the vain struggle to be Holy, you should walk in a large place at liberty; knowing that Jesus has already done it even when you can't see the results. Notice in the scripture that it says, *"...Holy and without fault **in His eyes.**"* Not ***in your deeds***, but in His eyes. No matter what act of sin you commit, you remain Holy in the eyes of God because how He sees you is not centered on your deeds. *"...it is a plan **centered on Christ**, designed long ago according to his good pleasure.(Eph 1:9)"*

Please understand that I am not giving you a license to go out and live a wretched life and say *"Nannie, nannie, nannie! I'm Holy anyway."* Any one who is truly a born again believer in Jesus is not trying to find a way into sin but instead is looking for every escape out of sin. My aim in teaching you this is to help you understand that God does not live in the realm of time as we do. He lives in eternity where the beginning, middle and end of the story all play out at the same time. That is why the text says that *"...he chose us from the beginning, and all things happen just as he decided long ago."* According to His own good pleasure, God already decided long ago that you would remain Holy in His eyes. He already knows the day and the hour that His Holiness will be manifested in your deeds, and He will be pleased to still call you His own while you are being processed and until that day is revealed.

So forget about this ridiculous struggle to make yourself Holy. It is not going to happen, and the superfluous focus on making yourself Holy is going to draw your attention away from what you should really be doing. You were created to commune with and worship God, you have been ordained to bear fruit and commissioned to spread the gospel of Jesus, son of the Living God. Yet, these two assignments are hard to fulfill when you feel as if it is your responsibility to be Holy and you know that you are not quite there yet. When you carry this responsibility you are consumed with the struggle, using all of your faculties to try and make it happen. Unfortunately, it leaves you unavailable to God for Him to use you as a vessel on the earth.

You feel as if you are not fit to witness and minister to people, and you are constantly waiting for some milestone moment in your Christian life to happen before you get started. Well, guess what? That milestone moment happened the day you gave Jesus your heart! When God sees that you are willing to go out and be a witness for Him, regardless of how you feel about yourself, He is going to empower you with a greater manifestation of His Holiness. This is because He knows how important it is for you to walk uprightly in order to be a good witness, but if you sit on the opportunity to do the work of ministry He will not be quick to endow you with more of His power.

So please, do not wear yourself out with the vain struggle to be Holy. Instead, rest in the love of Jesus and allow yourself to enjoy the freedom that He purchased for you with His Blood. You are already Holy in the eyes of your God and the more you understand that, the quicker you are going to see it manifest in your life. So, does that mean you should not pursue spiritual things? No, of course not! It just means that you have to pursue them with the right motive, working to acquire the most meaningful prize. You should never do spiritual things, or anything at all, with the intent of making yourself more Holy. Whatever you do, do it for the purpose of drawing closer to God in your personal relationship with

Him. If you do things with this motive, God will be able to prove to you more quickly that He has already made you Holy, and the enemy's effort to distract in this way will fail miserably.

2. Slothfulness

Slothfulness is another great enemy you will face. You may not know what the word *slothful* means. In modern terms, slothful means to be lazy and sluggish, but I do not want to use the word 'lazy' because the word lazy is used to define a state of physical sluggishness. However, the word slothful implies more than something that is simply physical. Lazy implies a physical condition, but slothful implies an internal condition. It can equivalently be defined as, laziness of the soul. *"Slothfulness casteth into a deep sleep; and an idle soul shall suffer hunger. (Prov 19:15, KJV)"* You can see in this scripture that slothfulness is clearly marked as a condition of the soul.

Slothfulness robs you of one of the things you will need more than anything else to successfully complete this process – motivation. We discussed earlier that the passion of our desires give us the will and the motivation to pursue our goals. Where slothfulness is present motivation is absent, passion is absent, effort is absent, planning is non-existent, desire is sluggish and ambition is lacking – that drive and push to get it done is not present. Slothfulness is a sure recipe for failure because *"...faith without **works** is dead (James 2:20, 26)"*, and there will be little to no works under the bondage of slothfulness.

"Slothfulness casteth into a deep sleep..." This text is warning you that slothfulness will turn you into a sleeping dreamer that never wakes up long enough to stop dreaming and put a plan into action that will bring your dreams to pass. That is why the Apostle Paul tells us in the book of Romans to, *"[Be] Not slothful in business; [be] fervent in spirit; serving God;(Rom. 12:11, KJV)"* We can read this same scripture also in the Amplified version of the Bible and gain further insight, *"__Never lag in zeal__ and in earnest endeavor; be aglow and burning with the Spirit, serving God. (Rom 12:11, AMP)"* This scripture in both versions again points out to us that slothfulness is a condition that has a much greater affect on you than simply physical laziness. The scripture encourages us to be full of

passion in heart and full of effort in body.

Some of the signs that slothfulness is in your life would include: physical laziness, lack of ambition, constant fatigue or sleepiness, a desire for things but no drive to pursue them, a sluggish response to critical matters, frequent daydreaming or the realization that you very seldom accomplish anything and fail to finish things that you do start. It will be virtually impossible to discipline your flesh if slothfulness is working against you. Discipline is a combination of effort, diligence and commitment, all of which are absent in a slothful soul.

Being slothful will leave your mind idle making it impossible to walk after the Spirit as well. That is why Proverbs 19:15, which we already read, says that *"...an idle soul shall suffer hunger."* The Word of Jesus is the Bread of Life. If you are not meditating on His Word, you are starving your soul and your spirit. Since the only two steps for deliverance in the flesh man are *discipline of the flesh* and *walking after the Spirit*, slothfulness makes deliverance in the flesh man completely unattainable and as you well know by now, if any one part of your being is left undelivered, you are not delivered at all because you will never be truly free!

Because sloth is a demon that attacks your soul (remember that is your mind, will and emotions), its attacks are particularly more damaging. Keep in mind that the soul is the bridge between the spirit and the flesh. Thus, because sloth works in your soul, that condition of sluggishness, laziness, apathy and idleness can easily be transmitted to your spirit and your body creating an overall condition of laziness in your entire being. If you are only dealing with physical laziness you can overcome that with the power of your mind and spirit. If you are feeling a little sluggish in your spirit only, you can overcome that through renewing of the mind and physical discipline. However, if your spirit, soul and body are all suffering slothfulness simultaneously, how can you overcome this?

Paul revealed to us the antidote to slothfulness in Romans 12:11, when we looked at it in the Amplified. He told us that we must ***"never lag in zeal"***. You must be full of zeal and burning with the fire of Jesus' Spirit. Zeal is inclusive of all of the characteristics I mentioned just a moment ago – motivation, passion, ambition and drive that leads to diligent works. At the same time though, slothfulness almost puts you in a catch 22 situation because you need to put forth some effort in order to get delivered from slothfulness and attain zeal, but you need to already have zeal in order to put forth any effort! However, if you should ever come under assault by the spirit of slothfulness or if you are already under assault, you need not be discouraged. God never leaves you without a way out. His power is still greater than any attack the devil can launch against you.

Do not forget that you have an almost effortless weapon in Christian fellowship. When slothfulness is in your life, it is an ideal time to use this weapon. We discussed earlier that the weapon of Christian fellowship is most beneficial in those times that you are stuck and need a boost. If you are bound by the demon of slothfulness, you are certainly stuck. Prayer can be used against this spirit too, but if this spirit has you so bound that you feel unable to pray, do not worry. You already learned that you do not always have to open your mouth to pray. Just the simple cry of your heart, expressing to God your desire to be full of zeal for the pursuit of Righteousness, will begin your liberation. Being aware that you are dealing with this spirit is very critical because once you are aware that this is the spirit you are fighting, you can cry out in your heart for the Holy Spirit to intercede on your behalf.

All throughout **Part II** of this book I have been highlighting the fact that success in this deliverance process is going to take great effort on your part. That is why slothfulness is such a dangerous enemy. Only a determined, intentional, diligent effort that is fortified with commitment is going to allow God to manifest His deliverance power in your life. You cannot be lazy; you cannot be sluggish; you cannot be idle or apathetic. Be watchful for this spirit. Assess yourself now to determine whether or not this spirit is a part of your life. If it is, then you already have the strategy for dealing with it. Once you get delivered from it or if you are not now bound by it, remain the victor over this spirit by: keeping your ambition fueled with passion, your mind fortified with the Word of Life, your efforts underlined with diligence and your heart colored with commitment. Do not daydream about your victorious life as a Christian, but instead *"...write the vision and make it plain...(Hab 2:2)"* and then skillfully execute it until your goal has been achieved. Keep your faith alive with works and you will never have to worry about the spirit of slothfulness.

3. **Loneliness**

To be alone would mean that you are somewhere all by yourself. The word alone describes the state of your physical body being separated from other people. It can also denote a lack of interaction with other people even though they may be nearby. However, similar to slothfulness, loneliness is an internal condition. You can be in a room full of people and still experience loneliness. The truth that loneliness is an intrinsic condition is even indicated by the fact that we consider loneliness not to be a spirit but instead an emotion. It can be just a temporary emotional condition, but it can also be a spirit that attacks you emotionally. In either case, loneliness is going to affect you emotionally, which means it is a condition not of the flesh but of the soul.

There are many emotions that can be detrimental to your walk with God and this deliverance process. This is true whether they are just sporadic emotional experiences or long-term demonic strongholds that manifest through certain emotions. Yet, I am emphasizing loneliness because it is the deadliest of all of the emotions when it comes to deliverance from sexual perversion. The need for companionship will continually draw you back into perversion or even keep you from ever leaving. In my own personal experience this was definitely the case. There were so many times that I wanted to try, so many times that I began to walk the road of sexual purity, but loneliness was always the u-turn in the road.

I shared with you earlier how so often times I did not even enjoy my sexual encounters with men. But, I did it anyway because I just did not want to be lonely. I had a preference as to what type of man I wanted to be with, but when you are suffering from loneliness, you will quickly toss your standards and preferences aside to fill the void. Anyone will do as long as you do not have to face loneliness. This was certainly true for me. I had no time to screen applicants. I was desperately lonely and needed a fix fast. My lack of selectivity, which you learned earlier is the spirit of promiscuity working in your life, led me into sexually perverse relationships time and time again.

The deception about using sexual perversion as a cure for loneliness was that I was trying to fix an internal problem using an external remedy. It cannot be done. It was like trying to use a topical rub to heal a broken leg. The sex medicated me, but it did not cure me. When the medicine wore off, I was looking for another dose right away. I did not understand at that time of my life that only Jesus can fill the loneliness void in a person's heart. I spent many nights lying in bed next to someone, yet still feeling lonely. There were also many occasions, which I used masturbation or sexual fantasy to medicate the loneliness. Even though I was still physically alone, the pleasure of the fantasies and the release of climax provided a temporary escape from my lonely reality. Yet, when I awakened from my fantasies, the loneliness was all the starker.

I do not think that there is anyone that does not feel lonely at times, but you need to be able to recognize when loneliness is no longer a fleeting emotional experience but instead is a serious demonic stronghold. If you feel lonely the majority of the time, even feeling lonely when you are with other people, then you know that this is a stronghold in your life. If you are willing to engage in sinful activities just to keep people around you so you will not have to be alone, you are bound by loneliness. If when finally alone, you have to have on the TV, radio or internet; if you keep your cell phone on all the time hoping for a call or spend a lot of time on the phone; if when you are not doing any of these other things you indulge in elaborate daydreams or fantasies (sexual or non-sexual), you are probably in bondage to the spirit of loneliness. If you are suffering from loneliness, it is partly because you do not like yourself and don't like to be in your own company.

The only – the one and only – cure for loneliness is to first of all, understand that God is the answer to your every need and to secondly, allow fellowship and oneness with Him to be your consuming desire. When your desire is for God only, you will never feel lonely because God is always with you. As matter of fact, He lives right inside of you! That is why He says in the book of Hebrews 13:5, that He will never leave you or forsake you. Developing this type of understanding and desire for God is not going to happen overnight. It does take time, but if you recognize what the true remedy for loneliness is, you can pursue that remedy instead of seeking out yet another temporary loneliness pain killer. Those pain killers never meet the expectation and lead to so much disappointment.

However, the truth of the matter is that loneliness is such an emotionally painful stronghold. It breeds a sense of desperation in you.

You just want to feel better. You do not want to hurt anymore. I believe that loneliness is one of the leading causes of suicide. When you feel lonely, you just want the pain to end. I do understand how you feel. I have been there, but medicating the pain is not going to solve your problem. In all truth, it is really only going to make things worse. Once I got married to my wonderful husband, I finally understood that only oneness with God was going to cure me of loneliness. I had a loving husband and a house full of doting babies and I still suffered loneliness! That is what finally opened my eyes to the truth.

Consuming emotional pain robs you of your joy, and I was tired of living a life of misery when I knew God had supplied everything I needed in order for me to live a fulfilled life. I made a determination to get to really know God and allow Him to become My All. The more I got to know The Lord, the more I could not help but to be consumed with my desire to commune with Him and be one with Him. Now there are times when I have to shoo people away from me so I can be alone (*smile*)! I cannot wait to get alone in the presence of my Healer and make love to Him.

Loneliness does not control me anymore and that is not because I am married. It is because I am consistently intimate with the Father. If you are suffering loneliness, I know that it hurts, but you are going to have to keep fighting through the tears. *"Weeping may endure for a night but joy comes in the morning (Ps 30:5)"*. There is going to be a stage of this deliverance process where you are going to be doing everything that the book says you should be doing, and you are still not going to feel any better, but keep on standing anyway. It will seem like you are going to be crushed under the pressure of loneliness, but persevere because as you do you are going to draw closer to God and begin to enjoy the wholeness that only He can provide. There is no easy cure for loneliness, but the harder you seek God the faster you will be healed. All of your spiritual armor and weapons will be needed to help you win this battle with loneliness, but the best strategy for combating it is to worship God. That experience of oneness with Him will obliterate any chance of loneliness being present in your life.

4. Anxiousness – not pacing your self

We already talked about this earlier in Chapter 9, Step 10, but it is definitely worth mentioning here once again since it is one of the top five enemies of the deliverance process. Anxiousness for deliverance will lead to frustration, and frustration will make you quit. Furthermore, not knowing how to pace yourself will put you on the *"Righteousness roller coaster"*. You will be **"Extraordinary Mega Christian"** one week, and the next week you will be **"Super Sin Sensation."** You have to have balance in your life. This process is not a short-distance sprint, it is a long-distance marathon. You need to map out a steady course and travel at a consistent pace. You must take one step at a time and rest along the way. I am not suggesting that you should not tenaciously and fervently pursue Righteousness. You certainly should. However, you should not be anxious about it. The Holy Spirit gave me a powerful one-liner that I say to myself when I begin to feel anxious. He said to me that *"Anxiousness is the enemy of preparation"*.

Anxiousness causes a chemical to be released in the body that interferes with mental clarity and focus. Thus for example, if you are anxious about taking the test, you are less likely to prepare well for it because you will be too nervous to concentrate on studying. Likewise, while you are so busy being anxious about deliverance, you will not be concentrating and focusing on what you need to do in order to walk therein. Where there is anxiousness there will be a deficit in preparation. So instead of being anxious, flow gracefully with the wind of the Holy Spirit. Do not put yourself on some rigorous deliverance regimen and be a slave driver over yourself, anxiously watching the clock to see if you have *arrived* yet. Such anxiousness will drive you nuts because you will be *arriving* everyday for the rest of your life. No one truly *arrives* until The Messiah our Lord *arrives* to take us home!

I have a personal testimony about deliverance from anxiousness. After I became born again, I used to really beat myself up over my personality flaws and some lingering sinful behaviors. I had so many personality flaws that I just could not stand myself. I would so often make these long, long lists of all of my faults. Making the lists would take hours sometimes. Then I would create these strict fasts and long consecrations to go on, determined to overcome all of my faults during that time. When I would initially implement the regimen, I would be really enthused about it. I would be really on fire and full of zeal. But, as I would anxiously check the calendar everyday wondering how much longer before I was going to see results, I would become frustrated.

The over exertion of energy that I expelled in the beginning would leave me lethargic very quickly. It would not be long before I would abandon the assignment, slump into a defeated mindset, meditate on my failure and flaws until I got sick of myself, lose all of my strength and fall into sin and depression, and would then start the entire exhausting cycle all over again! I did not understand back then that making long lists and naming and claiming everyday in anxiousness that I was not going to be mean or judgmental or lazy or *whatever* anymore, was not what I needed to do. Spending hours everyday evaluating my behavior was robbing me of the preparation time that I needed to really change. I needed to spend that time in God's Word and in His presence, but I instead spent so much time operating in anxiousness that I was not properly preparing my heart for change: *"**Anxiousness is the enemy of preparation!**"*

God began to deal with me about this anxiousness. He told me to get off of the Righteousness roller coaster, stop being anxious, stop creating these ridiculous regimens and to just enjoy my relationship with Him. So I did just that. I did not make anymore lists but instead learned how to move in His Spirit. He knew when I should fast, when I should pray, when I should go to church and when I should stay home. I submitted to the Holy Spirit and stopped marking off the days. So here is the victory report: Just a few weeks ago, as I was reading through one of my old journals, I saw one of those lists. I read the list and was amazed to see that nearly every personality fault and area of sinful struggle I had written down has been changed! God did it and I did not have to be anxious about it! I just made the right preparations and God stepped in and made the changes. Now I know first hand that The Lord does not need my anxiousness to get it done.

I simply learned how to pace myself. I repented for my daily failures, and I thanked Jesus for my daily victories. The failures became fewer and the victories became more. Remember that you have been chosen to bear fruit that remains. The fruit of the Spirit is love, joy, peace, **patience**... Where there is anxiousness there is not going to be the forbearance that comes with love; you will not have joy, you will not be at peace, and undoubtedly you will fall short on patience. **Relax!!!** You already know that victory is waiting (it is not going anywhere, it is **waiting**) for you at the end of the road. Allow yourself to enjoy the journey as you travel there!

5. Discouragement

Finally, I believe that the number one enemy to the deliverance process is going to be discouragement. Discouragement comes to take away your courage and your confidence and also to dishearten you. Discouragement comes to cause you to lose the heart and the morale to accomplish your goal. Discouragement comes to ensure that you give up the fight and accept defeat. There are two main wounds that discouragement will enter in through, which are failure and disappointment. One of the factors that add to discouragement's power is the fact there are so many channels through which discouragement can come. Who can name the number of different ways that we are disappointed or fail at something on a monthly, weekly or even a daily basis? Thus, there are countless opportunities for discouragement to enter into our lives.

As far as the entranceway of disappointment; people can disappoint you, circumstances can disappoint you, or you can disappoint yourself. However, the most detrimental form of disappointment is when it is directed toward God. When you feel like God has let you down you are in a dangerous place spiritually. I do not know if you have ever felt this way toward God. You may feel this way even now, or might in the future so we need to talk about this because this will definitely sabotage the deliverance process.

First of all, let me say that I believe that it is a normal part of your spiritual development to feel disappointed with God. God often times does not do what we want Him to and this can be upsetting. God never makes any mistakes and always does what is best, but the Bible teaches us that His ways are higher than our ways and that we cannot understand His plans *(Isa 55:9)*. It takes a lot of spiritual maturity to understand and accept the Sovereignty of God and until you do, you are going to feel let down when He does not do what you want Him to.

Yahweh is The Sovereign God. He can do whatever He wants to, whenever He wants to, however He wants to. He does not have to consult with anyone and He is justified in all that He does – point blank *(Rom 11:34-36)*! That is not always easy to accept when you feel like you need God to do something for you, and you know that He has the power to do it, but yet He does not do it. God's unwillingness to answer certain prayers in your life is an even greater let down when you are serving Him the best way that you can and giving Him your all. When you fall into this category, you feel like you *deserve* to have your prayers answered. Why did that close loved one die even though you prayed? Why did God allow you to be raped or abused? Why didn't you get the job or the house or the spouse or the money to go to college? These are legitimate needs, and yet God did not come through for you. It can be so bewildering. There are good reasons that these things happen, but most often times only God Himself understands those reasons.

The greatest danger in feeling disappointed toward God is that if that disappointment is not resolved, it will lead to anger. So many people are angry and bitter toward God. Once you become angry at God, you are no longer interested in what will please Him. No one really wants to please someone who has hurt and angered them. That is why this deliverance process can be completely devastated through disappointment toward God. The entire process is centered on building a relationship with and pleasing Him. If you have no desire to please Him, you will not have the heart to continue on in this process. When someone is angry at another person, they will often purposely try to inflict emotional pain upon that person as vengeance. Pleasing the person is usually the last thing on their mind. In the same manner, you may try to hurt God by living sinfully, in order to 'get back at Him'.

I am going to say to you again that you need to understand that **God is Sovereign**. All of creation is His; He made it and He still holds the owner's certificate. I do not care how uprightly you are living, God does not owe you anything. Even your ability to walk uprightly belongs to Him. Everything is His – your service, prayers, worship – whatever you consider yourself to be doing for God all belongs to Him anyway. I do not care how many injustices or hardships you have suffered in your lifetime.

The Lord owes you nothing!!! You also have to realize that as we discussed earlier, many of your prayers are not in line with God's will. They do not fit His plan or help to fulfill His purposes. You need to understand this in order to be able to accept His decisions. He loves you. He wants what is best for you, but He also has an entire universe to manage and every life and happening on this planet affects the balance of the entire universe and all of time. That is a rather big job (not for Him but certainly for us)! So how can anyone be arrogant enough to think that they know what is best more so than Elohim, The God who created all things?

Your desires (and your prayers) are based on what you know about yourself, your family, your friends, your past, your ideas about the future, your living environment... – in other words, your prayers are based on what you want and your very limited knowledge of life and the world. There are so many other factors to consider, so many things that you do not know. God has to operate based on what is best for all of creation, not based on what will make you happy! That is why we learn that His ways are higher than our ways and that no one can understand the scope of His great plan. He has a divine plan for creation and your desires are not always conducive to the coming to pass of His perfect plan.

Suffering on earth is a part of what helps us to understand our need for God, His goodness, satan's wickedness and why God is due all the glory, honor and praise. Therefore, we will all experience our share of suffering, but He will never allow you to suffer beyond what you can handle. Quite truly, the more you suffer, the more you can know that God has made you strong inside. Understanding this and seeking to love The Lord more is the only thing that is going to heal you of the disappointment that comes when He does not answer your prayers or allows painful occurrences in your life. Sometimes the Holy Spirit will tell you why, but often times He will not. You have to learn to just trust Him. You have to be willing to let Him use your life to bring Him glory, no matter what that means. Jesus suffered more than us all, but He never turned His back on God. He understood that His suffering brought the Father glory.

It is OK to feel disappointed, but it is not OK to become bitter toward God. You have to be certain that God loves you. The way that you can be certain of His love for you is simply by remembering that He gave His very own, one and only begotten Son to die, in order to save your life.

Would you sacrifice one of your children to die a gruesome, painful death for someone who hates you and treats you badly? I know that I wouldn't, but God did it for you, so you know for sure that He does indeed love you. Sometimes you need to just stop trying to figure out *'why'* and rest in God's love for you and His Omniscient ability to successfully manage what He has created. Allow Him to comfort you and you will be fine. This is how you can close the entranceway of disappointment.

The other doorway for discouragement is failure. There are many failures in life, but I am talking specifically about you failing yourself. Self-failure is a double entranceway because when you fail, you naturally feel disappointed as well. As far as this deliverance process is concerned, the failure that I am talking about is you falling into sin – failing to continually walk in uprightness. I can remember when I was going through this deliverance process. I used to feel so rotten when I messed up. There were many times that I just abandoned the entire pursuit because of one fall. What I did not understand then is that falling is a natural part of learning how to walk. We can learn this even from observing a baby. They fall many times when they are learning how to walk. Sometimes they cry, sometimes they get frustrated, but always they get up and keep on trying until they master the skill of walking uprightly.

Spiritual growth is the same way. You will fall along the way. Part of what makes these falls so seemingly unbearable is what we talked about earlier – that struggle to be Holy. If you continue to engage in this struggle, frustration and discouragement will certainly set in. When you feel like it is your responsibility to be Holy, you can't handle falling. What you do not understand is that <u>you need to fall</u>. The Bible tells us that *"...a righteous man falls seven times and rises again, but the wicked are overthrown by calamity (Pro 24:16, AMP)."* Notice that the scripture says *a righteous man falls*, not a wicked man but a righteous man. Seven is the number of completion and perfection. That means that God is going to allow you to fall as many times as it takes for you to be perfected in this area of your life and completely delivered! The scripture we just read could have just as easily been translated as, *"God's chosen children will fall as many times as is necessary to be perfected, but each time they will get up and in the end will remain standing surefooted on the path of Righteousness..."*

It is not bad to fall. It is only a problem when you stay down. Only the wicked wallow in sin making excuses as to why they cannot get up. That is why the scripture says that the wicked are overthrown by calamity. They do not get up. The very fact that you feel convicted about falling shows how righteous you really are. Once the Holy Spirit begins to control your life, you cannot stand to stay in sin. You just want to get up as quickly as you can. If you were not giving your ear to the Holy Spirit, you would not even care.

Paul tells us that we all have sinned and fallen short of the glory of God *(Rom 3:23),* and he was not talking to wicked people when he said this. He was talking to Christians. We are all going to fall sometimes, but falling is often times the best way to learn and the very best way to ensure that once you are fully delivered, you never turn back to sin. So do not focus on 'not falling' or 'not sinning'. Sin is unrighteousness and therefore if your focus is on 'not sinning', you are actually focusing on unrighteousness and satan. You already learned in Step 12 that your constant meditation should be of God. Therefore, let your focus instead be on building your relationship with God and becoming one with Jesus and thus being consumed by His nature. As you pursue Righteousness and intimate relations with God *'not sinning'* will be the natural subsequent and end result. You cannot continue in sin when you are one with God.

Honestly, no matter how uprightly you may be walking, your light is always going to show itself dim in comparison to the Light of the Holy One. The closer you get to the mark, the more you realize how far away from it you really are. So if your focus is on never falling or trying to be perfect, you will surely be discouraged. Remember too that *"...all things happen just as he decided long ago."* Even God allowing you to fall has been carefully designed by Him to fulfill His ultimate will. Just imagine if He had not allowed me to fall seven times. Would I be able to write this book right now? If this book has touched your life, it is only because I was perfected in falling. When you fall, do not be discouraged. Instead, receive God's forgiveness quickly, know that His grace is sufficient for you *(2 Cor 12:9),* get up, and continue on in the pursuit of deliverance.

These are the two doors for the spirit of discouragement. The biggest danger in discouragement, regardless of which door it enters in through, is that it tempts you to quit and give up the fight. When your courage, confidence and morale to continue in this process have been taken away, you begin to question yourself. *"Why should I even bother? Nothing is changing. Is it even worth it?"* You cannot allow these thoughts to consume you. You must arrest these thoughts immediately and answer yourself according to the Word of God. *"I should bother because I don't want to continue living in the misery of sin. Something is changing even when I can't see the results. Yes, it is worth it. My happiness is worth it, my eternal salvation is worth it and my Lord is worth it!"*

Encourage yourself by thinking on God's goodness in your life, the many blessings He has blessed you with and the progress that you have made so far. Meditate on the vision of you walking victoriously in deliverance. See the day that you fall in this area no more and just praise God for it now. Praising God is the most awesome cure for discouragement. It is an instant high for your soul that never gets old and will not leave you with a hangover! Discouragement will not stand a chance in the midst of your praise!

The joy of The Lord is your strength

Now that we have discussed the top five enemies that you will face in this process, did you notice something similar about all five of those enemies? They all seek to rob you of joy. Struggling, slothfulness, loneliness, anxiousness and discouragement will all rob you of your joy. Why such an adamant attack on joy? Joy is attacked because *"The joy of The Lord is your strength."* This is what the Bible tells us in Nehemiah 8:10. How can you stand strong in Righteousness without strength? The enemy is always going to strategize to take your joy away because he knows that if you have no joy you will have no strength. I do not know about you, but I personally have had some low moments in my life where I was so sad that I literally could not stand up. Have you ever felt this way? There is something about lacking joy that weakens you physically, mentally, emotionally and spiritually. Joy vitalizes your spirit and energizes your body. You can be really tired but yet full of joy and because of that joy have the energy to keep on going. You need joy in your life!

Where does joy come from? Did you know that there is a

difference between pleasure, happiness and joy? Pleasure is based on natural experiences, activities or interactions that cause a momentary emotional state of euphoria, happiness or joy-like feelings. Happiness is based on happenings, things going on around you, your environment, your health, your relationships or other natural circumstances working in your favor and bringing you pleasure for a more indefinite period of time (seasonal). Joy on the other hand has nothing to do with your experiences or natural circumstances. Joy is an internal condition of the spirit that comes from only one source – the Father's presence, "...***in Your presence is fullness of joy***, at Your right hand there are pleasures forevermore. (Ps 16:11b, AMP)" Pleasure is momentary and happiness is temporary, but joy can be everlasting!

    The joy that is available in The Lord's presence is not predicated on anything other than His sheer goodness and your constancy in seeking Him. You can have joy all day long without interruption because there is nothing that can *force* you out of God's presence. OK, that probably sounds crazy right? How can someone stay in God's presence **all** the time? Well, I did not say it would be easy, but I assure you that it is possible. Psalm 91:1 says, *"He who dwells in the secret place of the Most High shall remain stable and fixed under the shadow of the Almighty [Whose power no foe can withstand]. (AMP)"* Anytime you see a shadow, you know that whatever is casting that shadow is nearby. So this scripture lets you know that you can dwell in God's presence always, and when you keep God nearby satan will not be able to penetrate your spirit.

    Where is that secret place that this scripture talks about though – *"the secret place of the Most High"*? I believe that it is your heart. God's Spirit lives inside of you. He has chosen to make you His dwelling place. That intimate place in your heart is a secret place for you and God where no one else can enter in. It is your own personal Holy of Holies. Who can take it away from you since it is within your own heart? And since it is with you all day, everyday, no matter where you go or what you are doing, can you not dwell there constantly? Yes, you can! What could prevent you from doing so? Why do we think we have to perform some ritual to be in God's presence? He is with you all day long. All you have to do to be in His presence at any given time is simply ***acknowledge*** His presence. He is always longing to fellowship with you; always longing to hear your praises and pour His joy into you.

I know that you can do what I am telling you because I have experienced it. I have experienced joy in the midst of hardships and troubles; in the midst of sickness and persecutions; struggles and poverty. His joy has remained constant in me, <u>as long as I have remained constant in Him</u>. Then there are times that I allow myself to get busy. I will begin to forget to acknowledge God in my daily life. When I get like this, I begin to feel agitated when things are not going my way. I get frustrated and depressed. Things begin to look hopeless. I feel weak and it seems that life is just too much to bear. When I feel this way, I know almost immediately what the problem is. I know that I have not been acknowledging my Friend. I know that I have not been dwelling with Him in that secret place and giving Him the fellowship that He longs for.

The five enemies to deliverance that we just looked at all aim to draw you out of God's presence by consuming you with the negative emotional impact that they cause. They want you to focus your attention on the problem instead of the solution. If you do not enjoy yourself while you are going through this process, you probably will not last. See God in everything, and rest in the comfort of His arms always. Know that His hand is in everything and that all things are working in your best interest. Jesus is committed to helping you fulfill your destiny and satisfying you with a good life. When you know this and acknowledge this, you can have not only joy, but pleasure as well – the pleasures that are at the Father's right hand! Acknowledge Him in everything. Enjoy life. Laugh everyday as often as you can. Smile, sing, extend yourself to the service of others. Do not allow the enemy to draw you into an ambush by leading you out of God's presence where he knows you will be weak. Remember always that the joy of The Lord is your strength!!!

Dealing with re-visitations

We have talked so much about "total deliverance", but how will you know when you are truly delivered? Here is how you will know that you are victoriously free:

1) **When you no longer commit the acts.**
2) **When you no longer exhibit the spiritual characteristics.**
3) **When you are no longer *struggling* with the temptation (temptation will always loom near, but you should not be *struggling* with it).**
4) **When you are not afraid to boldly share with others what God has delivered you from in order to bless them.**
5) **When sexual demons steer clear of you.**

But, then what? You are all cleaned up and everything goes well and you live happily ever after – right? **NOT!** You didn't think the devil would make it that easy, did you? You can count on it – satan will come and try to re-claim you as his own. He will try to set you up. He will use old tricks and pull out some new ones too, but all you need to know is that you have the power! Before you are delivered satan has a stronghold set up in your life, but once you get completely delivered his stronghold has been torn down. You are no longer bound. He no longer has *control* over you. Before, you were enslaved and *had* to obey him. You could not say no even though you wanted to at times, but now you are free and have the right to make your own choices.

The enemy can bark, but he can't bite. He can try to influence you, but he can no longer control you as he was once able to. However, even after you are free and the wounds have been healed, the scars may remain; the residue may linger for a while longer, but do not let a scar, residue or an isolated attack put you back in bondage. The worse thing that you can do is settle into the mindset that you are still bound once Jesus has set you free. Whom the Son has set free is free indeed *(John 8:36)*! Just because you are attacked in this area from time to time or see the scars and residue that have been left behind, it does not mean that you are not set free. If you believe the lie that you are not set free, it will create an opening for the enemy to enter back in and build a new stronghold that will be stronger than the first one. And remember, in the event of a "slip up", the spirit of lust is always the first suspect because lust is the demon that can get even the strongest believers. Lust is the main culprit when someone walking in wholeness and true deliverance falls. *(Re-read the write up on lust if you do not remember why; this is very important to remember.)*

Deceiving you into thinking that you are not yet totally delivered and still under his control is just <u>one</u> of the tactics that the enemy will use in order to try and reclaim you as his own. Once you get delivered, those devils will keep coming back hoping to find an entranceway back into your life. Jesus teaches us this in the book of Matthew, chapter 12, verses 43-45. *"^{43}When an evil spirit leaves a person, it goes into the desert, seeking rest but finding none. ^{44}Then it says, 'I will return to the person I came from.' So it returns and finds its former home empty, swept, and clean. ^{45}Then the spirit finds seven other spirits more evil than itself, and they all enter the person and live there. And so that person is worse off than before. That will be the experience of this evil generation."*

Notice in the verse we just read that the enemy was only able to enter in because he came and found his former home empty. You have to stay full of the Holy Spirit, full of His Word and full of His presence – full of the truth that you are delivered and set free! You cannot leave any voids for the enemy to come and fill. That is why **<u>you must complete this deliverance process in totality</u>**! You cannot leave anything undone. The devil is going to be steaming mad that he has lost you and he is never going to stop trying to regain control over you, if he sees any possibility of being successful. **<u>Do not leave any possibility for the devil to re-claim you!</u>**

It can also be the case that you are deceived into thinking that you are fully delivered when you are not. Something you need to watch out for is how comfortable demons feel about approaching you. Whenever demons confronted Jesus in the Bible, they came to Him respectfully in trembling fear. After satan tested Jesus in the wilderness *(Luke 4:1-13)*, satan was determined to come back again when he caught Jesus in another weak moment, as the following scripture so reveals to us: *"That completed the testing. The Devil retreated temporarily, lying in wait for another opportunity. (Luke 4:13, MSG)"* However, even though satan was set to test Jesus again, Jesus never gave him another opportunity to do so. That is why The Lord says in John 14:30, *"...for the prince (evil genius, ruler) of the world is coming. And he has no claim on Me. [He has nothing in common with Me; there is nothing in Me that belongs to him, and he has no power over Me.] (AMP)"* Satan was never able to test Jesus again!

Therefore, you need to take heed if people that are operating in perversity feel at liberty in approaching you. This means that satan is still finding common ground within you, and that is why his demons of sexual perversion feel so at ease about approaching you. An occasional demon coming to confront you is not so much an issue, but when you are being frequently confronted by sexually perverse spirits; whether by human encounter, in temptation, in dreams or any other source, then you can know most assuredly that there is still an entranceway open. You need to seek God to find out what that entranceway is and get it closed as quickly as possible. Once you are completely delivered and every entranceway is closed, these demons will no longer feel such liberty in approaching you. Spirits of sexual perversion ought to hate and fear you now. Your old sex partners should not still be calling you and lust-filled people should not be frequently approaching you for dates and such. Please do not be deceived about this.

These are the ways that you can measure whether or not your deliverance is complete and the ways to deal successfully with re-visitations of sexually perverse spirits. The most important thing is to be mindful of the fact that you belong to God now and your life is a living testimony to others. Everyday that I walk in deliverance, I proclaim The Savior's glory and His deliverance power and you will do the same. Yet, there are times I see the enemy lurking. I know what to do in these times though. It is the same thing that you must do. First, be sure that you are completely delivered, and if you are just stand your ground and use your armor and your weapons because re-visitations will occur over and over again and *"... if you don't do well, sin is lying in wait for you, ready to pounce; it's out to get you, you have got to master it. (Gen 4:7b, MSG)"*

The conclusion of the matter

Sexual sin is one of the hardest sins to be liberated from. It sometimes seems impossible that you will ever be able to be freed from these spirits. But now you know that it is not impossible, and that **you can walk in total liberty and victory!** You have learned so much and are now so full of knowledge about living victoriously, yet now that you have acquired and apprehended the knowledge, you must apply it. I admonish you to remember the importance of a triune deliverance and working simultaneously on all of your being. The spirit, soul and body are all directly linked and what you do in one will affect the others.

Also, please do not forget to be mindful of the fact that discontinuing an act of sin physically does not necessarily mean that you are delivered from that spirit. True and complete deliverance must consist of these five manifestations: **1)** No longer committing the physical acts; **2)** No longer exhibiting the spiritual characteristics; **3)** No longer struggling the with the temptation; **4)** Being able to boldly share with others what God has delivered you from in order to bless them, and **5)** Being hated and revered by demons of sexual perversion and those whom they operate through. Consistently monitor your behavior to be sure that these spirits are not still operating in your life. This is important because as you have already learned, satan's primary goal in introducing sexual sin was to distort our intimate relationship with God. So, get delivered from the spirit, not just the act.

I say this especially to you who are married and those of you who would consider yourselves to be sanctified. You may have been reading this book just so you could learn how to help others, but be sure that you yourself do not have these spirits operating in your life, interfering with your interactions with other believers and your intimate relationship with God. And here is a warning for everyone: Regardless of where we are in this process right now, we all have to always keep before us the fact that we will never be free of the warfare between our flesh and the Holy Spirit. Deliverance, once accomplished, must be maintained daily. It is not a once and for all deal! Walk after the Spirit always and do not make the mistake of getting delivered and then falling asleep. *Watch and pray constantly so that you will not fall into temptation (Mat 26:41).*

You should already be familiar with **The Deliverance Workbook** by now, but on the following pages are located a few more appendixes that I did not instruct you on. I put my entire heart and soul into providing as much information and assistance to you as I could. I wanted this book to be more than just a book that you read and then stick on a shelf. I hope that it has been, and will continue to be, a personal coach to you as you continue on in this deliverance journey. So please, look at the appendixes and print out the charts and lists. Hang them somewhere that they will be visible as a constant reminder to you of what you should be doing. If you are not a born again believer in Jesus, Yeshua the Messiah, please read the epilogue that begins on page 277! I will explain to you there how to become born again. Being born again is the prerequisite for this deliverance process and without meeting that prerequisite requirement, it will not work for you.

Now, I want to make a personal request of sorts. Jesus said to one of His disciples, *"...and when you have returned to Me, strengthen your brethren. (Luke 22:32, KJV)."* So I ask you to please fulfill this mandate by compassionately remembering those that are still struggling with sexual sin once you yourself have been restored. Do not be like so many people in the church that get delivered and then become secretive and self-righteous! When I was going through this, no one would share with me there sexually perverse past and I felt so alone and helpless. That is why I was so intimate and personal within the pages of this book. So I am asking you to please follow my example, and make a commitment to yourself, to your God and to your fellow struggling friends, to go back and strengthen others once Jesus has completely delivered you.

Share your testimony openly and in all truth, <u>as often the Holy Spirit leads you to</u>. It will not always be appropriate to do so, but if you are going to err, I would encourage you to err on the side of telling it too often rather than err on the side of not telling it often enough! I will be truthful in saying to you that many people will scorn you for revealing your testimony, even as they have scorned me, but do not let that daunt you. The reality is that people who have no testimony or those who choose to deny their testimony are so jealous of people like you and I. So whenever they try to make me feel unworthy, I remind them of these words spoken by Jesus in Luke 7:47, *"I tell you, her sins – and they are many – have been forgiven, so she has shown me much love. But a person who is forgiven little shows only little love."*

Our sins and Jesus' forgiveness of those sins has afforded us the opportunity to love Him in a way that those kinds of self-righteous people will never be able to. I know that many people will get delivered from sexual perversion as a result of this book. I believe that my heart's desire to see people restored back to true worship of The Lord will come to pass, but my second greatest desire concerning this work is that it would create an opportunity for the total destruction of the shroud of secrecy that exists in the church concerning sexual sin. It is this secrecy that has empowered satan so greatly in this area and has kept people in bondage for so long. Your testimony can save someone's immortal life, so please partner with me my friend, in sharing your testimony.

As you finish the reading of this book, I know that your life is about to change forever. Writing it has certainly changed mine. Truthfully, I got delivered from many things as I wrote this book. The majority of the time that I was writing, I had no idea what I was going to write until my fingers tapped the keyboard. The Holy Spirit has truly written this book – not I. This book is so important that I almost died while I was writing it. I came under attack immediately after I began writing this book and the attacks continued even until the day I finalized this project. (You can read the preface to learn more about these attacks, if you have not already.) The enemy did not want me to write this book. He knew he would be in trouble, but yet I lived to finish it to the Father's glory, and you lived through hell to read it! Your life will never be the same after this!

I pray that my spirit has already and will continue to personally mentor you through the pages of this book. I say this because I realize that this book is a manual and you will need to refer back to it again and again as you continue on in this process. I thank you for allowing me to be the one (through the workings of the Holy Spirit of course) to lead you on this journey, and I am encouraged to know that the bondage that I suffered was not in vain. I purposefully left my title as an Evangelist and Prophetess off of this book, because I did not write this book as Clergy. I wrote it as a survivor, a victor and a friend coming back to help those still trapped!!! We are friends now and partners in deliverance. Thus, I welcome you to contact me through the information I will provide on the contact page in order to share your testimony of deliverance with me.

A final Prayer

Now close your eyes as you read this prayer. (I'm just kidding. You can't read and close your eyes at the same time! *Laugh*.) Seriously though, read this prayer **out loud** and move further into your journey to victorious freedom and newness, knowing that the Spirit of Jesus is with you!!!

Father Yah, I thank you for this book. I thank you Lord for providing a way through which I can see the Light of Your truth. I ask you Lord to forgive me for all of my sins Father. Please allow Your Holy Spirit to lead me as I commit myself to getting totally delivered from every spirit of sexual perversion that operates in my life. Expose and heal every entrance wound Father. Give me the boldness, desire, zeal and endurance to complete every step of this process without leaving anything undone. I thank you now for your grace Father. I don't plan on sinning anymore but if I do fall, I commit to receive your forgiveness and get up immediately and continue to seek your face God. You know my Lord that my intimate relationship with you has been perverted because of these demons in my life. Please restore me back to proper intimacy with you oh Lord. I will give your name the praise always and with your help will boldly tell of your deliverance in my life once it is complete, so that I may help others even as Laneen Haniah has helped me. In Yeshua's (Jesus') mighty name, I pray these things in the power of Your Holy Spirit and know that because it is a prayer prayed according to Your will that every word of it is already answered and will be completely manifested in my life. Amen. Hallelujah!

I Am Victoriously Free!

After being abused
I was lost and confused
But I am Victoriously Free!

My heart badly trampled
My life was in shambles
But I am Victoriously Free!

Though in hopeless despair
Did nobody care
But I am Victoriously Free!

Because of betrayal and lies
I learned to despise
But I am Victoriously Free!

I became wayward and wild
In my – inner child
But I am Victoriously Free!

My choices were wrong
And my suffering was long
But I am Victoriously Free!

In darkness I cried
In spirit I died
But Yeshua replied
And restored me inside
So I am Victoriously Free!

Because Yah reached His Hand
In Light I now stand
And I am Victoriously Free!

Until next time, please keep me in your prayers always and please help me promote this awesome deliverance manual in anyway that you can! I ❤ you!

Epilogue: Are you a born again believer?

So many wonderful truths have been presented throughout this book. However, the most wonderful truth of all is Yeshua/Jesus the Messiah! Yahweh God saves, but the promises of redemption, deliverance and salvation only belong to born again believers in His Son. If you are not born again, you will not be able to move forward in this deliverance process or your relationship with God or newness of life in general.

If you are not a born again believer or if you are unsure if you are, I believe that because you are reading this right now, The Father is drawing you into His sheepfold. For the Word of God tells us in John 6:44, *"For people cannot come to me (Yeshua/Jesus) unless the Father who sent me draws them to me..."* Today God is knocking on the door of your heart. He is drawing you, and so I want to explain to you how you can become a born again believer in Christ Yeshua/Jesus.

The Gospel of John chapter 3 *(AMP)*

"³Jesus answered him, I assure you, most solemnly I tell you, that unless a person is born again (anew, from above), he cannot ever see (know, be acquainted with, and experience) the Kingdom of God.

¹⁴And just as Moses lifted up the serpent in the desert [on a pole], so must [so it is necessary that] the Son of Man be lifted up [on the cross],

¹⁵In order that everyone who believes in Him (Yeshua/Jesus) [who cleaves to Him, trusts Him, and relies on Him] may not perish, but have eternal life and [actually] live forever!

¹⁶For God so greatly loved and dearly prized the world that He [even] gave up His only begotten (unique) Son, so that whoever believes in (trusts in, clings to, relies on) Him shall not perish (come to destruction, be lost) but have eternal (everlasting) life.

¹⁷For God did not send the Son into the world in order to judge (to reject, to condemn, to pass sentence on) the world, but that the world might find salvation and be made safe and sound through Him."

These are the words that were spoken by Yeshua/Jesus Himself. He let us know that we must be born again in order to be a part of God's Kingdom and that because of His sacrifice, everyone that believes in Him as the Son of God and the Savior of the world will be become born again and eventually be saved as a result.

I can only give you the basics here because the plan of salvation is discussed all throughout the New Testament. Therefore, I would have to write another entire book to cover it all, but I can offer you enough information and scriptures to at least get you started. In order to become a born again believer in Christ Yeshua/Jesus there are a few things that you must do:

1. First of all, as the scripture that we just read says *(John 3:16)*, you have to believe with all your heart that Christ Yeshua/Jesus is the Son of the Almighty True and Living God. You must believe the entire account of the gospel which is that Yeshua/Jesus is God Himself incarnated in flesh, was born of the virgin Mary; lived and walked the earth as a natural man doing great wonders by the power of the Holy Spirit; was then hung on a cross and crucified willingly as a sacrifice for your sins, and finally that He rose from the dead after three days with all victory and glory and ascended back to Heaven to sit at the right hand of the Father on the throne. (Please read in the Holy Bible in any one of the Gospels – Matthew, Mark, Luke, or John – to confirm these truths.) Yeshua/Jesus is there on the throne today, interceding for your sins and pleading your case with God.

"Therefore He is able also to save to the uttermost (completely, perfectly, finally, and for all time and eternity) those who come to God through Him, since He is always living to make petition to God and intercede with Him and intervene for them. (Heb 7:25, AMP)"

2. Once you believe in your heart that Yeshua/Jesus is *The Savior*, you have to make him *your Savior*. You must open up your mouth and invite Yeshua/Jesus into your heart. You must then cry out to God the Father: You must with penitence, humility and remorse ask God in Yeshua's name for forgiveness of your sins and be willing to allow God to work repentance in your heart. You have to make a commitment to diligently apply God's Word and walk uprightly before Him, offering your body up

as a living sacrifice. If you truly believe in Jesus, you will love Him for what He did for you, and if you love Him you will keep His commands. The true litmus test as to whether or not someone is truly a born again believer is the effort that they make to live according to God's Word.

"For it is by believing in your heart that you are made right with God, and it is by confessing with your mouth that you are saved. (Rom 10:10)"

"But if we confess our sins to Him, He is faithful and just to forgive us and to cleanse us from every wrong. (1 John 1:9)"

"And so, dear brothers and sisters, I plead with you to give your bodies to God. Let them be a living and Holy sacrifice – the kind he will accept. When you think of what he has done for you, is this too much to ask? (Rom 12:1)"

"If you [really] love Me, you will keep (obey) My commands. (John 14:15, AMP)"

3. Finally, you must be baptized in Yeshua's (or Jesus') name and receive His Holy Spirit. As soon as you do the first two steps, I believe that God honors your acceptance of Him into your heart, but it is important to, as soon as possible, go to a church to be baptized in Jesus' name (or Yeshua's name, but most churches don't use the name "Yeshua" and that is OK because we are still talking about the Savior and Son of God either way).

"^{15}And then he told them, "Go into all the world and preach the Good News to everyone, everywhere. ^{16}Anyone who believes and is baptized will be saved. But anyone who refuses to believe will be condemned. (Mark 16:15-16)"

"John baptized with water, but in just a few days you will be baptized with the Holy Spirit. (Acts 1:5)"

"Peter replied, 'Each of you must turn from your sins and turn to God, and be baptized in the name of Jesus Christ for the forgiveness of your

sins. Then you will receive the gift of the Holy Spirit.' (Acts 2:38)"

"⁹But you are not controlled by your sinful nature. 'You are controlled by the Spirit if you have the Spirit of Jesus living in you. (And remember that those who don't have the Spirit of Christ living in them are not Christians at all.)' (Rom 8:9)"

As far as water baptisms are concerned, you must be baptized at a church or have someone who is a Christian minister come to your home and baptize you in Yeshua's (Jesus') name and be fully submerged in water. However, you can ask God for and receive His Spirit anywhere, before or after you get baptized. *"...how much more will your heavenly Father give the Holy Spirit to those who ask Him. (Luke 11:13b, AMP)"* The Bible makes it clear that God will honor your request. I am also praying for you right now that if you become a born again believer as a result of reading this; that God will fill you with His Holy Spirit even as you pray right there where you are at, and that He will endow you with the gift of speaking in tongues immediately. You learn in the deliverance steps the importance of speaking in tongues.

You also learned that salvation is something that will be happening to you everyday until Yeshua/Jesus returns for you. Yet, in order for this to happen for you, you must stay connected to God and to the other members of the Body of Christ. You have learned (or will) that there is awesome power in Christian fellowship. Once you become a new believer, it is very important to go to a church that teaches the True Word of God. You need to fellowship with other mature believers as much as possible. Remember, you have been "born again". In other words, you start out as an infant just the same way that natural babies do. You are going to need a lot of care and guidance at this stage of your Christian walk. So seek The Lord for the guidance and the gifts of His Holy Spirit, go to a Spirit-filled, Word-teaching church often and read your Bible much everyday (especially the New Testament for getting started)!

Some people believe that if they give you a *'sinner's prayer'* to recite that you become born again by reciting the prayer. I mean no disrespect to anyone, but no where in the Bible do you see anyone become a believer in such a way (or at least I am not aware of such a scripture, if it does exist). However, the scriptures do make it plain that no one can become a Christian unless God has prepared the person's heart, and if your heart has truly been prepared then the Holy Spirit will give you the words to pray as you open your mouth. Therefore, I am not going to give you a nursery rhyme prayer to say.

All you need to do is speak your heart to Yeshua. Tell Him that you believe in Him and that you love Him and need Him. Tell Him about your sins and ask Him for forgiveness. Invite Yeshua into your heart to be your Savior and Lord forever. It does not have to be said in any special way, but it is important that it is sincerely coming from your heart. It cannot be *my* prayer; it has to be *your* prayer. So if you want to become a born again believer and be filled with the Holy Spirit right now, then please put this book down and begin to cry out to your Heavenly Father in the name of Yeshua/Jesus His Son. Tell Him what is in your heart and I welcome you in advance into the Kingdom of God, the Kingdom of Yahweh, as my new sister or brother in Christ!

Please contact the ministry to let us know that you have become born again! Use the contact info on page 307.

PART III:
THE DELIVERANCE WORKBOOK

What's a manual without a workbook to go along with it? I wanted to be sure to provide you with every necessary tool to help you successfully complete this deliverance process! In this workbook there are five appendixes that coincide with the information in **Part I** and **Part II** of the book. There are some essential exercises that you should complete. There are also several charts and lists that will give you quick access to some of the more pertinent information that is written in the book. You will be instructed on the use of Appendixes A, B and C within the chapters of the book. Appendixes C and D are included to provide you with some additional information and references.

I hope this workbook will help you along. Enjoy!

Appendix A:
The Spirits of Sexual Perversion Definitive Charts

On the following pages you will see four charts that give you a quick overview of the spirits of sexual perversion. The charts also enable you to assess your own sexual bondage by evaluating on a scale of 1-10, each spirit's current manifested operations in your life. Please do not try to do the evaluations without first reading the detailed assessments located in Chapter 6 (pg 53). The charts offer only a very quick overview and should not be used to make the final determination by themselves.

When filling out the evaluation section for each spirit, please do not forget to consider your spiritual life and whether or not this spirit is manifesting itself in your spiritual life (this concept is explained in-depth in chapters 5 and 6). It would be a good idea to evaluate the spiritual and natural manifestations separately. You can do this by circling a number from 1-10 for natural manifestation and underlining or highlighting a number from 1-10 for spiritual manifestation. I would also advise you to enlarge and print out these charts and keep them next to you as you are reading the assessment chapter. This will enable you to do your chart evaluations as you are reading. Do not forget to record the results in your journal book.

Spirits of Sexual Perversion Chart (A-C)

	Fornication	Masturbation	Adultery
Definition	Sexual intercourse or any type of sexual contact between partners who are not lawfully married to each other	The act of sexually stimulating oneself, usually until orgasm is achieved, without another person being involved	Voluntary sexual intercourse or other sexual contact, between a married person and a person other than their spouse
Assignment	To impart into us the idea that we can enjoy the pleasures of God without being committed to Him	To get us to feel like we do not need God; to give a false sense of empowerment and control	To cause us to be unfaithful to God and to selfishly use Him; to eventually cause total separation from Him altogether
Most Common Natural Characteristics	Lonely, attention seeking, self-pitying, low self-esteem, arrogant, insecure	Selfish, unemotional, unappreciative, very critical, hard on self	Needy, unpredictable, desperate, deceptive, backstabbing
Most Common Spiritual Characteristics	Inconsistent relationship w/ God, unreliable in church obligations, unfruitful, sinful lifestyle	Not true worshipers of God, unsubmissive to leadership, often complains about church leadership	Unfaithful to God, showy worshipers, jealous about the sincerity of others, religious but not Holy
Most Common Entranceways	Previous bad relationships, rejection, failure in life, childhood neglect, uncontrolled lust	Verbal abuse, feelings of inadequacy, stressful situations, childhood neglect, rejection	Lack of moral values in upbringing, neglectful spouse, fear of emotional pain
Currently how strongly is this spirit manifesting itself in your life?	1 2 3 4 5 6 7 8 9 10	1 2 3 4 5 6 7 8 9 10	1 2 3 4 5 6 7 8 9 10
Is this demon now, or has it been in the past, your strongman?	Yes, in the past Yes, right now No, not ever	Yes, in the past Yes, right now No, not ever	Yes, in the past Yes, right now No, not ever

Spirits of Sexual Perversion Chart (D-F)			
	Incest	Homosexuality	Prostitution
Definition	Sexual intercourse or other sexual contact between persons so closely related that law or custom forbids their marriage	Strong attraction toward persons of the same sex; sexual intercourse or other sexual contact with persons of the same sex	The act of offering oneself as a sexual partner in return for monetary compensation or some other favor or gift
Assignment	To cause us to have a distorted relationship with God, not being able to keep Him in proper perspective in our hearts	To keep us from understanding our true identity in God and prevent us from being able to conceive and give birth to His will	To affect our ability to see our value in Christ or simply as human beings therefore causing us to sell ourselves short
Most Common Natural Characteristics	Obviously abnormal, secretive, envious, stirs up strife, withdrawn	Stubborn, determined, defiant, argumentative, secretly depressed	Tough acting, emotionless, unpredictable, hypocritical, unable to form bonds
Most Common Spiritual Characteristics	Warped perception of God, strife stirrers in church, jealous at the elevation of others, deceived about own wickedness	Over exaggerated effort to show togetherness, unsure of identity in Christ, inconsistent behavior	Unstable walk with God, unable to receive His love, always expecting something in return for services
Most Common Entranceways	Defective display of love from someone close, loneliness, rejection	Sexual abuse, rejection, verbal abuse, confusion, a search for identity and acceptance	Abuse of any kind, no sense of self worth
Currently how strongly is this spirit manifesting itself in your life?	1 2 3 4 5 6 7 8 9 10	1 2 3 4 5 6 7 8 9 10	1 2 3 4 5 6 7 8 9 10
Is this demon now, or has it been in the past, your strongman?	Yes, in the past Yes, right now No, not ever	Yes, in the past Yes, right now No, not ever	Yes, in the past Yes, right now No, not ever

Spirits of Sexual Perversion Chart (G-I)

	Pornography/ Sexual Fantasy	Rape/ Pedophilia	Beastiality
Definition	Indulging in mental images, pictures, writings or films involving sexual intercourse or contact to arouse sexual excitement	The act of forcing another person (or child) to involuntarily submit to sexual contact or sexual intercourse	Sexual intercourse or any type of sexual contact with an animal
Assignment	To control our minds and subsequently our entire lives	To give committers a false sense of control through manipulation and violence	To draw people completely away from God ; aiming to take them to the point of no return
Most Common Natural Characteristics	Detachment from reality, procrastination, unorganized life, no goals only dreams	Eerie, short-tempered, manipulative, violent, withdrawn, childish acting, self-condemning	Unnaturally hateful, lacking affection, detached from humanity
Most Common Spiritual Characteristics	Fantasized relationship with God , double-mindedness, inactive in church activities	A sense of being better than God , controlling, desire to be surrounded by weak immature believers	Bordering on hating God , ashamed about feelings toward God , may blatantly worship satan or demons
Most Common Entranceways	Devastating uncontrollable circumstances, rejection, loneliness	Devastating and ongoing abuse and neglect in childhood, rejection	Being exposed to unnaturally hateful persons, satanic worship, lasciviousness
Currently how strongly is this spirit manifesting itself in your life?	1 2 3 4 5 6 7 8 9 10	1 2 3 4 5 6 7 8 9 10	1 2 3 4 5 6 7 8 9 10
Is this demon now, or has it been in the past, your strongman?	Yes, in the past Yes, right now No, not ever	Yes, in the past Yes, right now No, not ever	Yes, in the past Yes, right now No, not ever

Spirits of Sexual Perversion Chart (J-K)

	Sexual Lust	Lasciviousness	Promiscuity
Definition	A craving, longing, or desire to achieve sexual gratification through acts of sexual perversion	Extreme sexual lust; sexual lust completely unbridled and totally unrestrained	Lacking discrimination or selectivity, especially when referring to a number of different sexual partners
Assignment	To ambush an individual and take advantage of natural desires in order to draw them into sin and away from God	To totally consume an individual's mind, body and soul until they are unable to pursue God and are totally sold out to the sinful desires of the flesh	To assist other demon spirits (sexual demons as well as other types) in gaining access to one's life; ultimately it is assigned to distract and confuse
Most Common Natural Characteristics	Greedy, impatient, discontent, selfish, restless	Evil-natured, envious, untrustworthy, never satisfied	Confused, unsure of goals, must be around people, indecisive
Most Common Spiritual Characteristics	No real relationship w God, impatient in suffering, falls into sin often	No love for God, compromising the Word, very evil-natured although totally deceived	Confusion about calling, distracted from God's work, no quality time with God
Most Common Entranceways	Lack of self control, voluntary exposure, generational curses	Lack of self control, choosing to love the world and sin	Neediness, poor decisions, rejection, lack of selectivity
Currently how strongly is this spirit manifesting itself in your life?	1 2 3 4 5 6 7 8 9 10	1 2 3 4 5 6 7 8 9 10	1 2 3 4 5 6 7 8 9 10
Is this demon now, or has it been in the past, your strongman?	Yes, in the past Yes, right now No, not ever	Yes, in the past Yes, right now No, not ever	Yes, in the past Yes, right now No, not ever

Appendix B: Tracing Your Past

Step 2 of the deliverance process is *"Discovery"*. In this step we learn how to discover when and how spirits of sexual perversion entered our life and also how to determine the degree of each particular stronghold. Use the following questions to help yourself discover how spirits of sexual perversion entered your life. They may have entered into your life by more than one means. Note each path through which these spirits entered. Each entranceway has to be dealt with in a specific way. This exercise will help you to pinpoint more precisely which deliverance steps you will need to focus on most diligently in order to close every door or entranceway. You may want to enlarge and print out these questions so you will have more room to write your answers. You can also write the questions and answers in your journal book.

1. We talked about **generational curses** *(pg 163)*. In order to determine if generational curses play a part in your struggle with sexual sin, circle those acts of sexual perversion that have been committed by living or deceased members of your family.

Fornication   Masturbation   Adultery   Incest   Homosexuality

Prostitution   Sexual fantasy   Pornography   Rape   Pedophilia

Beastiality   Sexual lust   Lasciviousness   Promiscuity

2. Some generational curses are stronger than others. You can gain insight into the strength of a generational curse by determining how long the curse has been operating in your family and whether or not it operated on only one or both sides of your family. Determining the strength of a generational curse will help you be better equipped to combat it. In the chart below, write 'yes', 'no', or 'idk' (I don't know) under the appropriate heading ('Mom's side' or 'Dad's side'), in the space provided next to the name of each spirit. If you write 'yes', also write down the number of generations that spirit has been operating in your family. Start by tracing back as far as you can. For example, you may know the history of your great, great, great grandparents and their siblings. Count down each generation starting from them until you get to you,

your siblings and first cousins. If you have children, nieces or nephews they count as a separate generation as well.

	Mom's side	Dad's side		Mom's side	Dad's side
Fornication	Example: Yes 6	idk	Pornography		
Masturbation			Rape		
Adultery			Pedophilia		
Incest			Beastiality		
Homosexuals			Sexual lust		
Prostitution			Lasciviousness		
Sexual fantasy			Promiscuity		

<u>**To close the entranceway of generational curses, focus on Steps 6 & 9.**</u>

3. The second entranceway that we discussed in Step 2 is **involuntary exposure** *(pg 165)*. Involuntary exposure occurs when you are exposed to acts of sexual perversion in circumstances that are beyond your control. This can happen during childhood through your upbringing or at school. It can happen through sexual abuse. It can happen in a marriage situation when your spouse exposes you to such behavior or some other uncontrollable situation. Which spirits of sexual perversion were you exposed to through involuntary exposure? Circle each one.

Fornication   Masturbation   Adultery   Incest   Homosexuality

Prostitution   Sexual fantasy   Pornography   Rape   Pedophilia

Beastiality   Sexual lust   Lasciviousness   Promiscuity

4. Now for each spirit you circled, in your journal write as many details as you can think of concerning the circumstances of that exposure.

When, where, and how did it happen?

How did you feel at the time?

Did the exposure stir sexual impulses in you and/or did it disgust you?

How soon after the exposure did you begin to voluntarily participate in that act of sexual perversion, if you ever did?

To close the entranceway of involuntary exposure focus on Steps 6, 8 & 9

5. We also discussed in Chapter 8, **spiritual wounds** *(pg 168)*. Spiritual wounds give spirits of sexual perversion a much stronger foothold than generational curses or involuntary exposure. Generational curses and involuntary exposure only present an increased opportunity for influence, but spiritual wounds give demons a direct doorway to your soul. When using a spiritual wound as an entranceway, demons disguise themselves as a remedy for your pain or disease. That is why it is so important to determine what kinds of spiritual wounds exist in your life. Once you acknowledge those wounds, God Your Healer, can close those doors forever by giving you wholeness. Some of the most common spiritual wounds that allow spirits of sexual perversion into your life are:

sexual, emotional, verbal or mental abuse; childhood neglect; painful and failed relationships; devastating losses; rejection; lack of love, affection, and/or affirmation in life; or lack of acceptance by peers or loved ones.

All of those that I just mentioned lead to:

feelings of inadequacy; insecurity; low self-esteem and low sense of self-worth; depression; loneliness; self-condemnation; and hopelessness.

There are many more. These are just some of the more prevalent ones. Take a good, long, retrospective look at your life. Then, in your journal, answer these questions:

Which of these wounds or others do you carry?

How did those wounds get there?

Are you still angry about what happened to you?

Grieving is very important. Did you ever allow yourself to grieve properly over these hurts?

Have you forgiven those that hurt you or are you bitter (see pg 193)?

Are you angry at God?

Please take as much time as you need to answer these questions as thoroughly and as honestly as you can. This is probably the most important thing that you will have to do during this deliverance process. Even as you move on from Step 2, you will probably continually be gaining new insights and revelations concerning this topic. Always write down what the Holy Spirit reveals to you. Healing from spiritual wounds is discussed in more detail in step 2C *(pg 168)*.

To close the entranceway of spiritual wounds focus on Steps 6, 7 & 10

6. The last thing we discussed as far as how spirits of sexual perversion enter into your life is, **voluntary exposure**.*(pg 171)* Voluntary exposure gives demons the most direct and unrestrained access to your life, simply because with voluntary exposure they are entering with your permission. Promiscuity, which we discussed in the assessment chapter, is one of the most common forms of voluntary exposure. Write down the answers to the following questions in your journal. Writing it down plainly will help you see your need for God's forgiveness and help you make the decision to disassociate yourself from these influences in order to avoid any future voluntary exposure. It will also help you take responsibility for your actions and stop claiming ignorance or victimization. It will truly put you in the driver's seat.

Try to determine how many different people you have had sex or sexual contact with and also people that you have had close friendships with. What spirits of sexual perversion were operating in the lives of these people?

Think about the places, things, concepts, teachings and ideas you have exposed yourself to (through all sources). How much sexual perversion have you exposed yourself to in this way?

To close the entranceway of voluntary exposure focus on Steps 4,5,6 & 12

Appendix C: The Deliverance Process at a Glance

I wanted to give you a quick overview of the deliverance process. You can print out this list and put it in your journal book or hang it somewhere visible in your house or office. Keeping this list nearby will be a friendly reminder of what you need to be doing and will help you to maintain your focus. This is also one of the ways you can implement Steps 3 (*Renewing the mind*) and 12 (*Walking after The Spirit*).

Deliverance for the soul man

Step 1 – Confession/Acknowledgement: The very first thing that you need to do is to acknowledge within yourself that you have a problem. This step is about being honest with yourself.

Step 2 – Discovery: The second thing that needs to happen is the discovery of how demon spirits entered into your life. This is a very important step because it will give you the insight that you need to make sure those openings are closed forever. Let us do a recap of the four main entranceways for demons and how you can close those entranceways:

> Generational curses – Renounce generational demons because they have no right to afflict you once you become a part of God's family!
>
> Involuntary exposure – Renounce and bind these demons. Cover yourself in the Blood of Jesus and they will have to release you. They too have no right to afflict you.
>
> Spiritual wounds – First you must make sure that you have implemented forgiveness and are free of bitterness. You must allow yourself to grieve. Grieving must be done in the presence of the Father where you will be healed. Once healing has taken place, the demons will no longer have a place to reside within you.
>
> Voluntary exposure – These demons came because, through your actions, you invited them to come. You must confess your faults; allow God to cleanse you and determine to change your behavior.

Step 3 – Renewing the mind: The mind must be renewed in order for change to take place. Our mind is the control center of our being. Feed it the proper information from the Word of God and by all means please **keep** it free of corruption!

Deliverance for the spirit man

Step 4 – Confession/Admittance: After you have been honest with yourself and acknowledged that you have a problem, you need to be honest with God and admit to Him that you have a problem. Do not be shy with God; He already knows anyway; just lay it all on the table.

Step 5 – Penitence/Humility: Penitence is that next step after admittance. Not only must you admit your sins to God, but you must also experience brokenness and remorse over your sins. Penitence is about humility of spirit and there will be no deliverance without it.

Step 6 – Confession/Exposure: The third and final aspect of confession is exposure. This aspect of confession is about exposing your sins to an upright Christian. Do not forget the two reasons that you need to fulfill the exposure aspect of confession, 1) the protection of accountability, and 2) the power of intercession.

Step 7 – Forgiveness and letting go: Deliverance cannot take place if you refuse to forgive others because it will prevent Jesus from healing you. It will also cause your heart to be hard and embittered, making it impossible for the Holy Spirit to work with it. Finally, it will deny you God's forgiveness of your sins which will prevent you from connecting and fellowshipping with Him.

Step 8 – Spiritual Warfare: Putting on your spiritual armor: Do not forget about the five pieces of your spiritual armor, which will be used to defend yourself from the attacks of the enemy:

> The Belt of Truth for protecting yourself from the shame or guilt of your indecencies and sins with the truth of God's Word concerning forgiveness and deliverance.

> The Body Armor of Righteousness is about acquiring Righteousness through faith in Christ Jesus as your Lord and Savior and thus covering your entire body in His protective Blood.

> The Shoes of peace will protect your feet with the truth and joy of the gospel and your secure relationship with God, enabling you to

walk on the path of Righteousness without hindrance and stand on the battlefield without being moved.

The Shield of Faith will protect you from the fiery arrows of the enemy which are specifically designed to attack you in your weak areas. Believing God's Word is true will assure you that God can keep you even in your weaknesses.

The Helmet of Salvation is designed to protect your mind with the understanding that salvation is not a complete work until Jesus returns and will thus condition your mind to focus and to endure until the end.

Step 9 – Spiritual Warfare: Using your spiritual weapons: Let us also remember that God has given us mighty weapons of attack that enable us to go after the enemy and defeat him:

The Sword of the Word is used for close combat. By speaking God's Word you can cut the enemy right in his heart and send him fleeing with his tail tucked between his legs!

The Power of Praise can be used to confuse the enemy and render him defenseless. In his confusion, he will self destruct and actually end up helping you instead of hurting you!

Christian Fellowship can be used to come into agreement in prayer with other believers or to absorb strength from the anointing of other Christian men and women by just being in their presence or through the laying on of hands.

Praying and Fasting will be the most powerful weapon you have. Prayer is a direct link to God and is truly putting the battle in His hands. Fasting makes prayer more effective because it puts the flesh under subjection and makes you more submissive to the Holy Spirit in order for Him to do the praying through you.

Step 10 – Spiritual Warfare: Retreat and replenish: In every long war there are times when the warriors must retreat and replenish themselves. Do not forget to rest in the presence of God and be rejuvenated through true worship.

Deliverance for the flesh man

Step 11 – Discipline of the flesh: Deliverance in the flesh man is all about discipline. Let us recap on what we learned about discipline:

> Understanding Why Your Body Sins is very important. You have to realize that your skin, muscles, hormones, bones, sex organs or any other parts of your body, cannot control you! It is the sin nature of the flesh, which is the power of satan that causes you to sin. Satan is defeated, you can control your body!

> More About Discipline is the simple understanding that discipline is all about self-control in subjection to the Holy Spirit. Remember to set small discipline goals for yourself and not to put too much emphasis on discipline until you have implemented the steps for the spirit man and the soul man.

> More About Fasting is discussed simply because fasting is the best way to learn discipline. Remember that abstaining from food is not spiritual unless it is conjoined with other spiritual pursuits, so do not turn fasting into a diet.

Step 12 – Walking after The Spirit: Once deliverance has taken place in your life, it must be maintained daily by walking after the Spirit. Deliverance is not a once and for all deal. If you do not maintain it, you can lose it. Remember to protect the gateways to your mind. Keep them free of all contamination, corruption and sinful influences by meditating on God's Word constantly.

Conclusion

The 5 manifestations of total deliverance:
1) No longer committing the physical acts
2) No longer exhibiting the spiritual characteristics
3) No longer *struggling* the with the temptation
4) Being able to boldly share with others what God has delivered you from
5) Being avoided by demons of perversion and those whom they operate through

Appendix D: Tips on Fasting

The 10 requirements for spiritualizing fasting

1) Restricted eating: *Ezra 10:6, Ps 109:24, Dan 10:2-3, Luke 4:2*
2) Abstinence: *Lev 23:27, 1 Kings 21:27(AMP), Dan 6:18(AMP), 1 Cor 7:5*
3) Humility: *Lev 16:29-31(AMP), Ps 69:10, Isa 58:5, Joel 2:12*
4) Repentance: *Jud 20:26, 1 Sam 7:6, Dan 9:1-20, Joel 1:14; 2:12, Jonah 3:5 (AMP)*
5) Prayer: *Dan 9:1-20, Mark 9:29, Acts 13:3; 14:23, Luke 2:37(AMP)*
6) Worship: *Neh 9:1-3, Est 5:1(AMP), Dan 9:21, Luke 2:37, Acts 13:2*
7) Intercession: *Neh chap 1, Ps 35:13, Dan 6:18; 9:1-20, Acts 14:23*
8) Secrecy: *1 Kings 21:27, Mat 6:16-19, Luke 4:2*
9) Ministry: *Isa 58:6-7, Acts 13:2; 14:23*
10) Rest: *Lev 16:29-32 & 23:32*

Five general reasons for fasting

1) For religious rituals: *Lev 16:29 & 23:27-32(AMP), Neh 9:1, Zech 7:3-5, Luke 18:12*
2) Due to grief over tragedy or loss: *1 Sam 31:13, 2 Sam 1:12, 1 Kings 21:27, Est 4:3*
3) As show of repentance: *Jud 20:26, Isa 58:6-7, Joel 1:14 & 2:12, Jonah 3:5 (AMP)*
4) For favor or clarity from The Lord concerning prayers brought before Him:
   2 Sam 12:16, 2 Chron 20:3, Ezra 8:21, Neh 1:4, Est 4:16, Dan 9:3
5) As part of a corporate fast or on someone else's behalf: *Jud 20:26, 1 Sam 7:6, 1 Kings 21:9-12, Est 4:16, Jer 36:6-9, Jonah 3:5, Acts 13:2-3 & 14:23, Luke 5:33*

Six most common challenges when fasting

Another thing you need to know about fasting is when to quit *(Mat 9:14-15)*. Sometimes you may want to fast and you really are sincere about dedicating yourself to God in this way, but the timing for fasting has to be right, and God's grace has to be upon you to do it or else it will become a grievous task. Fasting can become a spiritual hindrance if it is done out of timing. Look for these signs to know when you should abort or modify the requirements of a fast you may be on. (This excludes any fast expressly mandated by God. *[Lev 23:27]*)

1) If you are crankier than usual and lashing out at people: The devil is taking advantage of the weak condition of your body to quench the fruit of the Spirit in your life.

2) If the weakness of your body is interfering with other assignments that God has

commissioned you to do (i.e. waking up at 5:00am every morning, praying two hours every day, going to church three times a week, etcetera): In this case, fasting has become a distraction and an act of disobedience.

3) If the weakness of your body is disabling you from performing on your job or serving your family: This will make you a bad witness to others and a poor example of The Lord's character of integrity.

4) If you cannot seem to stick to the fast and are frustrated and upset because of this: It has become a hindrance.

5) If you are not sure that God has commissioned you to fast and your health is severely compromised: You are no good to anyone dead or lying in a hospital!

6) And finally, if you are not adhering to the spiritual requirements of fasting: You are just wasting your time! *(Isa 1:13;58:3-4, Jer 14:12, Mat 6:16, Luke 18:10-14)*

Use wisdom when fasting and do not abuse it!

- Sometimes you just want to fast, other times God instructs you to fast. Do not alter in any way (including trying to make it more challenging), a fast incited by God. Stick to it just the way He gave it to you and He will see you through it. *(1 Kings 13:8-10 & 13:22)*

- Your sin-nature is always going to want you to abort a fast. You should never abort a fast that you are absolutely positive God has called you to – **not for any reason**.

- If you feel like you cannot make it through a fast, your first response should be to worship more. Worship will increase endurance and fruit.

- If you do have to end or modify a fast that you incited on your own, do not be discouraged. Just regroup, pray and try again. You will get it!

- No matter what type of fast you are on, try to always omit all foods with no nutritional value *(such as candy, caffeine, fried foods, chips and fast foods)* from your diet, until the days of the fast end.

- Because fasting is more about discipline and the spiritual aspects than the omittance of food, being pregnant or ill is not an acceptable excuse to avoid fasting. Reason being, you can always omit non-nutritional foods from your diet. *(Jud 13:7)*

- If you have any health conditions, make sure to take whatever precautions are necessary to stay healthy. Talk to your doctor.

- While you are fasting is not the time to do over-time on the job, spring clean, run a marathon, go to church seven days a week or stay up all night talking on the phone! You need to reserve your energy for those necessary obligations and spiritually enriching activities.
- Fasting can really devastate the body and therefore fasting too often is not healthy or wise. (Unless you go on partial fasts in which case you can still intake all the necessary nutrients.) *(Num 6:3-4, Dan 10:3)*
- Fasting from all food in-take for extended periods several times a year is an abuse. You will cause undue damage and health problems in your body. If you feel the need to continually go on these long hardcore fasts, you are not getting the point of fasting nor yielding the intended outcome!
- Fasting can become an object of worship and you can become addicted to it. Do not let this happen to you! Remember, it is only a means to an end.

Practical tips for a more successful fasting experience
- Drink plenty of water!
- If you are on a partial fast that permits juice, drink fresh vegetable juice and soy milk. These are great for protein and nutrients.
- To help rid your body of toxins while you are fasting drink a lot of water, do deep breathing outdoors, shower frequently and give yourself enemas (check with your doctor first though). This will help combat headaches, nausea, bad breath and other negative physical side affects.
- Try to get a little extra rest while you are fasting. If you can, take a day or two off of work (do this very rarely though), or try to fast on days when you know you can stay at home.
- If you are going to go on an extended fast (7 days or more) or you are a person that feels led by The Spirit to fast often, go on partial fasts instead of complete no-food fasts (unless God instructs you otherwise). It is important that your body is properly nourished just about everyday.

Appendix E: Deliverance Journal

You should buy yourself some type of notebook to use as a journal. God is going to reveal many things to you as you read this book. These few pages will not be enough to hold all of the precious revelations that He is going to pour into you. Use these blanks pages as a makeshift journal until you get another one or if you happen to get a revelation at a time that your journal book is not with you. Be sure to date each revelation but even more so try to remember to keep your official journal book with you at all times. Happy writing!

Contact the Author
(Please check website for up to date contact info)

Laneen and we at Heart Compassion Ministries, encourage you to contact us in order to share your testimony of deliverance and the impact that this book has had on your life! Please be sure to also let us know if you became born again as a result of reading this book. We would like to contact you. The following contact information can also be used to place book orders (see order form on the next page), send donations or make a request for a speaking engagement for Laneen Haniah or the Overseer of Heart Compassion Ministries, Emmanuel N. Haniah. *(Please always check website if information below becomes outdated.)*

Mailing address:
Heart Compassion Ministries
P.O. Box #151416
Dallas, TX 75315-1416

Phone number:
1-347-495-4555 (contact)
1-800-247-6553 (book orders only)

Website:
www.victoriouslyfree.org (Official website)

E-mail addresses:
For testimonials: *Iamfree@victoriouslyfree.org*

Questions or comments: *inquiries@victoriouslyfree.org*

Emmanuel Haniah or questions concerning Heart of Compassion Ministries: *EmmanuelHaniah@victoriouslyfree.org*

(PLEASE, no blank subject lines or your message may be spammed!)

Instant Messaging:
Laneen sometimes does On-line chat sessions and instant messaging using Yahoo!®. To send an IM add *'laneenhaniah'* to your friends list.

If you would like to purchase additional copies of this book please visit any major book retailer. If they don't have it in stock they can order it for you from www.atlasbooks.com. You may also order by phone at **1-800-247-6553,** On-line at www.victoriouslyfree.org or by mail by copying and sending this order form (please retain a copy for your own records) along with *check or money order **made payable to Victoriously Free! Publishing** to:

Victoriously Free! Publishing
P.O. Box #151416
Dallas, TX 75315-1416
Attn: Book order

(Please check website or call for current order information before mailing.)

Date _____   Phone # : _____

First Name _____   Last Name _____

Street Address _____   Apt. # _____

City _____ State _____ Zip _____

E-mail Address _____

Description	QTY	TOTALS
The Spirits of Sexual Perversion Handbook *($19.99 each)*		$
Tax ($1.70 per book NY & TX residents only)		
Donation to Heart Compassion Min *(Exclude S&H if making a donation of $50.00 or more.)*		
Shipping and Handling *(Please add $3.50/book or $2.00/book if ordering more than 5 books.)*		
Total		$

*There will be a $30.00 fee for each returned check.

Don't wait another day,
Don't wait another moment!
It's time to take your life back,
IT'S TIME FOR ANOTHER LEVEL!